For Security and For Peace

This book formulates a conceptual framework to analyse the Russian-Ukrainian conflict. It examines the strategies of the Baltic states and the attitudes of the societies of the Baltic Sea basin, directed not only towards limiting the consequences of the Russian-Ukrainian war but also towards restoring peace and ensuring future security in the region. It assesses the Baltic states during and after the conflict, discussing the problem of managing a coherent policy towards Russia and Ukraine, the challenges faced by states during and after the conflict, analysing the attitudes of societies and their evolution during and after the conflict.

The volume will be of interest to scholars and researchers of European studies and war, international relations, political science, peace and conflict studies.

Jolanta Itrich-Drabarek is a political scientist and professor at the University of Warsaw, Poland.

Marzena Cichosz is a political scientist, researcher and professor at the Institute of Political Science, University of Wrocław, Poland.

Danuta Plecka is a professor at the University of Gdańsk, Poland, and is editor of the series *Demokracja w Polsce po* . . . [Democracy in Poland after . . .] (2005, 2007 and 2015).

Anna Jach is a professor at the Jagiellonian University in Kraków, Poland. She works at the Department of Eurasian Area Studies, Jagiellonian University in Kraków, Poland.

For Security and For Peace
States and Societies of the Baltic Sea Basin and the Russian-Ukrainian War

Edited by Jolanta Itrich-Drabarek,
Marzena Cichosz, Danuta Plecka
and Anna Jach

LONDON AND NEW YORK

First published 2025
by Routledge
4 Park Square, Milton Park, Abingdon, Oxon OX14 4RN

and by Routledge
605 Third Avenue, New York, NY 10158

Routledge is an imprint of the Taylor & Francis Group, an informa business

© 2025 selection and editorial matter, Jolanta Itrich-Drabarek, Marzena Cichosz, Danuta Plecka and Anna Jach; individual chapters, the contributors

The right of Jolanta Itrich-Drabarek, Marzena Cichosz, Danuta Plecka and Anna Jach to be identified as the authors of the editorial material, and of the authors for their individual chapters, has been asserted in accordance with sections 77 and 78 of the Copyright, Designs and Patents Act 1988.

All rights reserved. No part of this book may be reprinted or reproduced or utilised in any form or by any electronic, mechanical, or other means, now known or hereafter invented, including photocopying and recording, or in any information storage or retrieval system, without permission in writing from the publishers.

Trademark notice: Product or corporate names may be trademarks or registered trademarks, and are used only for identification and explanation without intent to infringe.

British Library Cataloguing-in-Publication Data
A catalogue record for this book is available from the British Library

ISBN: 978-1-032-85125-9 (hbk)
ISBN: 978-1-032-90428-3 (pbk)
ISBN: 978-1-003-55804-0 (ebk)

DOI: 10.4324/9781003558040

Typeset in Sabon
by Apex CoVantage, LLC

The translation of the publication by Anna Jach, Monika Banaś, and Katarzyna Kosowska was supported by a grant from the Faculty of International and Political Studies as part of the Strategic Excellence Initiative Program of the Jagiellonian University.

Contents

List of tables	*vii*
List of contributors	*viii*
List of abbreviations	*xii*

Introduction 1
JOLANTA ITRICH-DRABAREK AND ANNA JACH

PART I
States and their initiatives 11

1 Values and 'anti-values' in times of war and peace 13
JOLANTA ITRICH-DRABAREK AND DANUTA PLECKA

2 The Baltic Sea states in the face of war and peace 26
JOANNA KOZIERSKA, JOANNA MARSZAŁEK-KAWA,
BEATA SŁOBODZIAN AND AGATA WŁODKOWSKA

3 Impact of the Russian-Ukrainian war on the Baltic
area's economy 41
KATARZYNA KOSOWSKA AND AGATA NIEWIADOMSKA

4 Sweden, Finland and the Russian-Ukrainian war and
prospects for its end 56
MONIKA BANAŚ

5 The vision of peace à la Putin: Russia's strategic objectives
towards the Baltic Sea states in the context of the war in Ukraine 70
MAGDALENA LACHOWICZ AND AGNIESZKA LEGUCKA

vi *Contents*

6 The role of states and international organisations in bringing
war crimes to account in the context of the Russian-Ukrainian
war: from documenting crimes to trying war criminals   83
AGNIESZKA FLORCZAK, ANNA JACH AND JOANNA ROSŁON-ŻMUDA

PART II
Social activism in Baltic Sea states   105

7 Societies of the Baltic Sea states in the face of security issues   107
PIOTR SULA, KAMIL BŁASZCZYŃSKI AND MICHAŁ KUŚ

8 Social activism for peace models in the Nordic and Baltic
Sea states   121
MAGDALENA LACHOWICZ

9 'When peace comes': activities undertaken in the Baltic
region states to preserve Ukraine's cultural capital   137
MAŁGORZATA MADEJ, MAŁGORZATA MYŚLIWIEC AND
KAROLINA TYBUCHOWSKA-HARTLIŃSKA

10 'It's not our war': social movements against state
involvement in aid to Ukraine   154
MARZENA CICHOSZ, ELŻBIETA SZYSZLAK AND
RENATA PODGÓRZAŃSKA

11 Between just and unjust war: social movements in Germany
and their attitude to the Russian-Ukrainian war   168
KATARZYNA KAMIŃSKA-KOROLCZUK AND MARLENA PIOTROWSKA

12 Between fear and courage: Russians vis-à-vis
the oppressive state   183
ANNA JACH AND MAGDALENA LACHOWICZ

13 Conclusion   200
DANUTA PLECKA AND MARZENA CICHOSZ

Index of persons   206

Tables

2.1	The number of refugees from Ukraine (as of June/July 2023)	30
6.1	Catalogue of war crimes committed in Ukraine by Russian troops after 24 February 2022	85
7.1	Opinions on safety and security in the Baltic Sea states – descriptive statistics	110
7.2	Opinions on challenges to the internal security of the EU in the Baltic Sea states	112
7.3	How secure or insecure do you feel about military defence?	114
7.4	Do you think your country currently spends too little on defence, too much on defence or about the right amount?	116
9.1	Non-EU citizens who had fled Ukraine and received temporary protection in the states of the Baltic region (end of June 2023)	138
9.2	Types of activities undertaken in the states of the Baltic region by state institutions, social organisations, private entities and volunteers in support of Ukrainian cultural capital in the period 2022–2023	141

Contributors

Monika Banaś is professor at the Faculty of International and Political Studies at Jagiellonian University in Kraków, Poland. Her research focuses on culture, politics and their mutual dependencies. She has published on migration and integration policies, political culture and political symbolism. Her research interests focus on migration and integration, migration trends in contemporary societies, welfare state, mutual dependences of economy and culture.

Kamil Błaszczyński, PhD, is a political scientist, researcher and lecturer at the Institute of Political Sciences of the University of Wrocław, Poland. He conducts research in the field of voting behaviour, social capital, youth civil participation and role of religiosity in political activity. He is also the deputy director of the Centre for Quantitative Research at the Institute of Political Science, University of Wrocław, Poland.

Marzena Cichosz, PhD with habilitation, is a political scientist, researcher, and professor at the Institute of Political Science, University of Wrocław, Poland. She heads the Social and Political Activity Research Unit. She conducts research in the fields of political marketing, the transformation of the political systems in Central and Eastern Europe, and the activity of social movements.

Agnieszka Florczak, PhD, is a political scientist, researcher and lecturer at the Institute of Political Sciences, University of Wrocław, Poland. He conducts research in the field of human rights protection, asylum policy and European integration. He is an expert of the Team Europe network operating at the Representation of the European Commission in Poland.

Jolanta Itrich-Drabarek is Professor at the University of Warsaw, Poland. She is a political scientist, holds a PhD with habilitation in social science and is a Member of the Scientific Excellence Council of the first term. She is the author of numerous scientific publications on the essence of a democratic state, the status of civil servants in Poland and Europe, civil service systems in the EU and worldwide, the role and place of public administration in a democratic state, internal security and ethics in the public sphere.

Contributors ix

Anna Jach, is a professor at the Jagiellonian University in Kraków, Poland, is a political scientist and historian. She works at the Department of Eurasian Area Studies in the Institute of Russian and East European Studies at the Faculty of International and Political Studies, Jagiellonian University in Kraków, Poland. She specialises in the 20th and 21st centuries history, with a particular focus on the history of the USSR and Russia, Polish-Russian relations, systemic transformation and the functioning of the non-governmental non-commercial sector, civil society in Russia.

Katarzyna Kamińska-Korolczuk, PhD with habilitation, is a political scientist, researcher, lecturer and the deputy director of the Institute of Political Science University of Gdańsk, Poland. Her main research interests include the issues of changes in political, party and media systems, state information policy and mediatisation of politics.

Katarzyna Kosowska is an assistant professor at the Institute of Russia and Eastern Europe at the Faculty of International and Political Studies of the Jagiellonian University, Poland. Her research areas include economy of the countries of the Eurasian region, economic models of the CIS countries, economic security and energy security of the post-Soviet countries, energy policy of the Russian Federation and economic relations between Russia and other CIS countries.

Joanna Kozierska, PhD, is an assistant professor at the Department of Political and Administrative Systems, Institute of Political Science, University of Wrocław, Poland. Her research work focuses mainly on the political systems of Central and Eastern Europe, with particular emphasis on the theory and practice of creation and functioning of coalition cabinets. She also conducts research in the field of elections and election campaigns.

Michał Kuś, PhD, is assistant professor at the Institute of Political Science, University of Wroclaw, Poland. His research interests: media and politics, media regulation. He is the project leader of Polish part of the European Journalism Observatory (EJO) project.

Magdalena Lachowicz, PhD, is an assistant professor at the Department of Eastern Studies, Faculty of History, Adam Mickiewicz University, Poznan. She is the researcher of issues of sociology of the nation, ethnic relations and regional movements in Eurasia, and history of the USSR, Ukraine and Russia of the 20th and 21st centuries. The scope of her research concerned the contemporary nationality politics of Central and Eastern European countries, with particular emphasis on Poland, Ukraine and Slovakia, and especially the functioning of the Carpathian Ruthenian group in the context of regional politics and global social processes.

Agnieszka Legucka, PhD with habilitation, is a senior research fellow of the Russia in Eastern Europe Program at the Polish Institute of International Affairs (PISM), Poland. She is an associate professor of security studies

x *Contributors*

at the Faculty of Business and International Relations in the Academy of Finance and Business Vistula in Warsaw. Her areas of expertise include Russian foreign and internal policy, security issues and conflicts in the EU's Eastern Neighbourhood, EU-Russia and NATO-Russia relations, Russian disinformation, and hybrid threats.

Małgorzata Madej, PhD, is a researcher and lecturer at the University of Wrocław, political scientist. Her main areas of scientific interest include citizens' participation in elections and decision-making processes, especially on the local level. She is deputy editor-in-chief of the *Polish Political Science Review*.

Joanna Marszałek-Kawa, PhD with habilitation, is a professor. She is the head of the Department of Political Systems at the Faculty of Political Science and Security Studies. Her main research interests include European parliaments, Asian issues, political systems and the constitutional systems of countries in the world.

Małgorzata Myśliwiec is a political scientist. She is associate professor, researcher and lecturer at the University of Silesia in Katowice. Her main areas of scientific interest include political systems of the EU and the Maghreb states (with particular emphasis on the political system of Spain and Morocco), processes of decentralisation and regionalisation in Europe, theory of nation and nationalism, regional and ethnoregional parties in Europe and public administration in European states.

Agata Niewiadomska, PhD in law, is an assistant professor at the Department of National Economy, Faculty of Management, University of Warsaw. She graduated in law, management and English philology from the University of Warsaw. She is the senator of the University of Warsaw.

Marlena Piotrowska, PhD, is a political scientist and assistant professor at the Department of Political and Administrative Systems, Institute of Political Science, University of Wrocław. The main areas of her scientific interests are social movements, political system in Germany, political careers and the role of women in politics.

Danuta Plecka, professor, she works at the University of Gdańsk. She was the editor of the series *Demokracja w Polsce po . . .* [Democracy in Poland after . . .] (2005, 2007 and 2015). She was the scientific director of the conference series *Administracja Publiczna* [Public Administration] (8 international editions). Her research interests oscillate around political systems, political culture and political civic competences.

Renata Podgórzańska, PhD with habilitation, is a political scientist and a professor of the University of Szczecin. Her research interests include an analysis of contemporary international relations with a particular focus on Poland's foreign policy, Poland's security policy and international conflict.

Contributors xi

She also investigates migration processes in today's world, the migration crisis in Europe and securitisation of the migration issue in Poland.

Joanna Rosłon-Żmuda, PhD, is an employee of the Institute of Political Sciences of the University of Gdańsk. Her research focuses mainly on issues related to international relationships.

Beata Słobodzian is an assistant professor at the Department of Political Systems, Institute of Political Science, University of Gdansk. Her research interests focus on the subject of European local government, with particular emphasis on Polish solutions, the political model, its transformations and modernisation.

Piotr Sula is associate professor at the University of Wrocław, Poland. He was one of the founding editors of *Polish Political Science Review*. He serves as the head of the Centre for Quantitative Research. He specialises in comparative politics, political parties and political competition.

Elżbieta Szyszlak is associate professor at the University of Wrocław, Poland, employed at the Institute of International Studies. Her areas of research interest include ethnic issues in the modern world, cultural security and cultural security of ethnic minorities.

Karolina Tybuchowska-Hartlińska, PhD with habilitation, is an employee of the Institute of Political Sciences, University of Warmia and Mazury in Olsztyn. Her research focuses mainly on issues related to local government, especially local elections, political participation, as well as social and political innovations.

Agata Włodkowska is a political scientist and holds a dr hab. degree in political science. Her key research areas concern international relations and security in Eurasia, Poland and Russia's foreign policy and feminist approach in international relations.

Abbreviations

2D	deterrence and dialogue principle
8xD	de-Ukrainisation, debanderisation, de-Europeanisation, de-ukranasification, demilitarisation, decriminalisation, decolonisation and decommunisation
AfD	Alternative for Germany (Alternative für Deutschland)
AGDF	Working Group Service for Peace (Arbeitsgemeinschaft Dienst für den Frieden)
AIM	Anti-involvement Movement
ALF	Anna Lindh Foundation (Lithuania)
ATM	Autonomous Trade Measures
BSV	League for Social Defence (Bund für Soziale Verteidigung)
CBSS	Council of Baltic Sea States
CDU/CSU	Christian Democratic Union/Christian Social Union
CEE	Central and Eastern Europe
Centre UA	Centre of United Actions
CEIDG	Central Register and Information on Economic Activity
CICED	Core International Crimes Evidence Database
CLT	Construct-Level Theory of Psychological Distance
CMI	Martti Ahtisaari Peace Foundation
CoE	Council of Europe
CPPCG or the Genocide Convention	UN Convention on the Prevention and Punishment of the Crime of Genocide
CSCE	Conference on Security and Cooperation in Europe
CSDP	The EU's Common Security and Defence Policy
CSO	Civil Society
CSP	Conducive Space for Peace (Denmark)
CSSP	Berlin Center for Integrative Mediation
DAAD	German Academic Exchange Service (Deutscher Akademischer Austauschdienst)

DCDPP	Development Cooperation and Democracy Promotion Programme
DDG	Danish Demining Group
DDoS	Distributed Denial of Service
DFG	German Peace Society (Deutsche Friedensgesellschaft)
Dialogue Group	Dialogue Group on Accountability for Ukraine
EBCO	European Bureau for Conscientious Objection
EC	European Commission
ECHR	European Court of Human Rights
EJN	European Judicial Network
EKD	Evangelical Church in Germany (Evangelische Kirche in Deutschland)
EP	European Parliament
EP	European Plan
EPLO	European Peacebuilding Liaison Office
EU	European Union
EUAM Ukraine	European Union Advisory Mission for Civilian Security Sector Reform Ukraine
Eurojust	EU Agency for Criminal Justice Cooperation
EÜVP	Estonian United Left Party (Objedinionnaja lewaja partija Estonii)
FAO	Food and Agriculture Organization
FDI	Foreign Direct Investment
FDP	Free Democratic Party
FRG	Federal Republic of Germany, Germany, West German
GA	General Assembly
GDP	Gross Domestic Product
GDR	German Democratic Republic, East German
Genocide Network	Network for investigation and prosecution of genocide, crimes against humanity and war crimes
GESIS	German Social Science Infrastructure Services
HRC	Human Rights Council
HRMMU	UN Human Rights Monitoring Mission in Ukraine
ICC	International Criminal Court
ICJ	International Court of Justice
ICMPD	Migration Outlook Eastern Europe and Central Asia
ICPA	International Centre for Prosecution of the Crime of Aggression
IdK	Internationale Kriegsdienstverweigerer
IEA	International Energy Agency
IHL	International Humanitarian Law

xiv *Abbreviations*

Ipsos	Institut Public de Sondage d'Opinion Secteur
IT	Information Technology
JEF	Joint Expeditionary Force
JITs Network	Network of National Experts on Joint Investigation Teams
KKP	Confederation of the Polish Crown (Konfederacja Korony Polskiej)
Levada-Center	Levada Analytical Center, Автономная некоммерческая организация Аналитический Центр Юрия Левады (АНО Левада-Центр)
LKNVOA	Association of Non-governmental Organisations of Contemporary Culture, Laikmetīgās kultūras nevalstisko organizāciju asociācija
LNG	Liquefied Natural Gas
LOORE	Estonian Creative Residency Network
LPI	Life and Peace Institute (Sweden)
MFA of Denmark	Ministry of Foreign Affairs of Denmark
MSB	Swedish Civil Contingencies Agency
NATO	North Atlantic Alliance Organization
NBI	Finnish National Bureau of Investigation
NCM	Nordic Council of Ministers
NEFCO	Nordic Environment Finance Cooperation
NGO	Non-governmental Organisation
NORDEN	five Nordic states: Denmark, Finland, Iceland, Norway, Sweden
NPOU	National Reconstruction Plan for Ukraine
NUPI	Norwegian Institute of International Affairs
ODA	Official Development Assistance
ODIHR	Office for Democratic Institutions and Human Rights
OHCHR	Office of the High Commissioner for Human Rights
OSCE	Organization for Security and Cooperation in Europe
OTP	Office of the Prosecutor
OUN-B	Organisation of Ukrainian Nationalists
PCA	Permanent Court of Arbitration
PfP	Partnership for Peace
PiS	Law and Justice, Prawo i Sprawiedliwość
PKK	Kurdistan Workers' Party
PSF	The Danish Peace and Stabilisation Fund
PTSD	Post-traumatic Stress Disorder
PZKB	Platform Peaceful Conflict Transformation
RES	Renewable Energy Sources

Abbreviations xv

RF	Russian Federation
RT	Russia Today
SALAR	Swedish Association of Local Authorities and Regions
SEK	Swedish krona
SIDA	Swedish International Development Cooperation Agency
SiE	Solidarity in Europe
Sikt	Norwegian Agency for Shared Services in Education and Research
SIPRI	Stockholm International Peace Research Institute
SMO	'Special Military Operation' (Russian: специальная военная операция, сво)
SPD	Social Democratic Party of Germany
StGB	Strafgesetzbuch – the German Criminal Code
SWIFT	Society for Worldwide Interbank Financial Telecommunication
TVRain	TV Rain (Телеканал "Дождь", ДО///ДЬ)
UN	United Nations
UN GA	United Nations General Assembly
UNESCO	United Nations Educational, Scientific and Cultural Organisation
UNHCR	United Nations High Commissioner for Refugees
UNICEF	United Nations International Children's Emergency Fund, United Nations Children's Fund
URC	Ukraine Recovery Conference
USSR	Union of Soviet Socialist Republics, Soviet Union
VCIOM	Russian Public Opinion Research Center
VK	Association of Conscientious Objectors, Verband der Kriegsdienstverweigerer
VPN	Virtual Private Network
VStGB	Völkerstrafgesetzbuch, The Code of Crimes against International Law
WFD	Weltfriedensdienst, World Peace Service
WFP	World Food Program
WISE	Wider Security Network (Finland)
YPG/PYD	Kurdish groups in Syria, the People's Defence Units and the Democratic Union Party

Introduction

Jolanta Itrich-Drabarek and Anna Jach

This monograph is the first attempt to systematically define and explain, across diverse contexts, the actions of states and societies during Russia's ongoing war with Ukraine. It aims to identify both commonalities and divergences among the Baltic region states bordering Russia, while offering a prognosis for achieving peace and security in the region. The authors' research focuses on identifying strategies, tactics, attitudes and models of state behaviour and social endeavour within these states whose aim is not only to restore peace within the region but also more importantly to ensure future security. Consequently, the study consciously follows mainstream peace research, while concentrating not only on state institutions but also on grassroots civil society initiatives. The focus is on the states of the region and their societies as key actors who live in the immediate vicinity of an ongoing full-scale armed conflict and are involved in it at varying levels of intensity and through different forms of engagement.

Since 24 February 2024, we have been observing and to some extent participating in an ongoing full-scale war, as Russia has invaded its neighbour, the independent and sovereign state of Ukraine. While Ukraine has borne the brunt of the armed conflict, its repercussions directly affect the entire European continent and influence the political landscape of nations worldwide. The conflict has been described in various ways, ranging from a 'clash of civilisations' to a struggle between the authentic values of the 'East' (sympathised with by the marginalised South) and the perceived decadence of the collective 'rotten West', which opposes everything the 'East' holds dear. Here, the 'East' is represented by the Russian Federation, while the West is symbolised by the United States, the North Atlantic Alliance and the majority of the countries of the European Union.

Russia's invasion of Ukraine has triggered a cascade of changes in the global economy, which have made it necessary to recalibrate global supply chains and trade flows. They also altered investor confidence and, most importantly, affected the region's energy and food security. Achieving energy independence from Russian gas and oil resources has gained prominence, alongside the prioritisation of climate protection and the implementation of 'Green Deal' policies. The start of wartime inflationary pressures has left its

DOI: 10.4324/9781003558040-1

2   *Jolanta Itrich-Drabarek and Anna Jach*

mark on these economies. The looming threat of spill-over and further escalation of the conflict has led to a reassessment of international security strategies, forcing states to strengthen their defence capabilities and, as a result, restructure their national budgets. In addition, the influx of war refugees, while potentially advantageous for the labour market, has increased costs for host countries.

All these consequences of the war primarily affected the states of the Baltic region, that is, Lithuania, Latvia, Estonia, Finland, Denmark, Germany, Sweden and Poland, located in central and northern Europe, which form both NATO's eastern flank and the borders of the European Union. Most of these countries share direct borders with the Russian Federation, while even those that do not are connected to Russia via the Baltic Sea. Russian influence is strong in many of these countries, some of which have significant Russian minority populations. The Baltic Sea, often referred to as the 'inner sea of NATO', has a special status in light of the recent NATO accession of Sweden and Finland. These countries have unique experiences shaped by their interactions with Russia, due to their geographical proximity, historical legacies and dependencies. It should be remembered that the experiences of the twentieth century have left an indelible mark on other European states as well, shaping perceptions of Russia as a country that, irrespective of its political system or regime, is viewed as, if not openly hostile, at least unstable and unpredictable in its policies. As a result, the states of the Baltic region hold a significant position in the geopolitical landscape, warranting a thorough examination of their roles, policies and public sentiments during the conflict. This monograph seeks to address the need to examine the processes aimed at ending the war, devising support mechanisms for Ukraine, and formulating preventive strategies for the future of Europe as a whole.

The primary objective of this research was to examine the strategies adopted by these states and the sentiments prevailing in their societies aimed not only at mitigating the effects of the Russian-Ukrainian war but also at restoring peace and ensuring future security in the region. The economic consequences of the war in Ukraine for these states, coupled with their citizens' perceptions of security mainly in terms of their own security and the military security of the respective states, became an important premise. The monograph analyses their strategies, focusing in particular on (1) their declared positions against the war; (2) declarations aimed at developing mechanisms to end the war and secure a lasting peace; (3) the activation of relief efforts, the dissemination of accurate information, the strengthening of security and the reintegration of post-war Europe; and (4). governments' commitment to managing the new reality of war-provoked turmoil in European markets, evidenced by: financial market downturns, commodity market panics, inflationary shocks, trade diversions, declining investor confidence, European population migrations (refugee inflows) and significant industrial challenges. In addition, the research examined social attitudes towards the Russian-Ukrainian war and the resulting social activities, as well as analysing reactions to the conflict itself, its underlying causes and perceptions of the policies of individual Baltic Sea states and Russia. A separate aspect was the diagnosis of the perception of this war as one of the first destructive conflicts in 21st-century Europe. A systematic study of public opinion before and during the outbreak of the Russian-Ukrainian war, particularly about perceptions of domestic security, has become relevant in this regard. Based on the adopted framework, the researchers also explored the post-24 February 2022 landscape focusing on (1) Russia's role as an aggressor state in external relations and as an oppressive regime striving for internal totalitarianism; (2) Ukraine's struggle amid the chaos of war, with the significant challenge of rebuilding a peaceful and democratic state and society; and (3) various crises with humanitarian, food, migration, energy, financial and other implications, not only in Ukraine but across the European continent.

Achieving the objectives required an examination of the core of the crisis caused by the Russian-Ukrainian conflict; a delineation of the involvement of the states of the Baltic region during and after the conflict; a discussion on the challenge of formulating a coherent policy towards both the aggressor and the victim; a discourse on challenges faced by states during and after the conflict; and an analysis of social attitudes and their evolution likewise.

The main research hypothesis of the monograph is as follows:

In response to Russia's aggression against Ukraine, the Baltic region states adjusted their domestic and foreign policies to prevent further escalation of the conflict and to facilitate the restoration of peace between Russia and Ukraine. This shift was motivated by the understanding that the war between Russia and Ukraine has destabilised the Baltic Sea region, changed social attitudes and set in motion numerous unregulated economic and social dynamics.

The authors have formulated the following auxiliary hypotheses:

Firstly, in modern societies during peacetime, an individual's hierarchy of values and the attitudes resulting from it are closely linked to the characteristics of society, and related to its level of development, sense of security and support for post-material values. However, in times of war, these values are strongly eroded or become marginal. Secondly, the war between Russia and Ukraine is prompting a reassessment of security strategies and policies across the political-military and socio-economic dimensions of the NATO member states in the Baltic region. This adjustment stems from the diverse yet complementary approaches adopted by these states with regard to extending political-military and socio-economic support to Ukraine. In addition, these states express different positions on Ukraine's potential membership of the EU and NATO as well as on prospects for future peace negotiations, including the status of the Crimean peninsula. Russia's invasion of Ukraine in 2022 precipitated economic instability, especially in the food and energy sectors, disrupting the global landscape and prompting a reconfiguration of global security dynamics.

The monograph discusses the posed research questions. How and why do universally accepted democratic values turn into 'anti-values' as a result

4   Jolanta Itrich-Drabarek and Anna Jach

of their instrumental use by parties to a conflict? Does the 'transplantation' of solutions from one state to another, under the banner of freedom, human rights and respect for others, really influence the progress of democratisation within societies and states? How does the international community react to armed interventions in the territory of another state on the pretext of combating fascism or defending the rights of minorities? What are the changes to security strategy and policy in the political-military and socio-economic dimensions of the NATO member states in the Baltic region? Will the most effective approach for the Baltic Sea states in addressing the energy, food, and financial crises involve rebuilding the market by guaranteeing a steady provision of essential resources and raw materials, diversifying trade routes, swiftly reconstructing financial and energy systems, and introducing innovative market solutions for international trade? What factors led Sweden and Finland to abandon their neutral status? How is Russia reshaping the concept of peace to pursue its global interests? What is the extent of the war crimes committed and what are the modalities of the multi-level system for documenting war crimes and efforts at prosecution, including updates on investigations initiated in international courts? How do formal and informal social activism initiatives manifest themselves in the states of the Baltic region during the Russian-Ukrainian war? What are the characteristics of anti-involvement movements (AIMs), which focus their activism solely on advocating an immediate peace agreement between Russia and Ukraine? Are there any initiatives by institutions, private groups, organisations and volunteers to promote Ukrainian-ness and Ukrainian culture, consolidate skills and social capital, and encourage the continuous creation of new Ukrainian culture in the region? In the context of the hybrid form of dictatorship that has characterised Russia since 2012, can acts of civil disobedience by Russian citizens inside Russia and by the Russian diaspora scattered across the states in the Baltic region have an impact on the restoration of peace between Russia and Ukraine? To what extent does the geographical proximity of the Russian-Ukrainian conflict influence the level of interest in security issues among the residents of the Baltic Sea states, particularly in relation to arms and defence issues? Furthermore, how does this proximity correlate with an increased percentage of individuals perceiving these events as significantly affecting their personal sense of security, and how does it shape their perceptions of their country's security?

The monograph posits that the theoretical approach encompasses both a conceptual framework and an explanatory model. The former addresses the challenges encountered by those states and societies in the Baltic region affected by the Russian-Ukrainian war as a subject for explanation, while the latter regards it as an explanatory model adopted by individual states and societies.

The study employs theories and research methods typical of the social sciences, including complexity theory, Ronald Inglehart's theory, Immanuel Kant's theories of 'democratic peace' and 'just war', reconstruction methods, comparative and predictive methods, and qualitative analysis to demonstrate the uniqueness and specificity of the phenomena under study. In addition, the authors of the opening chapter have developed their own theory, called 'authoritarian peace theory', based on the principles of democratic peace theory. This theory serves as a post-Bolshevik paradigm to explain how states with a façade democracy engage democratic states in war.

The study has used the science of complexity to address the research issues throughout the monograph. This approach has entailed drawing on a range of ideas, principles and concepts from diverse fields of knowledge, including chaos theory, cybernetics, complex adaptive systems, postmodern approaches and systems thinking (Ramalingam et al., 2008, pp. 4–5). By comprehending the individual components of the Russian-Ukrainian war, a holistic understanding of its entirety has been achieved. Viewing not only the conflict zone and the Baltic region but also Europe and the global landscape through the lens of their complexity highlights the various elements that shape socio-political reality, both in direct response to the conflict and in the longer term with regard to peace processes. Furthermore, the analysis of social movement activity was conducted on the basis of social movement theories, particularly the theory of resource mobilisation.

Ronald Inglehart's theory was applied to show that the hierarchy of an individual's values and the attitudes that result from them are closely linked to the characteristics of societies, including their level of development, sense of security and support for post-material values. These factors are connected to shifts in perceptions of social roles, changes in the quality of life and the degree of democratic consolidation. In each chapter, authors argue for the need for additional theories and methodologies.

The main focus of the opening chapter, 'Values and "Anti-values" in Times of War and Peace', is to explore the significance of both values and 'anti-values' during the crisis triggered by Russia's invasion of Ukraine. The authors aim to analyse the values relevant to the political ethos of societies in times of peace, and to examine their altered significance within the hierarchy in times of war. They argue that there is a strong correlation between an individual's value hierarchy, their resulting attitudes and the social characteristics associated with stages of development, perceptions of security and support for post-material values. This link is intertwined with changes in social role perceptions, changes in the quality of life and the level of democratic consolidation. However, this correlation takes on a different dimension during wartime, when universally accepted values can be turned into 'anti-values' depending on their instrumental manipulation by the parties to the conflict.

In Chapter 2, 'The Baltic States in the Face of War and Peace', the authors analyse the evolution of security strategies and policies in the political-military and socio-economic dimensions of NATO's Baltic members. The context of the analysis is the Russian aggression of 24 February 2022, the alliance's most recent strategic framework and the outcome of the Vilnius NATO Summit in July 2023. The chapter does not cover the activities of Finland and

Sweden, which are discussed elsewhere in this volume, but focuses on Lithuania, Latvia and Estonia (the Baltic states), together with Poland, Germany and Denmark. The chapter aims to consider the different military-political and socio-economic support strategies that these states have extended to Ukraine, and to analyse their divergent positions on Ukraine's potential EU and NATO membership, as well as on the future peace process, including the question of the Crimean peninsula. The authors find that the assistance provided by the Baltic NATO members to Ukraine, including political statements of support, the provision of military equipment, refugee assistance as well as political and financial involvement in its reconstruction efforts, has been one of their most significant contributions.

In Chapter 3, 'Impact of the Russian-Ukrainian War on the Baltic Area's Economy', the authors analyse the economic consequences of the conflict in Ukraine and examine its impact on the economies of the Baltic Sea states. The chapter discusses challenges related to energy and food security, as well as investment, provides an assessment of key economic indicators and forecasts potential future developments that may affect the economies of the Baltic Sea states, which is of particular importance, given the observed economic instability and the disruption to supply chains and transit of goods. This has caused trade diversion and undermined investor confidence in the region's markets. In addition, a pressing priority for the Baltic Sea states is to achieve energy independence from Russian resources, leading to increased efforts towards sustainable development and the implementation of the 'Green Deal' policy.

In Chapter 4, 'Sweden, Finland and the Russian-Ukrainian War with Prospects for Its End', the author seeks to identify the adjustments that Sweden and Finland have been contemplating to enhance the broader security of the Baltic region, thereby influencing the security dynamics of Europe and the global landscape in the 21st century. The chapter includes a qualitative analysis of the political and socio-cultural discourse surrounding Sweden's and Finland's accession to NATO, particularly in the context of policies that either oppose or express scepticism about the alliance's enlargement. The chapter also attempts to explain why neutrality and non-alignment are proving inadequate in times of global order realignment, and examines the implications of the phenomenon of the feminisation of foreign policy for peace-building processes.

In Chapter 5, 'The Vision of Peace à la Putin: Russia's Strategic Objectives towards the Baltic States in the Context of the War in Ukraine', the authors attempt to address how Russia is reshaping the concept of peace to promote its global interests. The chapter aims to analyse Russian propaganda concerning Ukraine, with a specific focus on the ideology of 'Russkiy mir' (*Русский мир*, Russian World), which not only asserts Russia's cultural supremacy over Ukraine but also serves as a rationale for intervening in the internal affairs of other countries where populations culturally aligned to Russia exist within their borders.

Introduction 7

In Chapter 6, 'The Role of States and International Organisations in Bringing War Crimes to Account in the Context of the Russian-Ukrainian War: From Documenting Crimes to Trying War Criminals', the authors aim to operationalise key concepts related to international crimes committed by the Russian Federation. They aim to provide an overview of the extent of the violations committed, both quantitatively and qualitatively, and to discuss the mechanisms of the multi-level system for documenting international crimes and the ongoing efforts at prosecution, including an update on the investigations initiated at the international courts. In addition, the authors intend to assess prospects for the establishment of a new ad hoc tribunal to deal with crimes of aggression. Furthermore, the chapter discusses the efforts of the states in the Baltic region to gather evidence and document international crimes committed in Ukraine, examines international cooperation among states in documenting such crimes after 24 February 2022, and evaluates the efforts of international judicial bodies to hold accountable those responsible for crimes committed after that date.

In Chapter 7, 'Societies of the Baltic Sea States in the Face of Security Issues', the starting point is the social perception of the Russian-Ukrainian war in terms of security, mostly in the context of citizens' sense of their own security and the military security of their states. Based on opinion polls carried out before and after the full-scale invasion of Ukraine – Round 10 of the European Social Survey, Eurobarometer and the SiE survey on solidarity in Europe – the chapter analyses the attitudes of the societies of Baltic Sea states towards security with regard to four issues: (1) the importance they attribute to living in a secure environment, (2) their views on the importance of war for the internal security of the EU, (3) their sense of security in the context of available military defence capabilities, and (4) their assessment of the adequacy of defence expenditure. The results clearly demonstrate that the geographical proximity of the Russian-Ukrainian conflict both impacts the degree of interest in security issues among the residents of the Baltic Sea states (arms and defence matters) and has raised the percentage of people considering these events to be a factor that significantly affects (rather negatively) both their own sense of security and their opinions on the security of their own country.

In Chapter 8, 'Social Activism for Peace Models in the Nordic and Baltic Sea States', the author analyses formal and informal models during the Russian-Ukrainian war, focusing on a comparative perspective across the states in the Baltic region. The study excludes the Russian Federation as it is the aggressor directly involved in the conflict. The author posits that a peace movement is broadly defined as a social movement dedicated to the realisation of ideals such as the cessation of war, with the primary aim of mitigating the effects of violence. It is therefore particularly interesting to examine cases of consolidation and the establishment of 'horizontal' networks aimed at creating support systems and safeguarding human rights. The aim is to present the models, forms and structures of social initiatives with explicitly anti-war

8 *Jolanta Itrich-Drabarek and Anna Jach*

and pro-Ukrainian tendencies manifested in the short and long terms, and in local, regional and transnational initiatives, including anti-war campaigns. The chapter also aims to describe the expressions of community-based activism, with a focus on the active involvement of those most affected by the conflict, namely Ukrainian war migrants.

In Chapter 9, '"When Peace Comes": Activities Undertaken in the Baltic Region States to Preserve Ukraine's Cultural Capital', the authors attempt to assess the initiatives taken by institutions, private groups, organisations and volunteers to promote 'Ukrainian-ness' and Ukrainian culture, as well as to foster skills and social capital, while creating new cultural work. The analysis focuses primarily on cultural domains such as music, literature and cinema. The authors argue that maintaining the identity and unity of the Ukrainian nation and its social capital is of particular importance in the face of challenges ranging from armed aggression to mass migration and the need to rebuild not only infrastructure but also social resources in the post-war period. In addition, the authors seek to assess the actions of public administrations and NGOs in the states of the Baltic region which have received the largest groups of refugees, to enhance Ukraine's post-war capacity to rebuild not only physical resources but also Ukrainian society.

In Chapter 10, '"It's Not Our War": Social Movements Against State Involvement in Aid to Ukraine', the authors undertake an analysis of the activities of social movement organisations (SMOs) openly protesting against state involvement in aid to Ukraine. The chapter seeks to elucidate the specific characteristics of movements commonly referred to as anti-involvement movements (AIMs). The authors argue that strategies, interactions with the environment and the institutionalisation of these movements are shaped by their emergence across several states in the Baltic region, each with different origins, socio-cultural developmental contexts (including ethnicity and history) and diverse relationships with political actors (including political parties).

In Chapter 11, 'Between Just and Unjust War: Social Movements in Germany and Their Attitude to the Russian-Ukrainian War', the authors attempt to describe the activities of German socio-political movements. Based on their experiences in the 20th century, these movements address emerging issues in the German political arena influenced by the Russian-Ukrainian war and propose possible solutions. The analysis examines various social formations, distinguishing their types and significance within the political landscape, while considering the implications of potential new activities that could influence the contemporary political space in Germany. This assessment is made against a backdrop of the evolving geopolitical landscape during the ongoing Russian-Ukrainian conflict. In addition, the chapter is contextualised within the changes taking place in the German political system following the initiation of the *Zeitenwende* policy on 27 February 2022. Consequently, the authors examine the activities of social movements and how German party elites interpret these processes within the state, alongside the evolving international context.

Introduction 9

The final chapter, 'Between Fear and Courage: Russians Vis-à-vis the Oppressive State', examines the dynamics of civil disobedience amidst the hybrid dictatorship characterised by spin and fear tactics (Guriev & Treisman, 2023) that has prevailed in Russia since 2012. This analysis is conducted against the backdrop of the ongoing full-scale Russian-Ukrainian war. The research covers two different groups: Russian citizens living in the country and the Russian diaspora in the states of the Baltic region. The authors examine various forms of civil disobedience within Russia, ranging from active anti-war campaigns to pro-Ukrainian initiatives advocating peace in the Russian-Ukrainian war. The chapter also investigates efforts to consolidate current dissidents and members of the diaspora, with a focus on strengthening existing centres outside Russian borders that advocate Russia's political transformation towards democracy. These efforts include the development of mechanisms to support anti-regime forces, such as conferences, debates, grassroots civic projects and ethno-political movements.

The analysis in this monograph is based on two main sources: the relevant norms of international law and national legislation including implemented international regulations. The extensive review of the literature, mainly popular-science, in each chapter, reflects the growing importance of the Russian-Ukrainian war. While many of the works reviewed may not be widely cited or recognised, they offer diverse scholarly perspectives on the issue, albeit often in a fragmented or casual manner. The analysis of definitions, models and explanatory frameworks highlights the need for nuanced interpretation and understanding, given their importance as explanatory indicators. The perspective on the perception of Russia's full-scale war against Ukraine is further enriched by statistical data reflecting the state of the economies of various countries in the war-affected situation, as well as by the results of public opinion polls conducted both before and during the outbreak of the conflict. Furthermore, evolving efforts to achieve a just peace, as outlined in this monograph, offer promise for future research. It is envisaged that the material presented here will serve as a reference point for scholars studying the crisis management of Russia, not only within the Eurasian region but also in the broader European context.

In conclusion, this monograph provides a robust methodological framework for assessing the validity of theoretical categories (the semantic fields of their definitions), explanatory frameworks and classification schemes. It presents a comprehensive literature review on the Russian-Ukrainian war and the role of the states and societies in the Baltic region in restoring peace. It formulates a conceptual framework that delineates the essence of the crisis caused by the conflict and provides insights into its study to determine the value of the latent qualitative variable, namely the start and end of the Russian-Ukrainian war. The monograph identifies a typology of the conflict termination scenarios prevalent in contemporary international relations and explains the sources of both similarities and differences in the behaviour of policymakers in different countries. It examines differences in social attitudes

10 Jolanta Itrich-Drabarek and Anna Jach

towards the war and peace-making, as well as differences between authorities and citizens in their approach to the conflict. Moreover, it describes the configurations of factors that influence specific patterns of behaviour by policy-makers and citizens throughout the duration and potential resolution of the conflict. Finally, it identifies the threats to human and civil rights during the ongoing conflict and explores the realities of accountability for war crimes after its conclusion.

References

Guriev, S., & Treisman, D. (2023). *Spin dyktatorzy. Nowe oblicze tyranii w XXI wieku*. Trans. A. Żak. Wydawnictwo Otwarte.

Ramalingam, B., Jones, H., Reba, T., & Young, J. (2008, October). *Exploring the Science of Complexity. Ideas and Implications for Development and Humanitarian Efforts* (2nd ed.). Overseas Development Institute. https://es.ircwash.org/sites/default/files/Ramalingam-2008-Exploring.pdf.

Part I
States and their initiatives

1 Values and 'anti-values' in times of war and peace

Jolanta Itrich-Drabarek and Danuta Plecka

Introduction

Values serve as a mechanism for justifying individual preferences, as well as social structure and change. They also provide explanations for actions (and their consequences) undertaken by states and governments in the political sphere. A similar role is assumed by 'anti-values', which often emerge during crisis situations, representing positive or negative responses from individuals and society to the national and international actions of the state. To comprehensively grasp both individual and social attitudes and behaviours, it is imperative to establish connections between individual and cultural differences and similarities regarding value preferences.

The starting point for our analysis will be the theory of Ronald Inglehart, who emphasised the existence of very strong connections between an individual's value hierarchy and the attitudes resulting, as well as the characteristics of individual societies related to their level of development, sense of security and support for post-materialistic values. This is associated with changes in the perception of social roles, quality of life and the level of consolidation of democracy. Economic development favours a departure from norms considered absolute and a shift towards rational, tolerant and participatory values. This theory takes on a different dynamic during wartime, when universally recognised values can transform into 'anti-values', depending on their instrumental use by conflicting parties and the destabilisation of existential security. During war, there is a noticeable tendency to retreat from the values inherent to a democratic regime in favour of an axiology tinged with authoritarianism, arising from the necessity of functioning in a reality requiring strong leadership. In our analysis, we will also incorporate Immanuel Kant's theory of 'democratic peace' and the concept of a 'just war', with St. Augustine being its precursor.

The focal point of our inquiry is to analyse the values pertinent to the political culture of societies during peacetime, and discerning shifts in their hierarchical significance during times of war. In accordance with Inglehart's perspective, we posit that the level of economic development achieved by a society precipitates a reordering of the hierarchy of importance from material

DOI: 10.4324/9781003558040-3

to post-material values. However, we acknowledge that such a trend may be reversed in the context of armed conflict. Furthermore, we ask ourselves whether what we define as values can be transformed into 'anti-values' contingent upon prevailing socio-political circumstances. If so, is there a potential for the reclassification of 'anti-values' as values in peacetime? The results of these investigations will subsequently prompt additional questions as to whether the war in Ukraine shows the characteristics of a 'just war'. Finally, in delineating the comparative nuances between 'democratic peace' and 'undemocratic peace', we aim to discern both the unique and shared values that underpin each.

Hence, our hypothesis posits that during times of peace, societies generally shift away from material values towards post-material values. However, this trend undergoes significant change during time of war, owing to different definitions of values and 'anti-values', depending on the prevailing political circumstances experienced by states and citizens. This phenomenon is intricately linked to factors associated with the political system characterising a community and the political milieu fostering either a 'democratic peace' or a 'non-democratic peace'. The ancillary hypothesis postulates that amid the ongoing Russo-Ukrainian war, a re-evaluation of concepts such as just war, state neutrality, refugee assistance and regional security has occurred in the states surrounding the Baltic Sea. This reassessment is attributed to the scale of the conflict as well as its dynamics and unpredictable course, and together these have collectively contributed to a shift in societal attitudes and the trajectory of political decisions made by the leaders of the states in question. Source-based reconstruction methods will be employed for this purpose. In the context of this chapter, the authors, drawing on democratic peace theory, have formulated their own version, named 'authoritarian peace theory', which serves as a post-Bolshevik paradigm aimed at explaining how façade democracies have engaged genuinely democratic states in war.

The political philosophy underpinning the theory of authoritarian peace has progressively permeated the sphere of its practical application in the 21st century, especially with regard to the foreign and security policies of China, Turkey and Russia. Consequently, an inquiry into the correlation between a state's political system and its actions in the international arena raises questions regarding implications in practice: Is it acceptable to divide the world into Russian, Chinese and American spheres of influence? To what extent does the implementation of solutions transferred from one state to another, championed under banners of freedom, human rights and respect for others, genuinely impact the democratisation processes within societies and states? Is intervention in the territory of another state through the use of armed force permissible under the pretext of combating fascism or defending minority rights? Just as the notions of 'restoration', 'rectification' or 'administration of historical justice' serve as pretexts for armed interventions, the consolidation of leadership power emerges as a primary foreign policy objective for both democratic and non-democratic states. The examination of how the language employed in communicating with the internal and external environments of states engaged in war influences their ethical perception is also crucial.

Reflections on the nature of values

Every political regime shapes its own value system, with the established institutions of the state undertaking the responsibility for socialising citizens based on accepted norms, thereby fostering recognition of specific values within a society. In the context of liberal democracies, these values revolve around a commitment to democratic institutions (including their representativeness), a pluralistic array of values, the accountability of those in power, inter-party and electoral competition, the separation of powers and the protection of minority rights. Additionally, it is pertinent to note that within a liberal democracy, the nature of political rivalry ensures the perpetual presence of one or more electoral players in opposition, an outcome resulting from sovereign decisions made by society. However, this reality does not imply an imminent threat of exclusion from the political arena; both the winner (the ruling party) and the loser of an election (the opposition) represent society in various spheres of its activity (Plecka, 2023). Tolerance, individualism, personal freedom, individual independence and, not least, the values of cooperation and compromise hold equal significance in this context (Bakker, 2020).

Democratic values play a crucial role in building an inclusive community. The characteristics inherent in a democratic regime facilitate discussions concerning the essence of the common good. Within this framework, accepted values impose responsibilities on community members, thereby promoting equal participation of all citizens in the exercise of power (Tam, 1998, p. 7). Consequently, the axiological system and resultant actions are not exclusive to the domain of political elites but extend to individual citizens who form this community. The proposed axiological system, upheld by democratic institutions, is subject to ongoing social scrutiny to align with optimal operational conditions. Through this process, individuals actively engage as part of the community, accept the preferred value system and establish a sense of identification with it. They build a community characterised by openness to 'otherness' and the absence of hostility towards other communities. Its foundational principle lies in the belief that relations can be shaped through compromise forged in negotiation. Consequently, discourse and commitment (Taylor, 1985, p. 188) supported by solidarity, reciprocity and co-responsibility emerge as pivotal elements in the formation of such a community. These features of an inclusive community reflect the values of liberal democracy at the societal level, facilitating peaceful coexistence with other democracies and non-democratic regimes. However, it is essential to acknowledge that this inclusive model of a community also has its inherent limitations.

At the opposite end of the continuum are non-democratic states in which the process of socialisation is based on values (perceived as anti-values in the

16 *Jolanta Itrich-Drabarek and Danuta Plecka*

democratic world) characterised by an iron-fist approach, brutality, no control over authorities and consequently, lack of citizen involvement, resulting in an absence of accountability for decisions made by political leaders. By rejecting value pluralism, these states embrace axiological monism leading to a dearth of political competition. Notably, in the 21st century, autocracies are not primarily established through military coups; rather, autocrats secure electoral victories by employing populist rhetoric rooted in post-truth narratives and social polarisation during campaigns. Recognising the challenge of garnering social legitimacy for authoritarianism in an era of widespread access to information, autocrats exploit the achievements of liberal democracy, subtly appropriating and dismantling the system. Moreover, in the context of the present research issue, autocrats strategically utilise a narrative that contributes to the construction of an exclusive community. Founded on the premise of its uniqueness, this community serves as an instrument for consolidating undemocratic power and opposing other communities.

Among the constitutive features of an exclusive community is the recourse to tradition, serving as a provider of specific tangibles and intangibles. At particular times, places and among specific individuals. This establishes the exclusivity of a community centred around a clearly defined common good. Autocrats employ this rhetoric to solidify their power within society and mobilise it to combat communities outside the sphere of exclusivity (MacIntyre, 2004, pp. 293–294). This is because these external communities lack the distinct characteristics of the exclusive community to which citizens are expected to be loyal, as it is only within this community that the preservation of standards derived from an axiological system allows survival in the most challenging moments of history. Moreover, it facilitates the definition of justice, which in an exclusive community is fundamentally derived from an understanding of the common good (Sandel, 1999, pp. 115–116). It is difficult not to notice that these values are wielded by both autocratic and seemingly democratic powers to justify engaging in warfare, a perfect example being Vladimir Putin and Russia's actions against Ukraine.

It is noteworthy that in a situation of social anxiety and uncertainty about the future, or in the face of extreme phenomena such as famine or war, the observable aspect is not merely a yearning for community but rather an extreme manifestation and confinement within a form of exclusivism. This exclusivism has clearly defined boundaries constructed from tradition (including language), historical experience and a collectively recognised lifestyle, that is, qualities that differentiate one group of people from another. This is accompanied by a belief in the superiority of community over individualism, as the experiences gained through the particularisms of a community. And its traditions enable individuals to comprehend themselves as human beings. War requires individuals to demonstrate loyalty to the community and believe in fulfilling their civic duties towards it. This forms the basis of an individual's moral presence within a specific community, which is an expression of the conviction that it is a value that shapes both present and subsequent generations, offering hope for victory over representatives of hostile communities. Undoubtedly, such attitudes are cultivated by the traditions of a specific community, providing the means to maintain unity across generations. This tradition is more enduring than any established legal norms as it transmits moral models and rules of conduct specific to a particular practice. It can be argued that these traditions constitute the capital of the community, especially relevant in times of war. They transcend individual aspirations, providing a sense of participation in a community whose functioning determines individual development based on bonds of solidarity and the definition of the common good. Thus, during warfare, an inclusive community naturally transforms into an exclusive one as the situation necessitates – people gather around values that were previously latent but become imperative for a military victory.

The phenomenon can be primarily attributed to a lack of individual existential security. Inglehart categorises this trend as 'xenophobic populist authoritarianism' (Inglehart, 1997, p. 78). It is an 'authoritarian reflex' resulting from a societal survival strategy, marked by a shift towards a strong personality, a relatively conscious curtailment of individual rights in favour of collective action, a stress on solidarity with others, adherence to social norms and compliance in actions. This often leads to a xenophobic inclination, with a notable emphasis on obedience to a political leader. The conditions of war intensify the tendency to distance oneself from post-material values, indicative of a perceived existential threat. Furthermore, concepts such as democracy, individualism, tolerance and openness to others become 'anti-values'.

The axiological systems adopted shape the attitudes of both liberal democratic and non-democratic states towards matters of war and peace. It should be remembered that each war dismantles a moral framework grounded in a specific value system. Furthermore, particularly in non-democratic regimes largely founded on social fear, war can assume a distinct value that encourages the adoption of populist rhetoric, the division of the world into 'us' and 'them', and the identification of an enemy both internal to its system and in the international arena. In such contexts, war comes as a value, with an axiological system conveyed by political leaders through propaganda mechanisms, significantly contributing to societies' heightened willingness to employ force in pursuit of political objectives. As previously emphasised, this results primarily from the acknowledged canon of values, which in liberal democratic states might be considered anti-values.

Liberal democracies ground their coexistence with other states on the principle of democratic peace (Kant, 2022). This concept originates from Kantian philosophy, positing a belief in an inner moral law where individuals interact with others in the manner they wish to be treated themselves. This inner moral law is founded on absolute tolerance and trust towards others, constituting the cornerstone of the axiological canon. Simultaneously, it delineates an ample boundary for individual freedom, recognising that such

18   *Jolanta Itrich-Drabarek and Danuta Plecka*

freedom ceases where another's freedom begins (Locke, 1994). Acknowledging the inherent imperfections in human morality, it becomes imperative to establish institutional guarantees to ensure practicality. This is closely linked to the creation of democratic institutions that uphold liberal values within society, while socialising both the masses and their leaders in the light of values such as rationality, personal freedom, individual autonomy, tolerance, interpersonal trust and the norm of reciprocity. In Immanuel Kant's theory of democratic peace, these values contribute to peace between states. The assumption is that the extension of these values beyond the borders of individual states contributes to the maximal possible presence of democratic states globally. This fosters peaceful coexistence on both normative and structural planes. The normative perspective acknowledges that democratic regimes are not inclined to engage in military actions against each other as norms of compromise and co-operation prevent the escalation of conflicts of interest and violent clashes. Conversely, the structural viewpoint assumes that the processes of political mobilisation within a society are intricate and institutionally constrained, naturally imposing limitations on the political leaders of two conflicting democracies. These constraints serve to prevent the violent escalation of conflict and the use of military means for its resolution (Maoz & Russett, 1993, pp. 624–638). Therefore, the democratic peace, arising from institutional constraints as well as the socialisation of societies and political leaders, evolves into a universal value, despite frequent criticisms on two levels. Firstly, it faces scrutiny for permitting military aggression against non-democratic regimes. Secondly, concerns are raised about its verifiability at the societal level.

Values versus the Russian-Ukrainian war

Situations in which democratic states initiate an attack on non-democratic regimes are plausible for several reasons. Firstly, they may occur when a democratic state ensures the transfer of its values to non-democratic counterparts. In such instances, political leaders are steadfast in their belief in the validity of their choices and the necessity to employ the 'ultimate measure' to safeguard the value of democracy. However, this poses the risk of a liberal democratic state adopting a superpower policy, driven by conviction in the arguments for democratic values, as well as temptation towards regional or global hegemony. While this vulnerability is more pronounced in non-democratic states, it is not entirely absent in democratic systems since it is intertwined with domestic politics, the pursuit of social interests and the electoral considerations of political leaders.

The second level of criticism against a democratic peace suggests that while its application and verification is feasible at the state level, individual preferences for an axiological system do not guarantee its preservation (Bakker, 2017). Liberal democracy, which upholds pluralism and tolerance as unequivocal values, assumes that individuals possess the right to formulate their own axiological systems. Although state institutions safeguard the democratic dimension, they can only guide individuals towards the most desirable system of values through socialisation and not coercion. Consequently, illiberal values may take root at individual or community levels within democratic regimes, potentially contributing to social tendencies that escalate conflicts both internally and externally. In this context, the attitudes of political leaders become crucial as they may be convinced of the righteousness of military action. In democratic systems, such decisions require public support and thus political leaders are obligated to provide compelling justifications regarding the necessity of taking military action. This creates a feedback loop, wherein public sentiment undeniably influences the decisions of political leaders, who in turn are compelled to present persuasive arguments to citizens when considering the use of the 'last resort' in conflict resolution.

Leaders of non-democratic states are similarly compelled to do some propaganda in favour of their decisions to conduct war. However, in democratic states, such decisions depend on public acceptance, whereas in non-democratic regimes, they are solely in the hands of leaders who either adeptly employ propaganda or impose their will on society. Importantly, these decisions are exempt from accountability to society, despite their frequent responsiveness to societal needs. A case in point is Russia's aggression against Ukraine, where Vladimir Putin did not seek to justify his decision to Russian society. Instead, over his years in power, he cultivated fertile ground in public consciousness by introducing propaganda slogans concerning the restoration of Russia's superpower status and underscoring commonality in language and territory (Rachman, 2022, p. 13).

Putin emphasised the inevitability of a clash between two political orders: liberal democracy and a non-democratic regime, attributing this to the 'unbridled abuse of force – military force – in international relations' by the United States (Troianovski, 2018). This declaration signified a willingness to take up arms against the order symbolised by liberal democracy, positioning it as a means of defending the exclusivity of the Russian community and countering perceived attempts, propagated for rhetorical purposes, to undermine Russia's greatness (Rachman, 2022, pp. 51–54). The nationalism embedded in Putin's narrative serves a dual purpose. On the one hand, it functions as a propaganda tool, around which he concentrates the public/community to mobilise resentment against an imagined enemy. On the other, the appeal to nationalism seeks to divert attention from internal issues, including privileges for oligarchs, economic deprivation affecting a significant part of society and, ultimately, an attempt to convince the people of the necessity of his continued leadership for collective welfare. The recourse to nationalism is primarily an effort to counter the perceived personal threat to power posed by the values promoted in liberal democracy.

This experience is related to the fear that the democratic values promoted contributed to attempts to overthrow autocratic regimes in certain regions of the former USSR in 2004–2005. This was the case in Georgia and Kyrgyzstan, and most significantly, in the successful overthrow of autocratic power in Ukraine during the Maidan Revolution. Putin did not interpret these events as expressions of independence but rather as actions orchestrated by US intelligence services, aiming to instil liberal democracy in Russia's neighbouring countries and ultimately in Russia itself (Rachman, 2022, p. 59). His apprehensions intensified in 2014 when Ukraine was about to sign an association agreement with the European Union. Under Putin's influence, President Viktor Yanukovych altered course, triggering subsequent waves of protests, Yanukovych's departure from Ukraine, and, in response to these developments, Russia's annexation of Crimea.

This event was the first step towards a full-scale invasion of Ukraine in February 2022. The annexation of Crimea in 2014 served as a test for liberal democracies, in which their ineffective response, through the imposition of relatively limited sanctions in reaction to the Kremlin's actions, emboldened Putin to escalate his activity against Ukraine. This exemplifies how a non-democratic state – Russia – has realised the basic principles of non-democratic peace. Firstly, this regards the principle that non-democratic regimes maintain a state of peace with other states, regardless of their system, when there is no external pressure from the international democratic environment to change the status of their exclusivity – essentially, the principles, norms and values internally recognised by these states. This occurs when democratic states lack the ambition to alter aspects of non-democratic systems. Putin's fear regarding the potential democratisation of Russia, that is, the imposition of values alien to an exclusive community grounded in nationalism, the scale and the power of the Russian state on the global stage, contributed to its attack on Ukraine. While it holds true that democratic states did not overtly condemn the Russian system, Putin perceived events and the actions of political leaders in democratic states differently – he noted the peril of 'infecting' society with democratic values.

Secondly, non-democratic states maintain a state of peace with others when they do not require the identification of an external enemy to pursue internal and ad hoc political objectives. During his tenure, Putin has attacked other states for domestic policy reasons. The Russian military intervention in Georgia in 2008 or the deployment of troops to Syria in 2016 were instances where military actions were designed to divert public attention from the escalating authoritarian standards within the country as well as from persistent issues such as corruption, the enrichment of oligarchs (Putin's allies) at the expense of the broader society, constitutional changes, the ageing of the population, economic conditions and fluctuations in oil and gas prices. Notably, these military actions were also intended to fortify his standing within Russia as a statesman ruling with a firm hand and exerting an impact on international politics. The attack on Ukraine was merely the initial stage of strengthening his position, which was to be consolidated by a swift and uncontested victory. The failure of the attack and the loss of the possibility of a quick triumph contributed to social unrest, resulting in arrests and

Values and 'anti-values' in times of war and peace 21

murders, thereby illustrating that Putin's authority, in addition to relying on populism, post-truth and propaganda, employs well-established authoritarian techniques of violence and repression against the dissatisfied, leading to the collapse of the myth of universal acceptance and success.

Finally, non-democratic states will not initiate an attack on a country with a consolidated democracy and a strong societal conviction, expressed by political elites, about the strength of the state in terms of democratic values. The attack on Ukraine was preceded by specific propaganda efforts, which not only laid the ground for justifying the 2022 attack but, above all, offered evidence of the absence of a consolidated democracy in Ukraine. In fact, it can be said that Ukraine was not so much in the process of consolidating democracy as it was only on a path to consolidation; in other words, the situation could be described as just a pre-consolidation of democracy. Putin capitalised on this situation by pursuing specific courses of action. Firstly, he highlighted historical ties: linguistic, ethnic, cultural and religious. These references were seemingly intended to underscore the uniqueness and exclusivity of belonging to a particular community capable of standing against others. Conversely, Putin often portrayed Ukraine as a failed state, an easy prey for cultural circles adhering to values of liberal democracy. Values that, according to the Russian leader, contradicted the axiological system inherent in the Russian sphere of influence, within which Ukraine was situated. The fear that Ukrainians might embrace democratic values allowed Putin to justify the aggression as a necessary act of self-defence.

This line of argumentation not only proves useful in international relations but also is employed for social mobilisation in safeguarding the values of an exclusive community, as Putin considers the Russian nation to be (Brzeziecki, 2023). From the perspective of the research problem under analysis, the clash of values, concurrently representing a clash of community models, appears inevitable. However, it would be overly simplistic to assert that Russia's attack on Ukraine was solely an attempt to militarily resolve a dispute over values. The conflict has also served as a struggle for spheres of economic and political influence involving both Russia and the democratic states supporting the Ukrainians. It is crucial to point out that for democrats, war is not a value but an act of aggression which poses a threat to human life, even a crime against the principles of peaceful co-existence among diverse societies in the international arena. Thus, war is viewed as a last resort, necessitating defence through all available non-military options for conflict resolution for as long as possible. In contrast, for autocrats, it serves as a tool for social mobilisation, a value around which they can construct propaganda promoting the greatness of their community, while also exploiting it for internal political purposes.

At the same time, it is noteworthy that modern warfare, facilitated by technological advancements, can exhibit extreme precision and align with the criteria of a 'just war'. Without delving into the historical context and analysing shifts in the assumptions of a 'just war', it is important to acknowledge

22 Jolanta Itrich-Drabarek and Danuta Plecka

that this concept became a value in the international arena due to social protests associated with the Vietnam War (Walzer, 2006, pp. 17–18). Similar to liberal democracy's 'democratic peace', the concept of a 'just war' comprises a set of sub-values essential for a comprehensive understanding of the phenomenon. The central value in this context is the protection of civilians, as a 'just war', by definition, restricts the use of force and coercive measures against individuals not engaged in combat. However, this principle extends beyond safeguarding civilians from military action or preventing mass murder. It encompasses a spectrum of military actions or inactions designed for the benefit of civilians, such as ensuring access to drinking water, providing electricity and maintaining a steady food supply. It is crucial to bear in mind that this value has inherent limitations as the standards derived from the principles of a 'just war' are subject to the decisions of political leaders. Therefore, a 'just war' may be employed as a form of propaganda.

Russia's aggression against Ukraine from the outset was a violation of the value of a 'just war'. Putin was well aware that military operations stood a better chance of success if they garnered support from various population groups residing in the conflict zones. Such support was partly secured only in Eastern Ukraine, which traditionally leans towards Russia. In other regions, however, hostile actions against the population were implemented to undermine civilian backing for the Ukrainian military's defensive efforts. Instances include numerous allegations of indiscriminate attacks, such as air strikes on a kindergarten in Ochtyrka, a children's and maternity hospital in Mariupol, and a residential area in Sumy (Amnesty International, 2022). Nevertheless, it was the images and reports of mass atrocities against Ukrainians in Irpin and Bucha that most profoundly shocked international public opinion (Ochab, 2022). Russia also faces accusations of employing cluster munitions, a practice prohibited in civilian-populated areas under the 2008 Convention on Cluster Munitions.[1] Furthermore, as Russian forces withdrew from specific areas, they left behind landmines, a breach of the principles associated with a 'just war' as these pose a threat to civilians. The acquisition of cluster munitions by Ukrainians from the United States and their use since July 2023 seems to place both Russians and Ukrainians on an equal footing here, even if, according to the Ukrainian side, cluster munitions are solely employed to reclaim national territory within internationally recognised borders and are not used in urban areas.

With the escalation of the conflict, Ukrainians have also ceased to apply the value of a 'just war' as their drone attacks have become more frequent. These attacks target not so much civilians but the infrastructure that serves them, such as refineries and power stations in Russia. This represents a notable transformation of values into anti-values and vice versa. Peace functions as a value as long as there is no imperative to defend it, at which point instruments typically associated with warfare come into play. One such instrument is the act of killing other people. In times of peace, someone who stands for human life, perhaps opposing practices like the death penalty, may find

Values and 'anti-values' in times of war and peace   23

themselves compelled to engage in killing during wartime to resist an invader and protect their community. However, this does not change the fact that there emerges axiological relativism, exemplifying the erosion of the moral order in the course of a war.

Also essential to a 'just war' is the assumption that military action will be succeeded by a restoration of the *status quo ante*, meaning that the situation existing before the aggression will be reinstated, eliminating the element of threat posed by the aggressor state from before the attack (Walzer, 2006, p. 115). Therefore, the responsibility falls on the international community to demobilise and disarm the aggressor's army while refraining from implementing changes in domestic policy, such as regime change or the socialisation associated with a different hierarchy of values. This acknowledgement stems from the recognition that such interference would also amount to aggression, a stance not endorsed within the framework of waging a 'just war'. An exception to this principle was observed in the actions taken in support of post-war Germany.

At present, all three principles of a 'just war' are contested by Jeff McMahan, who assumes that if every human being possesses designated human rights, then no one, not even a soldier, holds the right to kill another human being (McMahan, 2006). In essence, the contention is that it is impossible to fight for an unjust cause using just methods. This implies that if Russian soldiers exclusively target Ukrainian soldiers, they are still committing wrongdoing, even if adhering to the rules established by international law. Conversely, Ukrainian soldiers employ violence in self-defence to defend themselves, their fellow citizens and their state. Tomasz Żuradzki argues that the epistemic challenges faced by soldiers cannot serve as a contemporary justification for absolving them of the responsibility for fighting on the wrong side. He adds that with the development of education and the transmission of information, it is difficult to excuse someone for participating in a war that is clearly unjust (Żuradzki, 2010).

Conclusion

Russia's conflict with Ukraine has not only deeply unsettled these nations but also generated a profound shock among residents in the Baltic Sea basin. The region's strong historical memory of the events and aftermath of World War II has led to a resolute and unequivocal condemnation of the war as an evil that not only jeopardises the stability of the entire area but inflicts suffering upon millions of people. By characterising the war in Ukraine as a 'special military operation' aimed at combating 'Ukrainian fascists', Putin exploits a myth originating from the Great Patriotic War fought against the German fascists by the USSR, to which Russia traces its legacy. The term 'fascism' in Russia carries a potent negative emotional charge and is wielded by the Putin regime as the ultimate argument, pre-empting any discussion about the legitimacy of the war it is leading.

Contrary to the ongoing war pushing post-material values into the background, they continue to exert a significant influence on international opinion, particularly in the ethical assessment of the Russian-Ukrainian conflict.

The application of 'autocratic peace theory' to the analysis of the Russian-Ukrainian war has facilitated a thorough examination of the conflict. The findings suggest that non-democratic states maintain peaceful relations with other states (irrespective of their regime) when there is an absence of pressure from the democratic international environment to alter the status of their exclusivity, encompassing principles, norms and values internally recognised by these states. This state of peace prevails when democratic states lack the ambition to transform non-democratic entities. Non-democratic states also remain at peace when they do not need to seek an external enemy to pursue internal and ad hoc political objectives. Furthermore, non-democratic states will not succeed in capturing with their propaganda the minds of the populations of states with a consolidated democracy and a political elite grounded in democratic values.

Note

1 It should be emphasised here that neither Russia nor Ukraine is a party to the Convention.

References

Amnesty International. (2022, February 27). *Ukraine: Cluster Munitions Kill Child and Two Other Civilians Taking Shelter at a Preschool February 27*. www.amnesty.org/en/latest/news/2022/02/ukraine-cluster-munitions-kill-child-and-two-other-civilians-taking-shelter-at-a-preschool/

Bakker, F. E. (2017). Do liberal norms matter? A cross-regime experimental investigation of the normative explanation of the democratic peace thesis in China and The Netherlands. *Acta Politica*, 52(4), 521–543.

Bakker, F. E. (2020). The microfoundations of normative democratic peace theory: Experiments in the US, Russia and China. *Political Research Exchange*, 2(1), 2–31.

Brzeziecki, A. (2023, August 18). Rosja to nie jest państwo europejskie. *Gazeta Wyborcza*, 22–23.

Inglehart, R. (1997). *Modernization and Postmodernization* (p. 78). Princeton University Press.

Kant, I. (2022). *Krytyka czystego rozumu*. Onepress.

Locke, J. (1994). *Dwa traktaty o rządzie*. Wydawnictwo Naukowe PWN.

MacIntyre, A. (2004). Czy patriotyzm jest cnotą? In P. Śpiewak (Ed.), *Komunitarianie. Wybór tekstów*. Aletheia.

Maoz, Z., & Russett, B. (1993). Normative and structural causes of democratic peace 1946–1986. *American Political Science Journal*, 87(3), 624–638.

McMahan, J. (2006). The ethics of killing in war. *Philosophia*, 34, 23–41.

Ochab, E. U. (2022, April 3). As Russian troops retreat from Irpin and Bucha, more evidence of Putin's war crimes emerges. *Forbes*. www.forbes.com/sites/ewelinaochab/2022/04/03/more-evidence-of-putins-war-crimes-in-irpin-and-bucha-ukraine/?sh=66ab5c8f629a

Values and 'anti-values' in times of war and peace   25

Plecka, D. (2023) *O gentelmenach w polityce. Demokracja otwarta a polityczne kompetencje obywatelskie w kontekście kryzysu demokracji I prób jego przezwyciężenia*. Wydawnictwo Adam Marszałek.

Rachman, G. (2022). *The Age of the Strongman: How the Cult of the Leader Threatens Democracy Around the World*. Random House Ltd.

Sandel, M. (1999). The political theory of the procedural republic. In R. B. Reich (Ed.), *The Power of Public Ideas* (pp. 115–116). Ballinger Publishing Company.

Tam, H. (1998). *Communitarianism: A New Agenda for Politics and Citizenship*. Red Globe Press. DOI: 10.1007/978-1-349-26489-6

Taylor, C. (1985). Atomism: Philosophy and the Human Sciences. *Philosophical Papers, 3,* 4–16.

Troianovski, A. (2018, July 12). Branding Putin. *Washington Post*, 25–26.

Walzer, M. (2006). *Arguing about War*. Yale University Press.

Żuradzki, T. (2010). Etyka wojny a dopuszczalność zabijania. *Diametros, 25,* 12–14.

2 The Baltic Sea states in the face of war and peace

Joanna Kozierska, Joanna Marszałek-Kawa, Beata Słobodzian and Agata Włodkowska

Introduction

Russia's aggression against Ukraine in February 2022 forced NATO and its member states to redefine foreign and security policy. Four months after the Russian invasion, a NATO summit took place in Madrid on 28–30 June, where a number of ground-breaking decisions were taken, such as consent to the accession of Sweden and Finland and approval of the new NATO Strategic Concept. The expansion of membership to include these two states makes the Baltic an 'inland' NATO sea, strengthening the voice of Poland and the Baltic states, that is the countries that since 1991 have adopted a tough stance towards Russia, and emphasise the importance of strengthening the eastern flank against potential aggression from Moscow.

The most important change in comparison with the previous Strategic Concept of 2010 is the recognition of the Russian Federation (RF) as 'the most significant and direct threat to Allies' security and to peace and stability in the Euro-Atlantic area' (NATO, 2022, p. 4). Another important provision is the one concerning the possibility of aggression against the sovereignty and integrity of NATO member states as well as Russia striving to 'establish spheres of influence and direct control through coercion, subversion, aggression and annexation' (NATO, 2022, p. 4) and using conventional, cyber and hybrid means against NATO members and partners. The most recent strategy also pays attention to the Baltic Sea:

> In the High North, its capability to disrupt Allied reinforcements and freedom of navigation across the North Atlantic is a strategic challenge to the Alliance. Moscow's military build-up, including in the Baltic, Black and Mediterranean Sea regions, along with its military integration with Belarus, challenge our security and interests.
>
> (NATO, 2022, p. 4)

Apart from adopting the strategic concept for Baltic NATO members, another key decision was the one regarding an increase in the operational capabilities of NATO forces, that is a shift from a policy of deterrence to

DOI: 10.4324/9781003558040-4

The Baltic Sea states in the face of war and peace   27

enhanced forward defence. The latter involves a significant strengthening of NATO's eastern flank, including increasing the number of NATO troops in Poland and the Baltic states.

The past and the present

As the sole EU and NATO member which borders Ukraine as well as Russia and Belarus, Poland is the only one among the states discussed for which the Russian aggression of 24 February 2022 'has the dimension of existential reflection' (Ministry of Foreign Affairs of Poland, 2023, p. 2). The development of the situation in Ukraine remains equally relevant for the three Baltic states. A day before the war broke out, the heads of diplomacy from these three countries came to Kyiv for a two-day visit. On the day of the attack, they remained in the city and issued a strong statement, in which they committed themselves to 'do anything possible' (Rinkēvičs, 2022) to aid the Ukrainians. These four states from the beginning urged the allies to provide more military support, and in the following days they focused on pressuring European partners, including Germany, to cut Russia's access to SWIFT or to impose other economic sanctions and to grant Ukraine the status of an EU candidate. In Lithuania, a state of emergency was introduced from 24 February to 10 March. With the start of the military operations in Ukraine, all the Baltic states suspended the broadcasting of Russian media channels due to their bias and disinformation about the situation. In September 2022, the Latvian parliament changed the education law, significantly limiting Russian lessons in Latvian schools.[1] This was a continuation of earlier such activities (e.g. in 2018 teaching in Latvian became compulsory in schools for the Russian minority), and these have significantly intensified since the outbreak of the war. The Latvian Ministry of Economics decided that its officials will henceforth use only Latvian to communicate internally as well as externally, including to the media. In December 2022, the Estonian parliament decided to introduce obligatory teaching in Estonian to all kindergartens and schools.

Motivated by Russian aggression, each of the countries analysed updated their security strategies or developed documents aimed at increasing state security. Latvia, Poland and Lithuania still use strategies from the pre-invasion period (Polish and Latvian documents were adopted in 2020, and the Lithuanian one in 2021). These documents were considered sufficiently up-to-date; all of them recognise the RF as the greatest threat to state security,[2] while collective defence and the NATO deterrence strategy as well as defence cooperation with the United States are perceived as the main security guarantees (*Valsts aizsardzības koncepcija*, 2020; the National Security Strategy of the Republic of Poland, 2020; Seimas of the Republic of Lithuania, 2021). The Latvian strategy provides for a minimum defence spending of 2% of GDP, while the Polish one aims to achieve 2.5% GDP in 2024 (Szymański, 2020). Furthermore, in May 2022, Lithuania adopted a resistance training strategy. As a result of Yevgeny Prigozhin's rebellion in Russia, in June

28   *Kozierska et al.*

2023, Lithuanian authorities updated their border defence plan (asty/kab, 2023). In March 2022 Poland passed the Homeland Defence Act (*Ustawa z dnia 11 marca 2022 r. o obronie Ojczyzny*), whose provisions include additional financing for the Polish Army and increasing its size to approximately 300,000 soldiers (250,000 professional soldiers and 50,000 members of Territorial Defence Forces). In early 2023, Estonia adopted an updated version of the national security concept, referring to NATO's latest Strategic Concept.

In the context of the research topic, the most important provision is in defining Russia as the greatest threat to the national security of Poland. The document also includes a provision regarding increased defence spending in the subsequent years, reaching a minimum of 3% GDP, as well as the financing of non-military activities aimed at protecting the population (*Ustawa z dnia 11 marca 2022 r. o obronie Ojczyzny*).

The invasion of Ukraine also caused a revision of Denmark's security policy, and this included the announcement of a new security and foreign policy on 16 May 2023 (Ministry of Foreign Affairs of Denmark, 2023a).[3] This strategy is based on three priorities: (1) increasing the security of Denmark and Europe, (2) strengthening and creating global partnerships, and (3) building a strong and resilient society with regard to supply chains, energy security and critical infrastructure. These goals are an element of continued efforts to support Ukraine, as well as politically and economically to isolate Russia in the international arena. It was also announced that defence spending will have increased to 2% GDP by 2030, and that Denmark would join the EU's Common Security and Defence Policy (CSDP).[4] However, Denmark's security would still be based on close ties with the United States and NATO. Already in February 2022, Denmark began negotiations with the United States on a new defence agreement, providing for the possibility of stationing US armed forces and weapons there, which for Denmark would be a ground-breaking shift. One of the latest decisions was the announcement of the government's proposal for a new Defence Agreement for 2024–2033 (the previous one covered the period of 2018–2023). It provides for additional defence spending of 19.2 billion euros during the following decade. The document also emphasised the importance of Denmark's immediate neighbourhood in ensuring the country's security, which means the Baltic region, encompassing all Baltic states as well as the North Sea and the High North, including Greenland.

Although Germany shares no border with Russia or Ukraine, the events of 24 February 2022 were for German foreign and security policy a turning point (*Zeitenwende*),[5] with the RF's aggression proving the most important political event since the unification of Germany in 1991. For Germans, it is not only the symbolic ending of the post–Cold War era but also a confirmation of the failure of their *Ostpolitik*.[6] The outbreak of war forced Germany to redefine its international role as a civil power (*Zivilmacht*), to strengthen its military, to reform the *Bundeswehr* and to increase defence expenditure. To the latter aim, besides a commitment to spend 2% GDP on defence, an

The Baltic Sea states in the face of war and peace   29

earmarked fund of 100 billion euros was established to purchase the weapons and equipment most needed for the German armed forces.

A symbol of the *Zeitenwende* was the announcement in June 2023 of the National Defence Strategy, the first in the history of the Federal Republic of Germany (*Bundesregierung*, 2023). Its most crucial provisions include firstly, defining Russia as the greatest threat in the Euro-Atlantic area; secondly, perceiving NATO as an institution of key importance in ensuring Germany's security; thirdly, working towards maintaining close relations with NATO and the United States while simultaneously strengthening the European pillar of NATO so that it can operate independently. Germany is also interested in the *Bundeswehr* assuming a role as a pillar of conventional defence in Europe. As to defence spending, the document declares Germany's contribution of 2% GDP for NATO defence capabilities (*Bundesregierung*, 2023, p. 13). Importantly, Germany's goal is to avoid the direct involvement of NATO and the EU in the war.

In many of the member states, the debate on compulsory military service had already been ignited by the Russian annexation of Crimea in 2014. Lithuania returned to partial conscription in 2015, and a return to general conscription is considered. Latvian authorities have already taken this step, restoring compulsory military service from 1 January 2024.[7] This issue has been also debated in Germany, where social support for returning to compulsory military service (suspended in 2011) is high (61%) (Ipsos, 2023). Poland does not intend to reintroduce general conscription while Denmark has a compulsory military training for 18-year-olds that lasts from 4 to 12 months.

Another consequence of Russian aggression were decisions regarding aid for Ukraine, which included arms supplies. In terms of overall government support for Ukraine (as of 31 July 2023) the top two contributors are the United States and the EU (Kiel Institute for the World Economy, n.d.). Germany is third (military aid 17.1 billion,[8] humanitarian aid 2.48 billion and financial aid 1.3 billion),[9] with Poland in eighth place (3 billion, 0.35 billion and 0.92 billion, respectively) and Denmark in tenth (3.5 billion of military aid and 0.26 billion of humanitarian aid). Lithuania, Estonia and Latvia are 18th, 23rd and 25th, respectively. Purely in terms of military aid, Germany is 2nd, Denmark 5th and Poland 6th, while the Baltic states are 12th (Lithuania), 16th (Estonia) and 18th (Latvia).

However, considering GDP, the most significant military aid for Ukraine comes from the Baltic states and Poland. It should be highlighted that Germany's stance on supplies of military equipment was inconsistent, which could be interpreted as unwillingness to help the attacked state and has negatively impacted Germany's international image.[10] Explanations for delays in providing military aid included the danger of prolonging the conflict, which in turn increases the number of casualties; however, these delays were also criticised due to the growing number of victims among the Ukrainians exposed to the criminal activities of the Russian troops and the decreased chances of

30 *Kozierska et al.*

Table 2.1 The number of refugees from Ukraine (as of June/July 2023)

Germany	Poland	Estonia	Lithuania	Denmark	Latvia
1,076,680	999,690	48,580	48,160	41,305	38,145

Source: Statista (n.d.)

Ukraine winning the war. In this aspect, German policy follows the other states, predominantly the United States.

The expenses borne by the governments also include those connected to aid for refugees. As of the end of July 2023, Poland allocated 15.42 billion euros for this purpose, Germany 13.9 billion, Denmark 0.49 billion, Lithuania 0.43 billion, Estonia 0.38 billion and Latvia 0.38 billion (Kiel Institute for the World Economy, n.d.).

Germany remains one of the main and most attractive destinations for refugees from Ukraine (Table 2.1). Reasons include higher salaries and lower costs of living as well as demand for construction workers.[11] Germany is also the most popular destination (besides Finland, Spain and Italy) among Russian political immigrants. Since February 2022, the German state has granted almost 32,000 national visas to Russians.[12] In contrast to other states, the attitude among Germans towards Russians is positive due to historical sentiments and the fact that the younger generation of Russians is well integrated within German society (Domańska, 2023). Meanwhile, Poland, Lithuania, Latvia and Estonia have almost entirely ceased issuing entry visas for Russians. Exceptions are made, for instance, to the opponents of Putin's regime or for people who have to cross the Polish-Russian border due to their job such as lorry drivers and diplomats, as well as the holders of a Pole's Card and family members of citizens of Poland and other EU countries.

Military aid for Ukraine and the maintenance of Ukrainian refugees and Russian political immigrants are not the only burdens of the analysed countries. With the limitation of Russian energy supplies, the states of the Baltic region had to look for alternative energy sources and deal with high energy prices and rising inflation. For example, Germany decided to re-launch closed coal power plants and extend the life cycles of nuclear power stations despite the decision to abandon this type of power. It also concluded agreements on LNG gas deliveries from the United States, Norway, Qatar, Saudi Arabia and Canada. As of 1 April 2022, Russian natural gas stopped flowing into Latvia, Estonia and Lithuania, which resulted in the highest-ever increases in energy prices in these countries and the highest inflation rate in the EU. To disconnect from the Russian energy system, in August 2023, the Baltic states decided to integrate their energy systems with the EU grid (Tidey, 2023). The RF's aggression made it necessary to speed up the launch of the Baltic Pipe, which took place in September 2022, and of the North-South Gas Corridor. Naftoport, opened in 1991 in Gdańsk, to ensure to some extent energy security in the gas sector, and currently guarantees crude oil supplies, which is confirmed by statistical data. The Russo-Ukrainian conflict has also directly translated into the strengthening of energy transformation process in Denmark. In coming years, decreasing dependence on Russia and increasing energy self-sufficiency will be significant issues for many countries.

The future

Efforts to initiate peace talks between Russia and Ukraine have been underway since the very beginning of the conflict, with engagement from Belarus, Türkiye and China. However, none of these endeavours has been successful. One of the most important peace talks took place in Copenhagen (24 June 2023), involving 15 participating states, and in Saudi Arabia (5–6 August 2023), with over 40 states and institutions representing almost all world regions. Among the participants of the talks in Jeddah were the United States, China, Brazil and India as well as all the states of the Baltic region, except Russia. Despite such massive diplomatic involvement, the peace talks in Saudi Arabia brought no direct results. Any future peace process is likely to again require participation of global powers. Probably too, the Baltic states, unwilling to be a mere audience to these hypothetical negotiations, will attempt to become more active participants. The emerging suggestions of 'land for peace'[13] seem hardly acceptable for the states that are located closest to the conflict and consequently feel most threatened by Russia. The governments of Poland and the Baltic states clearly envision Russia's defeat as the end of this conflict. The representatives of these states emphasise that in order to ensure peace and stability in Europe, Ukraine's path to the EU and NATO should be quickly determined. They also maintain that Ukraine should make the final decision as to the terms of peace (Sejm Rzeczpospolitej Polskiej, 2023).

Meanwhile, Germany views this issue in a different light. During the peace talks in Jeddah, Chancellor Olaf Scholz called for the intensification of diplomatic efforts aimed at ending the conflict. At the same time Berlin wanted to play a significant role in future negotiations between Ukraine and Russia, and therefore limited the deliveries of weapons to Ukraine in several cases. An example here is the question of the supply of Taurus cruise missiles, the transfer of which to Ukraine was conditional on an exclusion of attacks on Russian territory (Larson, 2023). It should be noted that despite crises related to conflicts of economic interests and frustration caused by Ukraine's expectations (i.e. fast-tracking of its accession to NATO and the EU), the states of the Baltic region actively pursue diplomatic means supporting Ukraine in its pro-Western aspirations. Already on 27 February 2022, Mateusz Morawiecki, the prime minister of Poland, and Janez Janša, prime minister of Slovenia, proposed a plan for the rapid integration of Ukraine with the EU by 2030 in an official letter to Charles Michel, the president of the European Council. On 28 February 2022, the presidents of Bulgaria, Czechia, Estonia, Latvia,

Lithuania, Poland, Slovakia and Slovenia issued an open letter calling on EU member states to provide the maximum political support for Ukraine and to enable EU institutions to take steps to immediately grant Ukraine the status of candidate for the EU and open the negotiation process (Office of the President of the Republic of Lithuania, 2022). After that, multiple similar appeals were issued by the governments of the Baltic states and Poland. Ukraine's EU membership is supported also by Denmark and Germany, albeit their support does not seem as unconditional as that of Poland and the Baltic states. It should be mentioned that by June 2023, Ukraine had fully met only two out of seven conditions necessary to open accession talks with the EU.

Another question crucial for the states discussed is Ukraine's membership of NATO. The Vilnius summit of 11–12 July 2023 which raised this issue was of historical importance. Decisions were made regarding Sweden's accession, and a number of agreements were concluded to strengthen the security of the CEE region. Regional defence plans based on the existing strategy concepts and dedicated to the north (European Arctic and northern Atlantic), the south (the Mediterranean and the Black Sea region) and the centre (consisting of the Baltic Sea region, which is of interest to Poland, and Central Europe) were accepted as well. The regional plans provide for defence from the first days of any potential conflict, which is particularly important for the Baltic states as the previous NATO strategy assumed that in the case of an armed conflict these states would have to defend themselves against an attack on their own until the allies came to their aid. During the meeting, the provisions of the NATO strategic concept of (2022), including those concerning the threat from Russia as well as maintaining the rotational presence of battalion battle groups in Lithuania, Latvia, Estonia and Poland were restated, while the readiness to transform them into brigades was also agreed upon. Before the summit, Germany declared that it was ready to gradually deploy a 4,000-strong brigade in Lithuania as a permanent force. This decision demonstrates the evolution of Germany's stance on NATO's collective defence and an increase in its military involvement. Back in 2016, Germany had supported the application of deterrence and dialogue principle (2D) towards Russia and agreed only to the rotational presence of NATO forces on the eastern flank (in less than a brigade's strength). From 2022, they became the framework nation of the battalion in Lithuania and started to actively participate in military exercises in the Baltic states. The Vilnius NATO summit also upheld agreements from the Wales summit in 2014 regarding defence spending at the level of 2% GDP. According to the *Defence Expenditure of NATO Countries*, in 2023, expenditure at this level was reached by only 11 member states, including Poland (3.9%), Estonia (2.7%), Lithuania (2.5%) and Latvia (2.27) (NATO, 2023). In 2023, Germany declared defence spending below 2% at 1.57%.

One of the key topics of the Vilnius NATO summit was Ukraine's membership. No invitation was issued, nor was a clear prospect for membership delineated. However, the Bucharest commitments of 2008 regarding Ukraine

The Baltic Sea states in the face of war and peace 33

becoming a member of NATO were repeated. At the Vilnius summit, it was stressed that Ukraine's membership requires the acceptance of all its members, as well as meeting conditions, above all the end of the conflict. Lack of a uniform opinion on Ukraine's membership confirms the divergence of stances. Poland, Lithuania, Latvia and Estonia are in favour of a promise for Ukraine's accession and the alliance's guarantees for it. For these states, covering Ukraine with the guarantees of Art. 5 is one way to ensure long-term security in Eastern Europe (Sejm Rzeczpospolitej Polskiej, 2023). Germany is one of the states that view this issue differently, opting for the condition of ending the conflict and focusing on military aid. As to Ukraine's accession to NATO, Germany wants to make the decision only after the war ends (Bielecki, 2023).

Besides Ukraine's NATO membership, an issue that will be crucial in the future is not only to put an end to the conflict but also the post-war reconstruction of Ukraine. No matter when the war ends and which scenario will follow, the governments of the states providing political and military aid undertake activities aiming to develop the principles of economic co-operation. Its main goal will be to rebuild Ukraine. According to the World Bank report published in March 2023, the costs will amount to almost 411 billion dollars (World Bank, 2023), while the president of Ukraine, Volodymyr Zelenskyy, estimated that the reconstruction costs may exceed 1 trillion dollars (Presidential Office of Ukraine, 2022). The scale of war destruction in Ukraine is gigantic; no matter which calculation is more precise, the challenge will be immense, and the reconstruction process itself will be burdened by multiple threats. An obvious risk is the security of investments; hence the need for appropriate guarantees. It needs to be remembered here that corruption is a major problem in Ukraine which, in the 2022 Corruption Perception Index compiled by Transparency International, was classified in a distant 118th place (Transparency International, n.d.). According to the official data of the Ministry for the Economy in Ukraine, the value of the grey sector is 30% of the country's GDP (Piątek, 2022, p. 41). Another significant problem is that entrepreneurs interested in cooperating with Ukrainian entities in reconstruction efforts may encounter bureaucracy. There are also challenges related to conflicts of interest, such as the one on interstate relations connected to the trade in Ukrainian grain which flooded the EU market, causing serious problems to farmers in Poland, Hungary, Bulgaria, Romania and Slovakia. Four of these states (but not Hungary) have been providing significant (in proportion to their GDP) support for Ukraine (European Commission, 2023).

The challenge that will be the construction of a new post-war Ukraine will undoubtedly require close cooperation of the international community as well as an appropriate plan. Ukraine is a country with a population of almost 30 million, with rich mineral deposits and fertile soils. These natural resources and a strong agricultural sector will be competition for EU states.

In April 2022, President Zelenskyy approved the establishment of the National Council for the Recovery of Ukraine from the War. The main tasks

34 Kozierska et al.

of the council include developing a Plan for Post-War Reconstruction and Development; preparing proposals for the most important reforms, the implementation of which will be necessary during the war and in the post-war period; as well as preparing strategic initiatives and draft regulations, whose adoption and implementation will be necessary for the effective functioning and reconstruction of Ukraine in the war and post-war periods. The council prepared a draft National Reconstruction Plan for Ukraine (NPOU) and presented it during an international conference in Lugano in July 2022 (Ukraine Recovery Conference, 2022b). This plan described not only the reconstruction of Ukraine but also the transformation and modernisation of the state and its economy. It indicated the need to deepen integration processes with Europe, to ensure full access to the markets of the EU and G7 countries, and to create an environment conducive to the development of entrepreneurship and macro-financial stability. Conference participants, among them leaders of over 40 countries and international organisations, formulated seven main principles for the reconstruction of Ukraine (the so-called Lugano Principles). The most important of them are (1) focus on internal reforms (limiting the influence of oligarchs and combating corruption); (2) the rule of law; (3) gender equality; (4) sustainable development and (5) democratic participation of the Ukrainian society in the reconstruction[14] (Ukraine Recovery Conference, 2022a). Hence the reconstruction should be based on the principle *Build Back Better, Ukraine*. According to Ukrainian assumptions presented in Lugano, it is supposed to take place at two levels: regional, involving cooperation with foreign partners responsible for the recovery of individual regions; and industrial, aided by specific foreign investors. During the conference, Denys Smyhal, the Ukrainian prime minister, presented a map for the planned regional reconstruction, where governments of the Baltic region states were to agree to engage in the reconstruction of specific towns and regions. Poland together with Italy was to be responsible for the reconstruction of Donetsk, Denmark of Mykolaiv,[15] and Germany of Chernihiv. Lithuania, Latvia and Estonia also pointed to specific areas and activities they would like to support (Ukraine Recovery Conference, 2022a). During the second Ukraine Recovery Conference (URC, 2023), which took place in London in June, Oleksandr Kubrakov, deputy prime minister for restoration of Ukraine, head of the Ministry for Communities, Territories and Infrastructure Development, presented the Ukrainian vision of the reconstruction, pointing out that it has already begun on almost a full scale, especially with regard to roads, bridges and export corridors. He also underscored the need for financial, expert and technical support from international partners (Ukraine Recovery Conference, 2023).

At the URC conference in London, the German Minister for Economic Cooperation and Development, Svenja Schulze, stated that the costs of Ukraine's reconstruction should be covered by Russia, thus echoing the opinions expressed many months earlier by representatives of Poland and the Baltic states who demanded that the European Commission should accelerate work on using frozen Russian assets to support the reconstruction (Rankin, 2023).

The representatives of governments from the Baltic region states were active participants in both conferences. In Lugano those from Vilnius underlined the validity of sanctions against Russia, calling on the EU and all non-EU states which had imposed sanctions to establish a legal mechanism for seizing frozen assets and improving sanctions effectiveness. The German government pointed to the rebuilding of a free and democratic Ukraine as a shared goal, and to reconstruction, recovery and reforms as a strategic task for the EU in the coming years. Further emphasising their involvement in the rebuilding of Ukraine, Estonia expressed willingness to organising the Ukraine Recovery Conference in 2024 (Ukraine Recovery Conference, 2022b). Polish diplomats remarked that the reconstruction process should not be limited to standard reconstruction, aiming instead to lay a foundation for long-term development so that Ukraine can become a strong, citizen-friendly democratic European state. They pointed out that Poland wants to rebuild Ukraine in collaboration with the Ukrainians (Ukraine Recovery Conference, 2022b).

Despite the ongoing war, we should be aware that the process of revitalising Ukraine will be expensive and should be implemented on the basis of a plan. In the Baltic region states this topic is a subject of lively debate. Numerous conferences and meetings have been organised on possible involvement in the reconstruction of Ukraine. During economic congresses, politicians, practitioners and entrepreneurs seek the best solutions in which the primary goal is to create good conditions for local businessmen to operate in Ukraine as well as to develop an effective, transparent system for controlling the huge amounts of money that will be going there. Besides the summits in Lugano and London, one of the most important initiatives was the conference organised in Berlin (by the European Commission and Germany, which chaired the G-7 group) in October 2022. It was devoted not only to the restoration of Ukraine but also to its modernisation, for example, by consolidating activities that support Ukraine's efforts to become a member of the EU.

Apart from large international conferences, the Baltic region states have organised a number of smaller initiatives, often local in character. Their goal is to facilitate contacts of local business owners with Ukrainian officials and entrepreneurs. Examples include conferences such as 'Europe – Poland – Ukraine: Rebuild Together' organised in Poland by the Union of Entrepreneurs and Employers (Związek Przedsiębiorców i Pracodawców, 2023), the international conference 'Rebuilding Ukraine' organised in Lithuania on the initiative of its Ministry of the Economy, and 'Innovation' (Ministry of the Economy and Innovation of the Republic of Lithuania, 2022), and finally the conference 'Recovery Forum of the Zhytomyr region' organised by the Estonian Ministry of Foreign Affairs (Ministry of Foreign Affairs of Estonia, 2022). There are also other ways in which states can become involved in order to facilitate cooperation with Ukrainian parties; for example, the

German government created an internet portal *Plattform Wiederaufbau Ukraine*, where non-governmental organisations and agencies based in Germany can find information and contact data if they want to participate in the reconstruction (*Bundesregierung*, n. d.). The goal of this platform is to strengthen the German contribution and, above all, to help German entities become involved in this process.

Conclusion

Russia's aggression against Ukraine in February 2022 forced the states of the Baltic region to react quickly and extensively to the changing international situation. The highly unfavourable security situation in Europe provoked a change in the foreign and security policies pursued by these states and convinced them to seek support from the allies within the EU and NATO. This was particularly true in the case of Poland and the Baltic states who unequivocally perceived the conflict between the RF and Ukraine as a situation directly threatening their own security. The NATO summit in Madrid in June 2022 strengthened this conviction as Russia was recognised there to be the greatest threat to peace and stability in the Euro-Atlantic area. When the conflict broke out, the analysed states revised their own security strategies so that in changing conditions, they could better respond to new threats. Furthermore, Poland, Lithuania, Latvia and Estonia recognised that the acceleration of Ukraine's accession to the EU and NATO is a guarantee of the security in the region. These processes are also supported by Germany and Denmark, yet in these cases, the support depends on a variety of factors.

Since the beginning of the war, the Baltic region states have become a destination for Ukrainian refugees. This massive, sudden influx of people fleeing the war forced these countries to adapt quickly to secure funds for aiding refugees (food, housing, medical care and education).

The support provided for Ukraine is a significant burden on the budgets of the Baltic region states. The share of military, humanitarian and financial aid in their GDP ranges from 0.5% in the case of Germany to as much as 1.4% in the case of Lithuania. What should be remembered, however, is that these states see an opportunity for their economies that the process of post-war reconstruction of Ukraine can offer. The states demonstrate their interest in the activities undertaken in the international arena that are aimed at creating a new future together with Ukraine. They also involve themselves in peace initiatives although their opinions regarding chances for peace differ.

From the beginning of the conflict, various, more or less relevant formulas for peace have appeared, yet none of them has been implemented, even partially. This situation is to the detriment of Ukraine. As the conflict continues with no end in sight, the rest of the world may lose interest. The enthusiasm for defending Ukraine may diminish, while the internal interests of political

The Baltic Sea states in the face of war and peace 37

actors that so far have offered their unqualified support can and will determine the willingness to help and the scope of aid provided.

Concluding, the assistance provided to Ukraine by NATO member states of the Baltic region is among the largest, regardless of whether we are considering political declarations of support, help in supplying military equipment, accepting refugees or political and financial involvement in the process of Ukraine's reconstruction. Yet the future of such assistance may remain in doubt.

Notes

1 Russian-speaking minorities are a significant part of the population of the Baltic states: 6% in Lithuania, 32% in Latvia and ca. 27% in Estonia. Although a large part of these residents condemned the Russian aggression and expressed solidarity with the defenders of Ukraine, tensions with Russian and Belarusian minorities have significantly increased, particularly in Latvia and Estonia.
2 Lithuania named also Belarus and China as threats.
3 The previous version was published in January 2022.
4 Since the Maastricht Treaty came into force (1993), Denmark used the opt-out clauses on four dimensions of EU policy. One of them was CSDP.
5 The phrase was used by Chancellor Olaf Scholz during his historic address to Bundestag on 27 February 2022 (Press and Information Office of the Federal Government, 2023).
6 According to it, 'The security of Europe can only be built with Russia, not against it' (Gotkowska, 2022).
7 In Estonia and Denmark, military service is compulsory. After the Russian aggression, there have been voices that it should be extended: from 8–11 to 12 or 18 months in Estonia, and from 4 to 8–12 months in Denmark.
8 All amounts are given in euros.
9 Both aid actually provided and that which was only declared.
10 Until the announcement of the *Zeitenwende* policy, there had been a ban on sending weapons to regions with ongoing armed conflicts.
11 Germany is running an ongoing project for the thermo-modernisation of older buildings financed by the European Reconstruction Fund.
12 It allows its holder to stay in Germany for a longer period and take up work (SchengenVisaInfo.com, 2023).
13 NATO chief of staff, Stian Jenssen, even suggested that Ukraine should cede territory and become a member of NATO in order to end the war with Russia. However, he soon apologised for that speech, calling it a mistake.
14 Specific principles quoted in the final document of the conference are partnership, reform focus, transparency, accountability and rule of law, democratic participation, multi-stakeholder engagement, gender equality and inclusion, and sustainability.
15 In July 2023, Denmark announced the 1st Reconstruction Package of the Ukraine Fund of 615 million Danish crowns, whose main aims are assistance in rebuilding schools, hospitals, clinics, bomb shelters, water, heating and energy supply systems, as well as support for the population in war-afflicted territories, in particular the region of and the port city of Mykolaiv (Ministry of Foreign Affairs of Denmark, 2023b).

38 *Kozierska et al.*

References

asty/kab. (2023, June 28). Litwa aktualizuje plan ochrony granic, w razie konieczności szybsza reakcja wojska. *TVN24*. https://tvn24.pl/swiat/litwa-rzad-aktualizuje-plan-ochrony-granic-w-razie-koniecznosci-szybsza-reakcja-wojska-7193683

Bielecki, J. (2023, July 7). Minister obrony Niemiec, Boris Pistorius, o Ukrainie w NATO: Warunki ustalimy po wojnie. *Rzeczpospolita*. www.rp.pl/polityka/art38687171-minister-obrony-niemiec-boris-pistorius-o-ukrainie-w-nato-warunki-ustalimy-po-wojnie

Bundesregierung. (2023, June). *Wehrhaft. Resilient. Nachhaltig. Integrierte Sicherheit für Deutschland. Nationale Sicherheitsstrategie.* www.nationalesicherheitsstrategie.de/Sicherheitsstrategie-DE.pdf

Bundesregierung. (n.d.). *Plattform Wiederaufbau Ukraine.* www.ukraine-wiederaufbauen.de/ukraine

Domańska, M. (2023, July 4). Rosyjska emigracja polityczna nowej fali w Niemczech. Struktury, działalność, perspektywy. *Ośrodek Studiów Wschodnich.* www.osw.waw.pl/pl/publikacje/raport-osw/2023-07-04/rosyjska-emigracja-polityczna-nowej-fali-w-niemczech

European Commission. (2023). *Commission Staff Working Document.* https://neighbourhood-enlargement.ec.europa.eu/system/files/202311/SWD_2023_699%20Ukraine%20report.pdf

Gotkowska, J. (2022, March 30). The war in Ukraine: Consequences for the Bundeswehr and Germany's policy in NATO. *Ośrodek Studiów Wschodnich.* www.osw.waw.pl/en/publikacje/osw-commentary/2022-03-30/war-ukraine-consequences-bundeswehr-and-germanys-policy-nato

Ipsos. (2023, March 9). *Deutliche Mehrheit für Wiedereinführung der Wehrpflicht.* www.ipsos.com/de-de/deutliche-mehrheit-fur-wiedereinfuhrung-der-wehrpflicht

Kiel Institute for the World Economy. (n.d.). *Ukraine Support Tracker.* www.ifw-kiel.de/topics/war-against-ukraine/ukraine-support-tracker/

Larson, C. (2023, October 12). Why Germany is rattled about sending its Taurus missile to Ukraine. *Politico.* www.politico.eu/article/why-germany-scholz-rattled-sending-taurus-missile-ukraine/

Ministry of Foreign Affairs of Denmark. (2023a, May). *Foreign and Security Policy Strategy.* https://um.dk/en/foreign-policy/foreign-and-security-policy-2023

Ministry of Foreign Affairs of Denmark. (2023b, July 3). *Denmark Launches Support Package for the Reconstruction of Schools and Hospitals in Ukraine.* https://ukraine.um.dk/en/news/denmark-launches-support-package-for-the-reconstruction-of-schools-and-hospitals-in-ukraine

Ministry of Foreign Affairs of Estonia. (2022). *Second Recovery Forum of Zhytomyr region.* www.vm.ee/en/second-recovery-forum-zhytomyr-region

Ministry of Foreign Affairs of Poland. (2023). *Information on the Principles and Objectives of Poland's Foreign Policy.* www.sejm.gov.pl/media9.nsf/files/MPRA-CQUBZR/%24File/Information%20on%20the%20principles%20and%20objectives%20of%20Poland%E2%80%99s%20foreign%20policy.pdf

Ministry of the Economy and Innovation of the Republic of Lithuania. (2022). *International Conference Rebuild Ukraine in Vilnius.* https://eimin.lrv.lt/en/news/international-conference-rebuild-ukraine-in-vilnius

National Security Strategy of the Republic of Poland 2020. (2020). www.bbn.gov.pl/ftp/dokumenty/National_Security_Strategy_of_the_Republic_of_Poland_2020.pdf

North Atlantic Treaty Organization. (2022). *NATO 2022 Strategic Concept, Adopted by Heads of State and Government at the NATO Summit in Madrid 29 June 2022.* www.nato.int/strategic-concept/

North Atlantic Treaty Organization. (2023, July 7). *Defence Expenditures of NATO Countries (2014–2023).* www.nato.int/cps/en/natohq/news_216897.htm

Office of the President of the Republic of Lithuania. (2022, February 28). *Open Letter by Presidents in Support of Ukraine's Swift Candidacy to the European Union.* www.lrp.lt/en/media-center/news/open-letter-by-presidents-in-support-of-ukraines-swift-candidacy-to-the-european-union/37859

Piątek, M. (2022, October 31). Wizje odbudowy Ukrainy. Polskie firmy już biegną po kontrakty. *Polityka, 45*(3388), 41.

Presidential Office of Ukraine. (2022, November 29). *Ukraine Will Become a Role Model of Reconstruction – President Addressed the General Assembly of the International Bureau of Expositions regarding the holding of Expo 2030 in Odesa.* www.president.gov.ua/en/news/ukrayina-stane-vzircem-vidbudovi-prezident-zvernuvsya-do-gen-79513

Press and Information Office of the Federal Government. (2023). *Policy Statement by Olaf Scholz, Chancellor of the Federal Republic of Germany and Member of the German Bundestag, 27 February 2022 in Berlin.* www.bundesregierung.de/breg-en/news/policy-statement-by-olaf-scholz-chancellor-of-the-federal-republic-of-germany-and-member-of-the-german-bundestag-27-february-2022-in-berlin-2008378

Rankin, J. (2023, February 8). *EU Urged to Use Frozen Russian Assets to 'Cover Costs of Aggression' in Ukraine.* www.theguardian.com/world/2023/feb/08/eu-urged-to-use-frozen-russian-assets-to-cover-costs-of-aggression-in-ukraine

Rinkēvičs, E. [Edgars Rinkēvičs]. (2022, February 24). Joint statement with @eliimets and @GLandsbergis on the Russian aggression against Ukraine [Tweet]. *Twitter.* https://twitter.com/edgarsrinkevics/status/1496721181059203081

SchengenVisaInfo.com. (2023, August 8). *Germany Granted Nearly 32,000 National Visas to Russians Since February 2022.* www.schengenvisainfo.com/news/germany-granted-nearly-32000-national-visas-to-russians-since-february-2022/#google_vignette

Seimas of the Republic of Lithuania. (2021, December 16). *Resolution Amending Resolution No Ix-907 of the Seimas of the Republic of Lithuania of 28 May 2002 on the Approval of the National Security Strategy.* https://e-seimas.lrs.lt/portal/legalAct/lt/TAD/3ec6a2027a9a11ecb2fe9975f8a9e52e?jfwid=rivwzvpvg

Sejm Rzeczpospolitej Polskiej. (2023). *Joint Declaration by the Speakers of the Parliaments of Estonia, Latvia, Lithuania, and Poland One Year Since Russia's Full-Scale Military Invasion of Ukraine.* https://sejm.gov.pl/Sejm9.nsf/komunikat.xsp?documentId=5B3303AAD779A3F8C12589600002571E

Statista. (n.d.). *Estimated Number of Refugees from Ukraine Recorded in Europe and Asia Since February 2022 as of July 11, 2023, by Selected Country.* www.statista.com/statistics/1312584/ukrainian-refugees-by-country/

Szymański, P. (2020, February 10). Nowa strategia obronna Łotwy: priorytetem obrona powszechna. *Ośrodek Studiów Wschodnich.* www.osw.waw.pl/pl/publikacje/analizy/2020-10-02/nowa-strategia-obronna-lotwy-priorytetem-obrona-powszechna

Tidey, A. (2023, August 3). Baltic countries strike deal to disconnect from Russian power grid earlier than expected. *Euronews.* www.euronews.com/my-europe/2023/08/03/baltic-countries-strike-deal-to-disconnect-from-russian-power-grid-earlier-than-expected

Transparency International. (n.d.). *Corruption Perceptions Index.* www.transparency.org/en/countries/ukraine

Ukraine Recovery Conference. (2022a, July 4–5). *Conference Materials.* www.urc-international.com/conference-materials

Ukraine Recovery Conference. (2022b, July 4–5). *National Statements.* www.urc-international.com/urc-2022

Ukraine Recovery Conference. (2023, June 21–22). *URC 2023 Information.* www.urc-international.com/urc-2023-info

40 *Kozierska et al.*

Ustawa z dnia 11 marca 2022 r. o obronie Ojczyzny. Dz.U. 2022, poz. 655. https://isap.sejm.gov.pl/isap.nsf/DocDetails.xsp?id=WDU20220000655

Valsts aizsardzības koncepcija 2020. (2020). www.mod.gov.lv/sites/mod/files/document/AiMVAK_2020.pdf

World Bank. (2023, March 23). *Updated Ukraine Recovery and Reconstruction Needs Assessment.* www.worldbank.org/en/news/press-release/2023/03/23/updated-ukraine-recovery-and-reconstruction-needs-assessment

Związek Przedsiębiorców i Pracodawców. (2023). *Konferencja "Europe – Poland – Ukraine. Rebuild Together 2023".* https://zpp.net.pl/events/event/ii-edycja-konferencji-europe-poland-ukraine-rebuild-together/

3 Impact of the Russian-Ukrainian war on the Baltic area's economy

Katarzyna Kosowska and Agata Niewiadomska

Introduction

In February 2022, Russia initiated a war against Ukraine representing the greatest military conflict since World War II. The long-established peace and economic order was disrupted by an armed clash between the two nuclear powers, and the consequences are being increasingly felt not only by the Baltic states but also by the major European countries. Changes in the global economy have affected both the need to adjust global supply chains and the direction of trade, as well as levels of investor confidence, but above all have undermined energy and food security in the region. Energy independence from Russian gas and oil resources has become important, but it is also vital to prioritise climate preservation and the adoption of 'Green Deal' policies. The negative impact of rising producer stock costs and the concomitant increase in commodity prices has intensified inflationary pressures, further accentuating negative consequences for their economies. The possibility of further Russian escalation in the conflict has prompted the need to restructure thinking about international security and, at the same time, the need for states to rearm and, therefore, change the structure of national budgets. The influx of war refugees has resulted in increased costs for host countries which, while potentially beneficial for the labour market, also poses a significant financial burden.

The aim of the chapter is to present the economic consequences of the war in Ukraine for the Baltic states. Although it is indisputable that any war implies long-term negative effects and despite the application of sanctions against Russia, which has not been effectively isolated, this armed conflict has also highlighted the positive aspect of increased cooperation between economies and the demonstration of solidarity with Ukraine. Based on these factors, the research hypothesis is that the war in Ukraine has caused economic instability, particularly in the food and energy sectors, challenging the globalised world and leading to a new pattern of global security.

DOI: 10.4324/9781003558040-5

The war in Ukraine and the threat to food security

Russia's invasion of Ukraine has a number of serious consequences, particularly in terms of food security. Both countries are among the world's main exporters of wheat, barley and sunflower oil. Prior to the outbreak of the war, Ukraine had produced nearly half of the world's volume of sunflower oil and the economy being in the top ten in terms of production of sunflower seeds, sunflower oil, sunflower cake and meal, walnuts, rapeseed, maize, barley, wheat, soybeans and butter had the opportunity to export about 70–80% of agricultural products (Bułkowska & Bazhenova, 2023). According to data from the International Grains Council, cereal production in the 2022/2023 season decreased by 28% compared to the same period in 2021/22. At the same time, exports also decreased by 9%. Forecasts for the following 2023/24 period are not encouraging, despite predictions of a slight increase in production of 6%; however, exports are still expected to fall by as much as 16% (IGC, 2024). The expected increase in agricultural prices to come is rooted in a reduction in production and exports from both conflict economies. In addition, simultaneous increases in the cost of fertilisers and energy raw materials may have a negative impact on prices, especially that Russia and Belarus jointly accounted for 52% of potassium fertiliser export to the EU in 2020 (Ambroziak et al., 2022). The value of agri-food product exports from Ukraine to Poland in terms of value almost tripled between 2021 and 2022, reaching €2.8 billion. The continuation of international trade in agri-food products will be determined primarily by the further course of the conflict and the possibility of supplying goods both by sea through ports on the Black and Azov Seas and through solidarity routes (OSW Team, 2023).

More than 90% of Ukraine's grains, oilseeds and oils are exported by sea, therefore it is crucial to maintain the permeability of distribution channels. For this reason, it was extremely important to launch the grain corridor in 2022, the so-called Black Sea Corridor, as well as to strengthen EU partnership with Ukraine in terms of trade. The abolition of quantitative duties and quotas turned out to be positive for Ukrainian exports, but on the other hand, it caused serious disruption in regional agricultural markets where a surge in imports from Ukraine contributed to oversupply, which consequently triggered downward pressure on prices (Bułkowska & Bazhenova, 2023). It also caused farmers' protests in many EU countries, including Baltic Sea states such as Poland, Germany, Czechia, Slovakia, Lithuania, Latvia and Hungary. At the same time, concerns about the quality of imported products have increased, especially regarding so-called technical grain (Kacprzak & Zawadka, 2023).

From the beginning of the Russian invasion until 1 August 2022, the blockade of Ukrainian ports posed a significant barrier. Stabilisation of the situation with regard to fears of an imminent food crisis was guaranteed by signing of an agreement on the temporary liberalisation of road freight transport between the EU and Ukraine (Gajadhur, 2023) in June 2022 and the simultaneous development of infrastructure at the border, followed by an agreement to unblock Black Sea ports in July 2022 (Michalski et al., 2022). Despite the absorption of supply shocks and positive international reaction, the decline in agri-food commodity prices still does not show a downward trend in the consumer price index for food. This is a result of high energy costs and also unfavourable exchange rates (Bułkowska & Bazhenova, 2023). High prices of exported goods also mean higher revenues. Thus, Russia's attempt to restrict Ukraine's trade opportunities may not only trigger higher profits but at the same time negatively affect food security. As the FAO estimates that a prolonged conflict may translate into an increase in the number of malnourished people by 8–13 million in 2022/2023 which provides a political argument allowing accusations against the West for causing this (Ambroziak et al., 2022).

Favourable import conditions meant that the volume of products imported from Ukraine was increasing; this could not be observed in case of Ukraine's share in total Polish exports, which decreased to 2%. Rising inflation compounded by rising food prices and a negative balance of trade with Ukraine led Poland to restrict imports of selected products from the war zone. However, the Regulation of the Minister of Development and Technology was quickly repealed in favour of an EU Commission Regulation introducing prohibitive measures concerning certain products originating in Ukraine (Commission Implementing Regulation (EU) 2023/903, 2023). This legal regulation, in force until 15 September 2023, led to a restriction of cereal exports, that is, wheat, maize and sunflower from Ukraine to Poland, Romania, Bulgaria and Slovakia. In addition, the European parliament extended the suspension of tariff quotas on goods from Ukraine until 5 June 2024. Further cooperation on trade between EU countries and Ukraine will take place taking into account high quality requirements and compliance with, for instance, sanitary standards for products imported to the European market. Given the destruction of agricultural equipment and crops in the war zones, a decrease in food exports can be expected in the coming months. Moreover, such a trend will continue even after the end of the conflict due to the reintroduction of trade restrictions and barriers between the EU and Ukraine (Ambroziak et al., 2022). A position still favourable to Ukraine's interests, regarding the continuation of the EU's tariff suspension, has been presented by the European Commission in an announced draft regulation extending the autonomous trade measures (ATM), which is to be in force until 5 June 2025. The draft is still under consultation and, as it is not entirely satisfactory, the Polish minister of agriculture and rural development has already presented demands. The new proposal maintains solutions allowing for the application of so-called regional protection measures, but unlike the standards currently in force, there will be no need to prove the existence of disorder in the entire EU, but just in one country or region and, in addition, the whole procedure for activating protection measures is to be carried out in a shorter time than it has been so far. At the same time, the Ministry of Agriculture and Rural

44 *Katarzyna Kosowska and Agata Niewiadomska*

Development has doubts about limitations on protective measures to selected agricultural commodities but not to all, including those whose imports were liberalised even before they came into force, for example on oilseed rape or soft fruit. A separate special safeguarding measure is envisaged for imports of poultry meat, eggs and sugar, where the EC automatically reinstates customs duties on trade in these products once the established import limit is exceeded. There are doubts about limiting the powers of states to introduce necessary measures to protect the life, health and safety of people, animals and plants, if imports from Ukraine pose a threat. The Ministry also points to the need to clarify, in the EU-Ukraine agreement, which is currently being negotiated, conditions for the import of cereals from Ukraine, taking into account the licensing mechanism (Ministerstwo Rolnictwa i Rozwoju Wsi, 2024). However, any adaptation of the agreements and further cooperation on trade will depend primarily on the development of the armed conflict.

Investments

Russia's invasion of Ukraine has translated into amplified inflationary pressures, as a result of rising prices for many commodities (including agriculture, energy, metals) and disruptions to supply chains. The outbreak of the conflict led to an increase in the price of a barrel of Brent crude oil from 90 dollars to 130 dollars, but it is now below 90 dollars (Kępka & Pająk, 2022). The price increase in the Baltic Sea countries was caused by disrupted supply chains and disruptions in production processes caused by the pandemic but also by the sanctions imposed by the EU on Russia and Belarus which resulted in reduced economic cooperation with these countries. It should be noted that until the outbreak of the conflict, Russia was the largest export market for Lithuania (7.3%) and Estonia (6.4%) and an important import partner for these countries, with 12.1% of Lithuania's total imports, 11.6% of Estonia's and 9.1% of Latvia's coming from Russia. Belarus was the 11th export market for Lithuania (3.0% of total exports), the 20th for Latvia (1.1%), and the 28th for Estonia (0.5%). In terms of imports, it also played an important role as the 9th import market for Lithuania (3.5% of total imports), the 12th for Latvia (2.4%) and the 10th for Estonia (3.4%). The increase in consumption as a result of the influx of refugees from Ukraine, and also the wage-price spiral resulting from the shortage occurring in the labour market (average gross wages in the first quarter of 2021 increased by 14% in Lithuania, by 9% in Latvia and by 8% in Estonia), proved to be important for inflation. If this is accompanied by a depreciation of national currencies (against the dollar), it can further accelerate inflation (Gołębiewska, 2022). In the first year of the war, the Baltic states had the highest inflation rates: Estonia (19.4%), Lithuania (18.9%) and Latvia (17.2%). Poland ranked fourth with an inflation rate of 13.2% while the other Baltic Sea countries recorded price increases fluctuating between 7 and 8.5%. In 2023, inflationary pressure weakened: the highest rate – 10.9% – was in Poland and the inflation rates for Lithuania,

Latvia and Estonia were around 9% (Eurostat, 2024). Economies are constantly trying to curb inflation, but the reality is that successfully tackling inflation in some economies will mean the threat of recession in others. After 2022, there was a sharp decline in the living standards of German citizens – the result of a fall in the real value of wages and the government's failure to take effective action to put the brakes on energy price rises in 2022.

In the first 18 months of the armed conflict, the largest increases in food prices took place in the Baltic states: in Lithuania (23.9%), Latvia (19.5%) and Estonia (17.6%). In Poland and Germany, food prices rose in the range of 12.6–13.8%. For the Scandinavian countries, the inflation rate did not exceed 10% (Fulvimari et al., 2023). Between 2021 and 2023, the largest increases in the percentage of the population affected by severe material and social poverty were in Germany with a jump from 4.3% to 6.9%, and in Denmark, from 3.1% to 4.9%. A high value for this indicator was also found in Lithuania (6.0%) and Latvia (6.2%) (Eurostat, 2024).

Weak currencies and the proximity of the Baltic Sea countries to a war-torn economy have negatively affected investor sentiment and actions. Foreign direct investment (FDI) is an extremely important element for any economy, given that in Germany, for example, it accounts for 20% of GDP. It should be Europe's primary goal to create a business-friendly environment by investing in research and innovation in economies while supporting digital and green investments. The consequences of the war are clearly leaving their mark in this respect. Already in 2022, effects such as the energy, geopolitical and economic crises negatively impacted the number of jobs generated by FDI in Europe, reduced by 16%. On the other hand, as the authors of the report 'How can Europe attract next-generation inward investment?' pointed out, there was a 14% increase in the number of planned foreign investments in 2023 compared to the previous year. Challenges include instability in the banking sector, rising interest rates and inflation still above its target (Teigland et al., 2023).

Baltic countries such as Lithuania, Latvia and Estonia reflect the trend of investing in the digital sector as this should drive economic growth in the coming years. After a period of uncertainty among investors, Baltic countries are regaining confidence and therefore the potential for FDI is also increasing. Almost 60% of companies planned to establish or expand their operations in these countries in 2022, which was 7% ahead of the European average. Investors appreciate the region for its political and administrative stability, effective governance and relative availability of labour resources, as well as its favourable start-up ecosystem, while remaining relatively cautious due to the war in Ukraine. The year 2023 brought a slowdown in the markets, with Estonia in particular suffering a 3.5% economic decline. The negative impact of the increasingly weakening prosperity of the trading partners of these economies translated into a decline in private sector investments, which was compensated for by public investments. Investor sentiment and expectations in relation to the Baltic Sea countries seems to be mixed. Whereas assessment of Lithuania's investment attractiveness is positive, investors assume a decline in Estonia and Latvia in coming years. Juxtaposing this with the number of reported investment projects, changes can be observed in the architecture of global investment distribution. A slight increase in this respect was recorded by Eastern and Central European countries, including Germany and Poland, which is not surprising after the shock period caused by Russia's military attack on Ukraine. The perceived growth is the result of the reconfiguration of global supply chains and the trend to seek price-competitive areas for manufacturing. According to data from the 2022 FDI intelligence report, Poland ranked fifth in Europe in terms of the number of greenfield projects; almost 500 projects were announced which accounted for 7.2% of all such projects in the European market (Druchin et al., 2023).

Between 2021 and 2022, the value of investment as a proportion of GDP increased for two Scandinavian countries, Sweden (from 25.6% to 27.2%), Finland (from 23.6% to 24.2%), and for Germany (from 21.8% to 22.5%). Although Estonia lost its leading position, it still retained a high level, indicating positive trends in development (25.3%). In comparison, at the end of 2021, the value of investment as a proportion of GDP in the EU as a whole was 22% (Eurostat, 2024).

Not insignificant for FDI was the influx of refugees from war territories. The enormous cost of aid to state budgets is obvious, as the Kiel Institute for the World Economy points out, Poland has spent 3.35% of its GDP, or around EUR 20.73 billion, while the German economy has spent EUR 21.44 billion since the beginning of Russia's invasion of Ukraine which equates to 0.55% of its GDP. On the one hand, the influx of people from war zones is an ongoing cost for the respective economies in terms of enabling access to education or healthcare, but at the same time, it means filling a gap in the labour market.

According to the Office for Foreigners, one year after the start of the armed conflict, more than one million Ukrainian nationals benefitted from temporary protection in Poland, 87% of which were women and children (Urząd ds. Cudzoziemców, 2023b). The number of applications for a residence permit in Poland submitted by Belarusians also systematically increased to over 100,000. The wave of Belarusian migration to Poland began after the rigged presidential elections in August 2020 and continued after the Russian attack on Ukraine in February 2022 (Urząd ds. Cudzoziemców, 2023a). Young and economically active people settled in Poland in the largest numbers, primarily from the IT sector, which was a priority industry in Belarus (Gródek-Szostak et al., 2021). Eurostat data for (2024) shows that the largest proportion of Ukrainian refugees is currently in Germany, with 1.3 million, representing more than 30 % of all Ukrainians who left their homeland because of the war. Poland was second with 957,000 refugees. The three Scandinavian countries of the Baltic Sea basin together host around 150,000, the same number as the three Baltic states combined (Eurostat, 2024). In 2022, of the 15.2 million people working in Poland, 3.8 % were foreigners, a year earlier, the share was only 1.6 % (Dębkowska & Wojt-Knyżewska, 2023). According to data from the Central Register and Information on Economic Activity (CEIDG), between the beginning of 2022 and the end of 2023, more than 44,500 Ukrainian companies had started a business in Poland, which means that almost 70% of active business activities registered in Poland by foreigners belonged to Ukrainian citizens (Skwirowski, 2024). Next to Ukrainians, the second most numerous and professionally active group are Belarusians, and between January 2022 and mid-2023, they established 11,700 companies in Poland. Of the approximately 8,000 companies in the 'Information and Communication' area, 86% are engaged in IT activities, 11% in professional, scientific or technical activities, while less than 5% are engaged in construction (Bankier.pl, 2023). There are currently around 850,000 Ukrainian refugees in Germany, the second-largest nationality group after Turkish citizens. Half of all Ukrainians have jobs below their qualifications, however, a majority are attending language or integration courses in order to become more mobile in the labour market. In the future, they are likely to fill the employment gap, which is expected to reach seven million by 2034 (Frymark, 2023).

The repercussions of the war are felt in every area of the economy. Helping to counter the refugee crisis is the Baltic Sea Region Interreg Programme 2021–2027, which brings together nine countries, including Poland, Denmark, Sweden, Lithuania, Latvia, Estonia, Finland and part of Germany. The programme aims to support business initiatives from the Baltic Sea countries in order to create a more innovative region that supports sustainable development, environmental protection and also leads to an improved quality of life for its inhabitants (Europejska Współpraca Terytorialna, 2024). The European Regional Development Fund has earmarked EUR 250.98 million to support the programme (Schwarz, 2023) and its support for Ukraine opens up opportunities for closer cooperation between Ukrainian organisations and those of the Baltic Sea Region countries. Although the Interreg Baltic Sea Region does not provide separate funding for Ukrainian organisations, it allows them to participate as an associate organisation in projects and to take part in various project activities. At the same time, the programme actively seeks opportunities to use regional funding instruments to support Ukraine. Examples of the effects of the activities are projects such as the BSI_4Women project, operating in Poland, Norway, Denmark, Estonia, Lithuania, Latvia and Sweden, helping refugee women from Ukraine to start a business (Kolosowa, 2024).

It is also worth mentioning European defence spending as a consequence of the Russian invasion of Ukraine. In 2022, Europe spent €240 billion on defence programmes, 6% more than in the previous year. Of the eight Baltic Sea states, only one country – Finland – reduced defence spending, the others all increased and the greatest was in Sweden, with an increase of 30.1%. Lithuania came second with an increase of 27.6%, followed by Denmark (+8.5%), Poland (+5.5%) and Germany (+5.4) (European Defence Agency,

2022). Due to their geographical location, the Baltic states are the most vulnerable to attack from Russia and for this reason, Lithuania, Latvia and Estonia have assumed major increases in their war budgets for coming years. Latvia's defence budget is expected to be more than €1 billion in 2024 and €1.1 billion in 2025. In Estonia's budget, defence spending is planned at €1.33 billion, with the government allocating €5.6 billion between 2024 and 2027. Lithuania's defence budget, on the other hand, will be €2.09 billion, or 2.77% of GDP, in 2024 (Lachert, 2024).

Baltic Sea states facing the 2022 energy crisis

The Russian-Ukrainian conflict started in 2022 was preceded by a year of very high natural gas prices on the European market, a consequence of the game played by the Russian gas giant Gazprom. In 2021, Russia's oil production reached 528 million tonnes, making the country the second-largest oil producer in the world after the United States (Enerdata, 2023a). At the same time, Russia remained the second-largest producer of natural gas after the United States with a production of 793 bcm (Enerdata, 2023b). In the context of the turmoil in the EU energy market, it is extremely important to note that Russia was the largest exporter of both oil and natural gas to the European market. These raw materials accounted for 44% and 28% respectively of the EU's total extra-agreement imports (Eurostat, 2024). The Russian invasion of Ukraine and the sanctions imposed on the aggressor caused an additional price shock in the energy commodity markets, manifesting itself in their sharp rise. As a consequence, EU countries were hit by an energy crisis.

Following the launch of the war in Ukraine, Russia decreased gas supplies to Europe by implementing a new payment system for gas exports. Certain countries, described as 'unfriendly', were cut off from gas supplies at the beginning, on the pretext of requesting ruble settlements for the gas that was delivered (Mikulska & Pronińska, 2022). EU countries that refused ruble transactions – including Poland – were deprived of access to Russian gas as early as April. Only one month later, Finland was cut off as a result of its application to join NATO (Łoskot-Strachota & Hyndle-Hussein, 2022). In the following months, Gazprom obstructed the supply of its largest customer, Germany (Kardaś, 2022), and gradually terminated supplies through the Nord Stream 1 pipeline (Menkiszak, 2022). It is worth noting here that Russian natural gas has occupied a central place in Germany's energy security strategy and also as a transition fuel in the German *Energiewende*. Among the Baltic Sea states in 2019, the ones most dependent on Russian gas (in terms of internal consumption) were Finland (94%), Latvia (93%) and Estonia (79%). Russian gas also covered almost half of Germany's internal consumption (49%). In contrast, the country most dependent on imported energy resources (in terms of internal consumption) was Lithuania (Eurostat, 2024).

In these circumstances, the Baltic Sea states had to confront the vision of long-term supply disruptions from their main oil and gas supplier, as well as

Impact of the Russian-Ukrainian war   49

considering cutting themselves off completely from Russian supplies. Concerns about energy security have increased among Baltic Sea countries, both in economic terms (fears about the economic availability of energy for citizens and concerning the consequences of expensive energy on raw material markets for the economies of importer countries) and geostrategic, and therefore the physical availability of raw materials necessary for the production of energy in its various forms (Pronińska, 2023).

During the first 18 months of the conflict, Estonia had the highest increase in electricity prices at 131.5% while for the other two Baltic states, it oscillated around 40%. For the Scandinavian countries, electricity prices increased by 64.5% in Denmark, 36.2% in Finland and 48.6% in Sweden during the period, while in Poland prices increased by 10.7%, and Germany by 16.7% (Fulvimari et al., 2023). The increase in electricity prices was accompanied by an increase in natural gas prices. In the first 18 months after the outbreak of the war, Estonia remained the country most affected by the increase at just over 150%. Denmark (138.4 %) and Latvia (103.7 %) recorded high jumps in prices as well, while for Germany and Poland the average increased by around 40% (Fulvimari et al., 2023).

Against the backdrop of rising energy and electricity commodity prices, the value of the share of the energy budget allocated to households in individual EU countries has increased. Households in Latvia and Estonia allocated the largest share of their budget to energy (above 14%), in Poland and Lithuania, the share ranged from 12.1–12.6%, but in contrast, German and Danish societies spent around 9% (Fulvimari et al., 2023). In Germany, for heating energy, the share of expenditure that must be spent increased dramatically for lower-income groups, reaching 19% in 2022 and the number of households paying more than 10% of their income on energy increased from 26% to 43% in 2023 (Lutz & Becker, 2023).

In response to rising energy prices, countries with particularly vulnerable populations have launched a variety of financial assistance packages for households and the industrial sector. Since the start of the energy crisis, €651 billion have been allocated and set aside in European countries to protect consumers from rising energy costs. Of the €540 billion accruing to the EU, €158 billion has been reserved exclusively by Germany (Sgaravatti et al., 2023). Among the countries of the Baltic Sea area, in the period September 2021–January 2023, the largest percentage of GDP for protecting households and companies from the energy crisis was allocated by Lithuania with 5.1%, Germany with 4.4 % and Latvia with 3.3 %. In value terms, Germany remained the undisputed leader with €157.7 billion; Poland came second with €12.4 billion and Sweden third (€6.8 billion) (Sgaravatti et al., 2023).

The economy in the face of an energy crisis

On the back of the wave of high energy prices, industrial activity in the Baltic Sea states slowed noticeably. The greatest slowdown was observed in metals and chemicals production, where the percentage decrease was in the double digit range. In addition, industries such as glass, paper, coke and petroleum products, which are characterised by high energy consumption during production, were affected (Druchin et al., 2023).

Concerns about deindustrialisation were especially acute in Germany, a country that was particularly dependent on Russian gas supplies and where, in addition, industrial production accounts for more than 20% of GDP. In German industry, the energy-intensive chemical sector was the biggest problem and as a result of the crisis, its production is planned to be transferred abroad. In the non-energy-intensive sectors, production was maintained, partly due to companies' efforts to improve energy efficiency (Chen et al., 2023). Between September 2021 and October 2023, the average activity of energy-intensive sectors fell by 17.4%. During this period, Polish industry proved more resilient to energy perturbations, as the activity of energy-intensive sectors decreased by only 6.4% (Druchin et al., 2023). During the wave of the crisis, steel mills, chemical plants and ceramics plants were ramped down or stopped, factory closures were accompanied by group lay-offs and about two-thirds of Polish companies indicated that energy costs accounted for more than 10% of their operating costs while almost all reacted to increased energy and fuel costs by increasing prices for products or services (Kąsek, 2022). In most cases, this translated into reduced demand as forced to save, Poles began to buy only necessities. The small Estonian economy was hit hard by rising energy prices and supply disruptions. GDP contracted by 1.3 % in 2022 and economic activity slowed considerably, nevertheless, the labour market remained stable (European Commission, 2023). The energy shock also weakened Lithuania's economy where disruptions in supply chains and high energy prices put pressure on costs, reduced productivity and the competitiveness of certain sectors and held back investment. In addition, the decline in private consumption in 2022 due to impoverished households and reduced consumer confidence was a major concern. As a result, Lithuania's economic growth in the fourth quarter of 2022 was negative, with annual growth slowing to 1.9% (Jóźwik, 2023). Under these conditions, the Baltic governments prepared programmes of financial support and compensation for price increases, as well as social benefits to reduce the risk of poverty and social exclusion. In Latvia, partial reimbursement of costs incurred due to energy price increases were also given to industry and in total Latvia allocated EUR 400 million for this purpose (Paszkowski & Kuczyńska-Zonik, 2022).

Tackling the energy crisis

Given that Russia was the main supplier of energy resources to the European market, it became necessary to look for new solutions to limit the effects of the existing energy crisis and to seek new suppliers of oil and natural gas to the EU market. In March 2022, the International Energy Agency prepared a ten-step plan to minimise the risk of natural gas supply disruptions over the next two years which mainly points to the need to reduce gas consumption, to seek alternative suppliers and find alternative sources of natural gas (International Energy Agency, 2022). In May 2022, the EC launched the REPowerEU Plan, that is an instrument to rapidly decouple Europe from Russian fossil fuels by 2030 and accelerate the energy transition in the EU. Within the framework of the REPowerEU Plan, valued at €300 billion, the actions of EU countries are to be implemented in three areas: diversification of energy supply, reduction of energy consumption and production of energy from renewable sources (European Commission, 2022b). However, the first step of the EU authorities to improve the energy security of member states was to increase the supply of liquefied natural gas (LNG) from the United States and Norway, strengthen cooperation with Azerbaijan, negotiate gas agreements with Egypt and Israel, resume the energy dialogue with Algeria and co-operate with Qatar and Australia (Pronińska, 2023).

In response to the energy crisis, Germany's gas consumption dropped by 18% in 2022 (Amelang, 2023). In addition, Germany was redoubling its efforts to develop renewable energy sources (RES), betting on LNG, a temporary revival of coal-fired power plants and a limited extension of operation for nuclear power plants (Kędzierski, 2023). On 1 May 2022, the Poland-Lithuania interconnector started commercial operations, increasing the optionality and resilience of the entire Baltic gas market. The gas interconnector enables the flow of LNG, increasing energy security in the region by connecting the Baltic and Finnish markets with the Polish one. The project strengthens the region's energy independence and enhances the use of the Klaipeda LNG terminal in Lithuania and the Świnoujście LNG terminal in Poland (European Commission, 2022a). Poland expects to achieve a 29.8% share of RES in gross final energy consumption by 2030 while new RES sources are to take the place of decommissioned coal-fired power plants. Poland will aim to phase out coal from households by 2040 and the first large nuclear power plant is expected to be commissioned between 2030 and 2035 (Zielińska, 2023). Latvia aims to generate more than 60% of its electricity and 58% of its heat from renewable sources by 2030 and it is worth mentioning that Latvia has the largest hydroelectric power plant in the Baltics. Nine new solar power plants and the largest solar park of photovoltaic panels in the Baltic will be built to increase energy independence (Szafrański, 2023). Sweden's electricity system is based on nuclear and hydroelectric power which account for the vast majority generated (approximately 80%). The remaining energy comes from wind farms and biomass. There is currently an ongoing debate in Sweden on the construction of new nuclear power plants and the restoration of reactors in the southern part of the country (Paszkowski, 2023). In 2022, more than 60% of Denmark's electricity will come from RES, with offshore wind dominating. Currently, Denmark has not yet moved entirely away from fossil fuels, but plans indicate a reduction in the future as it plans to quadruple energy production from onshore wind and photovoltaics by 2030 (Z energią o prawie, 2023). Finland had already made significant progress in the share of renewable energy by 2021, exceeding 40%, and biomass and wind energy play a key role in renewable energy production. Finland is currently planning to expand its nuclear power plant and wind farms. During the energy crisis, the Lithuanian LNG terminal played an important role in meeting the country's needs and the Incukalns storage facility in Latvia is important to ensure supply during the autumn-winter season (Gibała, 2023).

Conclusion

The Russian invasion of Ukraine has caused a lot of turmoil on European markets, including those of the Baltic Sea countries. It initiated, declines in financial markets, panic in raw material markets, inflation shock, changes to trade directions, a decrease in investor confidence, population migration in Europe (refugee wave) and serious industrial problems. The consequence of the Russian-Ukrainian war was a serious crisis in the energy and food markets.

The armed conflict between the two leading producers and exporters of cereals and oilseeds could not fail to translate into a decline in food security in European countries. The blockade of ports in the Black Sea, the destruction of Ukraine's agricultural infrastructure and restrictions on grain exports imposed by Russia have and will continue to have a negative impact on food markets in the coming years. The food crisis was brought to a halt thanks to global cooperation, under pressure from which Russia agreed to end the blockade of the Black Sea ports in Ukraine. However, a large part of Ukrainian cereals ended up in Poland, hitting Polish farmers' incomes and becoming the cause of numerous protests.

Over the last two decades, Russia has successfully implemented its energy strategy towards the EU, focused on the maximum possible dependence of EU countries on its energy resources. Russian aggression against Ukraine has caused the biggest energy crisis in many years, destroying the existing energy structure of the European market and the foundations of the region's energy security. Disturbances or in some cases the suspension of gas supplies to Europe and price inaccessibility paralysed the economies of some Baltic Sea countries, especially, for a short time, those specifically dependent on one large supplier for natural gas and oil. The energy crisis in the form of the negative impact of the deficit and high prices for energy raw materials is a test for the Baltic Sea states and poses a huge challenge for EU member states. The optimal response to the energy crisis and its positive aspect will be the reconstruction of the energy market: the ability of countries to ensure the continuity of energy supplies, diversification of routes, rapid reconstruction of the energy system and new solutions for the energy market.

References

Ambroziak, Ł., Gniadek, J., Sierocińska, K., Strzelecki, J., & Wąsiński, M. (2022). Kryzys podażowy na rynku żywnościowym jako efekt inwazji na Ukrainę. *Polski Instytut Ekonomiczny.* https://pie.net.pl/wp-content/uploads/2022/06/Kryzys-podaz‖cowy-20.07.2022-kopia.pdf

Amelang, S. (2023, March 17). Transition state of play – Germany is emerging from the energy crisis. *Clean Energy Wire.* www.cleanenergywire.org/germany-net-zero-transition-energy-crisis

Bankier.pl. (2023, September 7). *Obywatele Białorusi coraz częściej otwierają firmy w Polsce. Oto najnowsze dane.* www.bankier.pl/wiadomosc/Obywatele-Bialorusi-coraz-czesciej-otwieraja-firmy-w-Polsce-Oto-najnowsze-dane-8607080.html

Bułkowska, M., & Bazhenowa, H. (2023). Direct and indirect consequences of the war in Ukraine for polish trade in agri-food products. *Zagadnienia Ekonomiki Rolnej/Problems of Agricultural Economics, 376*(3), 66–90. DOI: 10.30858/zer/170892

Chen, Y., Lan, T., Mineshima, A., & Zhou, J. (2023, July). Impact of high energy prices on Germany's potential output. *IMF Selected Issues Paper* (SIP/2023/059), Washington, D.C. https://www.imf.org/en/Publications/selected-issues-papers/Issues/2023/07/24/Impact-of-High-Energy-Prices-on-Germanys-Potential-Output-536837

Commission Implementing Regulation (EU) 2023/903 of 2 May 2023 Introducing Preventive Measures Concerning Certain Products Originating in Ukraine. (2023, May 2). *OJ L 114I, 2.5.2023,* pp. 1–4. http://data.europa.eu/eli/reg_impl/2023/903/oj

Dębkowska, K., & Wojt-Knyżewska, A. (2023, June 1). Coraz więcej cudzoziemców pracuje w Polsce. *Tygodnik Gospodarczy PIE,* 22/2023, 6–7.

Druchin, S., Klucznik, M., Miniszewski, M., Rybacki, J., Sajnóg, S., & Sułkowski, M. (2023). Kondycja branż energochłonnych w Europie Środkowej i Wschodniej dwa lata po szoku energetycznym. *Polski Instytut Ekonomiczny.* https://pie.net.pl/wp-content/uploads/2024/02/Branze-energochlonne.pdf

Enerdata. (2023a). *Dobycha syroj nefti.* https://energystats.enerdata.net/crude-oil/world-production-statistics.html [access: 15.04.2024].

Enerdata. (2023b). *Dobycha prirodnogo gaza.* https://energystats.enerdata.net/natural-gas/world-natural-gas-production-statistics.htm [access: 15.04.2024].

European Commission. (2022a). *EU Action in Response to the Energy Crisis.* https://commission.europa.eu/strategy-and-policy/priorities-2019-2024/european-green-deal/eu-action-address-energy-crisis_en

European Commission. (2022b). *REPowerEU: A Plan to Rapidly Reduce Dependence on Russian Fossil Fuels and Fast Forward the Green Transition.* https://ec.europa.eu/commission/presscorner/detail/en/IP_22_3131

European Commission. (2023). Country report – Estonia. *Publications Office of the European Union.* https://economy-finance.ec.europa.eu/system/files/2023-06/ip230_en.pdf

European Defence Agency. (2022). *Defence Data.* https://eda.europa.eu/publications-and-data/defence-data

Europejska Współpraca Terytorialna. (2024, March 26). Program Interreg Region Morza Bałtyckiego 2021–2027. *Serwis Programów Europejskiej Wspólnoty Terytorialnej i Europejskiego Instrumentu Sąsiedztwa.* www.ewt.gov.pl/strony/o-programach/programy-interreg-2021-2027/program-interreg-region-morza-bal-tyckiego-2021-2027/, [access: 15.04.2024].

Eurostat. (2024). https://ec.europa.eu/eurostat/web/main/data/database [access: 15.04.2024].

Frymark, K. (2023, August 25). Ukrainians are slowly adapting to life in Germany. *Ośrodek Studiów Wschodnich.* www.osw.waw.pl/pl/publikacje/analizy/2023-08-25/powolna-adaptacja-ukraincow-w-niemczech

Fulvimari, A., Temursho, U., Vaitkeviciute, A., & Weitzel, M. (2023, May). Economic and distributional effects of higher energy prices on households in the EU. *European Commission*. https://op.europa.eu/en/publication-detail/-/publication/f872114d-81db-11ee-99ba-01aa75ed71a1

Gajadhur, A. (2023, November 29). Speech during the first session of Polish Sejm on 29-11-2023. *Sejm Rzeczpospolitej Polskiej*. www.sejm.gov.pl/sejm10.nsf/wypowiedz.xsp?posiedzenie=1&dzien=6&wyp=128

Gibała, M. (2023, September 3). Finlandia radzi sobie bez rosyjskich surowców. *Biznes Alert*. https://biznesalert.pl/finlandia-energetyka-rosja-gaz-oze/

Gołębiewska, M. (2022, August 4). Wyczekując piku. Inflacja w państwach bałtyckich. IEŚ Commentary 670. *Instytut Europy Środkowej*. https://ies.lublin.pl/komentarze/wyczekujac-piku-inflacja-w-panstwach-baltyckich/

Gródek-Szostak, Z., Kotulewicz-Wisińska, K., Lisiakiewicz, R., & Zysk, W. (2021). W poszukiwaniu bezpiecznej przystani. Perspektywy pracowników białoruskiego sektora IT w Polsce. *Centrum Polityk Publicznych. MISAP, Uniwersytet Ekonomiczny w Krakowie*.

International Energy Agency. (2022, March). *A 10-Point Plan to Reduce the European Union's Reliance on Russian Natural Gas*. www.iea.org/reports/a-10-point-plan-to-reduce-the-european-unions-reliance-on-russian-natural-gas

International Grains Council. (2024, March 14). *Supply & Demand*. www.igc.int/en/markets/marketinfo-sd.aspx [access: 15.04.2024].

Jóźwik, B. (2023, July 12). Spowolnienie wzrostu gospodarczego i perspektywy na przyszłość: analiza prognoz dla Litwy. IEŚ Commentary 902. *Instytut Europy Srodkowej*. https://ies.lublin.pl/komentarze/spowolnienie-wzrostu-gospodarczego-i-perspektywy-na-przyszlosc-analiza-prognoz-dla-litwy/

Kacprzak, I., & Zawadka, G. (2023, April 14). Ziarno z Ukrainy nadal się sypie. *Rzeczpospolita*. www.rp.pl/polityka/art38316541-ziarno-z-ukrainy-nadal-sie-sypie

Kardaś, S. (2022, June 17). Rosja: kolejne ograniczenie dostaw gazu do Europy. *Ośrodek Studiów Wschodnich*. https://www.osw.waw.pl/pl/publikacje/analizy/2022-06-17/rosja-kolejne-ograniczenie-dostaw-gazu-do-europy

Kąsek, L. (Ed.). (2022, October). *Reakcja polskiego biznesu na szok energetyczny* 2022. ING Bank Śląski.

Kędzierski, M. (2023, January 12). Germany: How the gas sector changed in the crisis year of 2022. *Ośrodek Studiów Wschodnich*. www.osw.waw.pl/en/publikacje/osw-commentary/2023-01-12/germany-how-gas-sector-changed-crisis-year-2022

Kępka, A., & Pająk, N. (2022). Wpływ wojny w Ukrainie na wysokość inflacji w Polsce. *Studia Ekonomiczne, Prawne i Administracyjne, 2022/4*. https://sepia.uniwersytetradom.pl/wp-content/uploads/sites/63/2023/04/SEPiA_2022-4_Kepka-Pajak_2.pdf

Kolosowa, I. (2024, January 24). Building connections to Ukrainian organization. *Interreg Baltic Sea Region*. https://interreg-baltic.eu/top-news/building-connections-to-ukrainian-organisations/

Lachert, J. (2024, January 6). Nie tylko Polska się zbroi. Oni również. *wnp.pl*. www.wnp.pl/przemysl-obronny/nie-tylko-polska-sie-zbroi-oni-rowniez,791589.html

Lutz, C., & Becker, L. (2023). Effects of energy price shocks on Germany's economy and private households. In R. Bardazzi & M. G. Pazienza (Eds.), *Vulnerable Households in the Energy Transition* (pp. 11–28). Springer.

Łoskot-Strachota, A., & Hyndle-Hussein, J. (2022, May 23). Wstrzymanie dostaw rosyjskiego gazu do Finlandii. *Ośrodek Studiów Wschodnich*. www.osw.waw.pl/pl/publikacje/analizy/2022-05-23/wstrzymanie-dostaw-rosyjskiego-gazu-do-finlandii

Menkiszak, M. (2022, July 15). Zatrzymanie gazociągu Nord Stream 1. *Ośrodek Studiów Wschodnich*. www.osw.waw.pl/pl/publikacje/analizy/2022-07-15/zatrzymanie-gazociagu-nord-stream-1

Michalski, A., Nieczypor, K., & Wiśniewska, I. (2022, July 26). Zboże pod ostrzałem: porozumienie o odblokowaniu portów czarnomorskich. *Ośrodek Studiów Wschodnich.* www.osw.waw.pl/pl/publikacje/analizy/2022-07-26/zboze-pod-ostrzalem-porozumienie-o-odblokowaniu-portow-czarnomorskich

Mikulska, A., & Pronińska, K. (2022, May 3). Poland and Bulgaria gas cutoff: 'Closing time' for Gazprom's Eurozone cash flows. *Forbes.* www.forbes.com/sites/thebakersinstitute/2022/05/03/poland-and-bulgaria-gas-cutoff-closing-time-for-gazproms-eurozone-cash-flows/

Ministerstwo Rolnictwa i Rozwoju Wsi. (2024, January 31). Komentarz MRiRW po publikacji przez Komisję Europejską projektu rozporządzenia przedłużającego autonomiczne środki handlowe (ATM) dla Ukrainy. *gov.pl.* www.gov.pl/web/rolnictwo/komentarz-mrirw-po-publikacji-przez-komisje-europejska-projektu-rozporzadzenia-przedluzajacego-autonomiczne-srodki-handlowe-atm-dla-ukrainy

OSW Team. (2023, April 11). The EU increases its agri-food imports from Ukraine: Causes and reactions from Central European states. *Ośrodek Studiów Wschodnich.* www.osw.waw.pl/en/publikacje/osw-commentary/2023-04-11/eu-increases-its-agri-food-imports-ukraine-causes-and

Paszkowski, M. (2023, June 22). Wyzwania sektora elektroenergetycznego w Szwecji. *IEŚ Commentary 879.* https://ies.lublin.pl/komentarze/wyzwania-sektora-elektroenergetycznego-w-szwecji/

Paszkowski, M., & Kuczyńska-Zonik, A. (2022, February 2). Konsekwencje kryzysu cen energii energetycznej w państwach bałtyckich. IEŚ Commentary 512. *Instytut Europy Środkowej.* https://ies.lublin.pl/komentarze/konsekwencje-kryzysu-cen-energii-energetycznej-w-panstwach-baltyckich/

Pronińska, K. (2023). Świat i Europa w obliczu kryzysu energetycznego: konsekwencje wojny, sankcji i rosyjskiej broni energetycznej. *Rocznik Strategiczny, 2022 /2023,* 145–167.

Schwarz, K. (2023, October). European Regional Development Fund (ERDF). *European Parliament.* www.europarl.europa.eu/factsheets/en/sheet/95/europejski-fundusz-rozwoju-regionalnego-efrr-

Sgaravatti, G., Tagliapietra, S., Trasi, C., & Zachmann, G. (2023, June 26). National Fiscal policy responses to the energy crisis. *Bruegel.* www.bruegel.org/dataset/national-policies-shield-consumers-rising-energy-prices [access: 15.04.2024].

Skwirowski, P. (2024, January 25). Ukraińcy coraz chętniej zakładają firmy w Polsce. *money.pl.* www.rp.pl/biznes/art39740191-ukraincy-coraz-chetniej-zakladaja-firmy-w-polsce

Szafrański, B. (2023, August 1). Łotwa zwiększa udział zielonej energii. *CIRE.PL Centrum Informacji o Rynku Energii.* www.cire.pl/artykuly/serwis-informacyjny-cire-24/lotwa-zwieksza-udzial-zielonej-energii

Teigland, J. L., Bax, H. J., & Lhermitte, M. (2023, June 21). How can Europe attract next-generation inward investment? *EY.* www.ey.com/en_pl/attractiveness/ey-europe-attractiveness-survey

Urząd ds. Cudzoziemców. (2023a, December 7). Obywatele Białorusi w Polsce – raport. *gov.pl.* www.gov.pl/web/udsc/obywatele-bialorusi-w-polsce--raport2

Urząd ds. Cudzoziemców. (2023b, February 24). Obywatele Ukrainy w Polsce – aktualne dane migracyjne. *gov.pl.* www.gov.pl/web/udsc/obywatele-ukrainy-w-polsce--aktualne-dane-migracyjne2

Z energią o prawie. (2023, August 31). *Miks energetyczny Danii.* https://zeop.pl/miks-energetyczny-danii/ [access: 15.04.2024].

Zielińska, A. (2023, March 7). Energetyczny plan na nowo. Polska zmienia kluczowe cele. *Money.pl.* www.money.pl/gospodarka/energetyczny-plan-na-nowo-polska-zmienia-kluczowe-cele-7003395710954272a.html

4 Sweden, Finland and the Russian-Ukrainian war and prospects for its end

Monika Banaś

Introduction

Wars, armed conflicts and violent confrontations are as old as the world. Human experience shows that they do not vanish with the progress and development of civilisation. Numerous attempts have been made to explain this phenomenon, attributing it to a range of psychosocial, economic, religious and cultural factors and interpretations worthy of note can be found in the works of Feliks Koneczny, Samuel Huntington and Fernand Braudel.

Emphasising the civilisational diversity of nations and human communities, Koneczny distinguishes seven civilisations: Arab, Byzantine, Brahmin, Chinese, Latin, Turanian and Jewish. Civilisations engage in competition, particularly in contact/border areas but they refrain from intermingling as this poses a risk of weakening. In the absence of equality and lack of struggle, the less developed civilisation, favouring aggression and military force, is likely to prevail. Furthermore, Koneczny argues that each aspires to expand and propagate the cultural patterns characteristic of that civilisation (2002).

Huntington adopts a comparable approach, identifying nine distinct civilisations: Western, Latin American, Orthodox, African, Islamic, Hindu, Buddhist, Chinese and Japanese. He places special emphasis on regions where different cultural systems intersect, as these areas manifest unique dynamics resulting from processes of cultural diffusion (2000).

Both scholars identify zones with a significant potential to generate conflicts: the border areas of civilisations where two or more axiologically normative systems meet. This tendency arises from the inherent nature of these systems; manifested in human actions, they seek expansion through cultural influence (soft power), military (hard power), or a combination of both (smart power) (Nye, 2009).

The three types of action are integral components of civilisational 'grammar', a concept introduced by Braudel (2006), later referenced in the text.

Russia's attack on Ukraine was marked by diversionary acts that extended across multiple levels and incorporated a substantial disinformation component, transforming the conflict into a hybrid war (Clark, 2020; Hofmann, 2022). Media accounts, narratives emerging from circles close to the

DOI: 10.4324/9781003558040-6

combating parties, as well as statements from the leaders of those countries, collectively form a cultural map offering insights into the prospects for enduring peace in Europe.

The effectiveness of verbal communication, especially through elaborated narratives, is evidenced not only within the humanities but also across sociology and politics (Austin, 1962; Crow & Jones, 2018; Polkinghorne, 1988; Polletta & Callahan, 2017; Shenhav, 2006). The conflict waged through words, images and stories, parallels the physical war. The former, if effective, captures the minds of individuals, while the latter poses a significant threat to societies, even those who opted for neutrality or non-alignment, such as Sweden and Finland.

This chapter aims to present the factors shaping Sweden's changing international status, marking its departure from neutrality, and Finland's abandonment of its non-alignment policy. An interdisciplinary perspective which employs methodological and exploratory tools from political science and cultural studies will provide a comprehensive understanding of the complexity of external and internal dynamics within the European socio-political landscape in the early 2020s. Additionally, the chapter will strive to address fundamental questions concerning the potential impact of these changes on the possibility of non-violent developments.

Anticipating an escalating threat from the Russian Federation, in 2018, every household in Sweden received from the authorities a brochure offering essential information on preparing for potential aggression and emphasising the importance of relying solely on information from Swedish state sources (Myndigheten för samhällsskydd och beredskap, 2018, p. 7). In Finland, whose direct neighbour is the Russian Federation, the situation differs slightly. The Finnish state and society have maintained a perpetual state of readiness to defend their territory, which stems from the experience of the Winter War in 1939 when the Soviet Union attacked the country.

From neutrality and non-alignment to NATO

The Nordic countries, including Sweden and Finland, constitute a group of international actors often inclined towards similar approaches, particularly on political matters. This inclination is a result of factors such as geographical proximity, cultural affinities and strong ties within the Nordic community. Characterised by relatively modest populations, the combined populace of all five Nordic states and the three special status territories of Greenland, the Faroe Islands and the Åland Islands not exceeding 28 million in 2022 (Nordic Statistic Database, 2023), these societies foster intra-regional collaboration to strengthen their collective agency on the global stage. This cooperation was evidenced by the formation of the Nordic Council in 1952, serving as a consultative forum for national parliaments and autonomous territories, and the establishment of a common labour market for the NORDEN region under the Helsinki Convention in 1962.[1] Intra-regional initiatives aimed at

58 Monika Banaś

consolidating national potential are complemented by engagements on the international arena where the Nordic countries exhibit diverse approaches to the same issues. Illustrative instances include EU membership (Sweden, Denmark, Finland) and the adoption of the euro (Finland). Until February 2022, NATO membership was another instance of divergent approaches to defence alliances. While Norway, Denmark and Iceland were NATO members, Sweden and Finland remained outside. Sweden's stance was rooted in its fidelity to the concept of neutrality articulated in the doctrine of 'freedom from alliances connected with a strong conventional defence' (Noreen, 1983, p. 47), a principle it had sought to uphold since the mid-19th century. In contrast, Finland refrained from NATO membership due to concerns about the potential reaction of the USSR, a state which may have perceived such affiliation as a direct threat to its interests protected by the earlier Treaty of Friendship, Cooperation and Mutual Assistance (FCA, 1948). This 'Nordic balance', a nuanced constellation of varied arrangements and alliances with diverse partners, was modified over time to align with emerging opportunities and circumstances, and served as a concept and strategy to ensure the general security of the Nordic states and their societies. Built on the fundamental assumption that stability in the region could be maintained within a bipolar system dominated by the United States and the USSR, the Nordic balance involved some actors aligning with US power (Iceland, Norway, Denmark), while others remained neutral (Sweden) or maintained proximity to the Eastern bloc (Finland) (Brundtland, 1966; Noreen, 1983; Rieker, 2006).

The fall of the Berlin Wall (1989) and the dissolution of the Soviet Union (1991) profoundly transformed the political map of Europe and, indeed, the world. The year of 1989 became a caesura of a new era for several nations including Poland, Slovakia, Czechia, Germany, Lithuania, Latvia, Estonia, Belarus, Ukraine and other states that had been liberated from Soviet hegemony. This wind of change reached NORDEN too, affording opportunities for more assertive decisions, particularly evident in the case of Finland. Nonetheless, an important concept for shaping Nordic defence policy developed from the strategic insights of Thorvald Stoltenberg, the Norwegian foreign minister (1987 to 1989 and 1990 to 1993) and the father of Jens Stoltenberg, the Secretary General of NATO since 2014. In 2009, Thorvald presented a strategic draft aimed at formulating a cohesive Nordic policy on the subject. The primary motivations behind this initiative, commissioned by the governments of individual member states, were threefold: (1) the withdrawing of the US military base in Iceland in 2006, (2) the escalating dispute over access to Arctic mineral deposits at the North Pole in 2007, and (3) the Russian invasion of Georgia in 2008. The latter in particular prompted the Nordic states to reassess their security policy in response to Russia's recurrent aggressive stance (Banaś, 2012, pp. 340–342).

The Stoltenberg report outlined a 13-point strategy for pooling resources to enhance the security of the Nordic states.[2] Following multilateral consultations and negotiations, unanimity in NORDEN was reached on six points including the establishment of a common Nordic satellite system, cybersecurity collaboration, enhanced cooperation among foreign services, joint military training, the prosecution of crimes against humanity, and the creation of a Nordic stabilisation task force, participating in UN peacekeeping missions, among other initiatives. However, divergent perspectives emerged on several levels, such as the defence of Icelandic airspace, the monitoring of territorial waters, establishing a rapid response force, maritime security, marine infantry, responses to natural disasters and the signing of a Nordic declaration of solidarity (Stoltenberg, 2009). The latter postulate faced particular resistance from the majority of parties (except Sweden), an opposition attributed to a preference for a more flexible relationship, unencumbered by written commitments.

Despite notable divergences in the positions of individual states, the Stoltenberg report garnered a favourable reception, laying the groundwork for comprehensive multilateral talks aimed at formulating a cohesive Nordic strategy to safeguard security in its widest conception. This strategy aligns within the broader institutional framework encompassing Europe and NATO (Haugevik & Sverdrup, 2019).

Concepts aimed at integrating Nordic potential are not new. Historical attempts towards (re)unification trace back to the 10th century under the reign of the Danish King, Harald Blåtand (Bluetooth), followed in subsequent centuries by initiatives such as Margaret I's establishment of the Kalmar Union. In contemporary times, specifically in 2009, Swedish historian Gunnar Wetterberg presented a concept in which Norden, a federation comprising Nordic states, would emerge on the world map in 2040, responding to the dynamics of the global scene. This united entity would have a common government, parliament, currency, institutions to facilitate economic harmonisation among member states, a unified foreign and defence policy, and a shared representative on international forums. Matters pertaining to taxation, social welfare, primary and secondary education, and cultural policy would remain the sole responsibility of member states (Wetterberg, 2010). The concept of a Nordic Federation has gained substantive attention, evidenced by extensive debates within the Nordic Council, the Nordic Council of Ministers and the Nordic media. Proponents emphasise this model of resource consolidation as an inevitable necessity amidst escalating international competition and growing tensions among global actors (states, organisations and corporations). In contrast, opponents express concerns regarding the potential weakening of EU structures and ties with the West (Banaś, 2012).

In the context of the Russian-Ukrainian war, this concept retains its relevance. The consolidation of the capabilities of individual Nordic states, in cooperation with allied or like-minded actors, appears a sensible course of action. Indeed, the security paradigm of the Nordic region can be based on the dual approach of fostering intra-regional cooperation while concurrently enhancing relations, including military engagement, with external actors opposed to Russian aggression. In this context, the decision by Sweden and Finland to join NATO aligns with the processes outlined.

The neutrality status of Sweden and Finland had long been a theoretical construct (Rieker, 2006, pp. 64–75, 91–101) and in practical terms, both countries engaged in operations under the NATO umbrella on a partnership basis. For instance, Swedish units participated in safeguarding Icelandic airspace (Haugevik & Sverdrup, 2019, p. 6), while Finland provided support to NATO forces in missions across the Balkans, Afghanistan and Iraq (NATO, 2023). Russia's attack on Ukraine in February 2022 became a turning point, marking the end of the era characterised by the official neutrality of Sweden and the non-alignment of Finland. Swedish neutrality, which means an absolute refusal to participate in war, and Finnish non-alignment, leaving an option of military participation, did not merely postpone but strategically awaited an opportune moment to unequivocally declare their affiliation to the group of allied states with whom they had long collaborated. Since the mid-1990s, Sweden and Finland have actively participated in NATO's Partnership for Peace (PfP) and the UK-led non-NATO Joint Expeditionary Force (JEF), initiatives aimed at consolidating and enhancing the defence capabilities of ten northern European partners.

Sweden and Finland's simultaneous application for membership in the North Atlantic Alliance on 18 May 2022 served as a definitive indication to the international community of the two countries' extensive security collaboration and their readiness to fully join the coalition resolutely opposing Russia and the latter's allies. For both Sweden and Finland, as with other NATO members, Article 5 of the treaty holds particular significance. The article stipulates that an attack on any of the pact's signatories is considered an attack on the entire bloc, prompting a response, including a military one, from the member states of the alliance (Article 5 of the Washington Treaty).

At the NATO summit in Madrid on 29 June 2022, both candidate countries received formal invitations to join as members. This decision was bolstered by arguments emphasising the need to protect Sweden and Finland, strengthen the alliance itself, and enhance security within the Euro-Atlantic region (NATO, 2022). The concept of 'Finlandisation', hoped for by Russia, became an unrealistic wish, supplanted by the prospect of a 'NATOisation' of Finland and Sweden.

The official invitation extended to the candidates was preceded by a series of extensive, often fraught negotiations. Türkiye's withdrawal of objections to the membership of the two countries was contingent upon the fulfilment of several conditions including the extradition of individuals considered by Türkiye to be terrorists and residing in Sweden or Finland, cessation of support for Kurdish dissidents, and the lifting of the embargo on arms supplies to Türkiye. Meanwhile, Hungary cited its hesitancy due to the strong criticisms voiced by both Sweden and Finland against the government of Viktor Orban and its policies on the international arena. These criticisms articulated, for instance, in the European Parliament, alleged violations of the rule of law in Hungary and the suppression of free media (Reuters, 2023; RFE/RL, 2022; Szakacs, 2023; 'Turkey rejects NATO offer', 2022).

Sweden, Finland and the Russian-Ukrainian war 61

It appeared that the intricate dynamics in Türkiye-Sweden and Türkiye-Finland relations would find resolution with the signing of a trilateral memorandum during the Madrid summit. Within the memorandum, the involved parties agreed among other stipulations that Sweden and Finland would cease their support for the YPG/PYD (Kurdish groups in Syria, the People's Defence Units and the Democratic Union Party), recognise the PKK (Kurdistan Workers' Party) as a terrorist organisation, extradite individuals identified as terrorists by Türkiye, and combat disinformation harmful to national interests (Trilateral Memorandum, 2022). Following several months implementing these agreements, no hindrances seemed to stand in the way to membership for the two Nordic countries, as NATO Secretary General Jens Stoltenberg announced subsequent to his visit to Ankara in November 2022 (Bilginsoy & Cook, 2022). However, a setback in the accession process came from Türkiye once more. This was caused by several events in Stockholm in January 2023, including the ostentatious display of effigy of President Erdogan and the burning of a copy of the Quran by the Swedish-Danish radical, Rasmus Paludan (UN Body [S4] Condemns Quran Burning in Sweden, 2023). Sweden's decision to permit this event, criticised not only by Turkish authorities, for whom Islam holds significant socio-religious importance, but also by other international actors (including the UN), was justified on the grounds of freedom of expression and the democratic principles underpinning the country. Freedom of speech and opinion, enshrined within the broader framework of liberal democracy, constitute the cornerstones of the Swedish multicultural framework. Although such an incident occurred in Sweden, it did not happen in Finland, where all public acts of burning objects are prohibited. This contrast prompted Türkiye to proceed with Finland in subsequent negotiation stages and consequently, the accession process was split into two separate tracks: Finnish and Swedish. This led to the ratification of Finland's accession protocol by the Turkish parliament on 30 March 2023 and the country's admission to NATO on 4 April 2023.

Türkiye's objections to Sweden's membership, in addition to the aspects mentioned, harboured a less pronounced dimension related to Türkiye's purchase of 40 F-16 aircraft from the United States. While President Joe Biden supported the agreement, the stance of the US Congress remained unclear, and the transaction could not proceed without its approval (Pamuk & Shalal, 2022).

Hungary delayed the ratification of the Swedish and Finnish accession protocols for reasons previously delineated, further underscored by Prime Minister Orban's assertion that Türkiye's demands should be met (Reuters, 2023). The hesitancy exhibited by certain members of the Hungarian parliament stemmed from the fact that Türkiye, one of NATO's strongest partners, had serious reservations regarding the alliance's expansion. Others highlighted the challenge posed by the length of the Finnish-Russian border, after Finland's NATO membership, one of the longest to defend. Additionally, some voices of indecision, impeding the accession process, underscored Türkiye's

62   Monika Banaś

influential position and emphasised the importance of respecting its stance on the matter (Bayer, 2023).

Türkiye's and Hungary's ties with Russia played a significant role in shaping the trajectory of these negotiations. As of August 2023, both countries have maintained close relationships with the Russian Federation. Instances include Russian investments in Hungary's nuclear power plant infrastructure and the provision of gas and oil to both states. Türkiye in particular has longstanding economic connections with Russia as a key trading partner ('*Europe's Energy Crisis*', 2022; Gosling, 2023; Ministry of Foreign Affairs of Republic of Türkiye, 2022; Tanis, 2022; Toksabay & Hayatsever, 2023).

Hungary and Türkiye played a key role in the accession process of Sweden and Finland. By expressing reservations, they impeded the procedure, leading to tensions and rendering the entire accession process challenging within the global context. While Türkiye, as a NATO member, tried to assume the role of a mediator or a bridge between the Western powers and Russia, Hungary, also a NATO member, did not possess such competence. The Hungarian stance appeared more inclined towards leveraging the circumstances to convey to its critics within the EU, that these countries should respect the policy of the Orban administration, even if they consider it populist or undemocratic.

The stances taken by Türkiye and Hungary leaned towards favouring Russia's interests. Despite the Russian Federation's opposition to the accession of Sweden and Finland, President Putin asserted that upon joining NATO, the Nordic countries would not pose a threat to Russia provided that NATO refrained from deploying forces and establishing infrastructure on their territories (Reuters, 2022). This statement, although transparently strategic, served to portray Russia as a party compelled by Western forces (through NATO) to defend itself by actions counterproductive to de-escalating the conflict, referred to in Russian terminology as a 'special military operation in Ukraine'.

The difference in perspectives on this matter is evidenced in May 2022 by Sanna Marin, the Prime Minister of the Finnish government:

> The only country that is threatening Europe's security and openly waging a war of aggression is Russia.
> (Prime Minister Sanna Marin, source: https://valtioneuvosto.
> fi/en/-//10616/speech-delivered-by-prime-minister-sanna-
> marin-at-parliament-s-plenary-session-on-16-may-2022)

and by Ann Linde, Swedish Foreign Minister, in June 2022:

> A dark new chapter has begun in the history of Europe. On 24 February, Russia launched an unprovoked, illegal and unjustifiable war against its neighbour, the democratic state of Ukraine. The Russian threat to the European security order will persist for a long time to come.
> (Minister of Foreign Affairs, Ann Linde, Statement of
> Government Policy in the Parliamentary Debate on
> Foreign Affairs, Friday, 10 June 2022)

Cultural foundations for political-military actions: Sweden, Finland, Russia

Actions in the political realm and those executed through military means are shaped by specific value systems that mould minds in individual and collective forms. This process is framed by culture. While numerous attempts have been made to define culture, delving into them is beyond the scope of this discussion, however it is worth highlighting one perspective relevant to our discourse. Culture, functioning as a collective shaping force on the mind, explains human attitudes, behaviours, actions, beliefs and values. The diversity inherent in culture creates more or less distinct constellations, which in turn form a broader construct: civilisations (Huntington, 2000).

When analysing the attitudes and behaviours of individuals, a concept of cultural dimensions is proposed by Geert Hofstede, and while this framework is not devoid of limitations, it serves as a valuable tool for presenting the mechanisms that underlie collective actions within communities. Hofstede delineated six fundamental dimensions: power distance (acceptance of unequal distribution of power), individualism (an individual's self-image is defined by I or We), long-term orientation (relations to the past, the present and the future), masculinity (problem solving via dialogue or competition and confrontation), uncertainty avoidance (preference for status quo) and indulgence (gratification) (Hofstede, 2010).

A comparison of the four countries, or more precisely of their societies, gives the following graph:

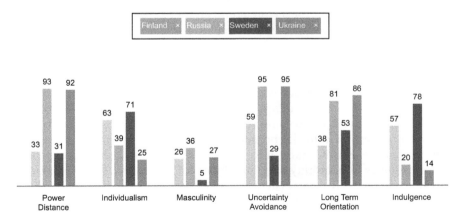

Graph 4.1 Cultural dimensions by Geert Hofstede.

Source: www.hofstede-insights.com/country-comparisontool?countries=finland%2Crussia%2Csweden%2Cukraine*

64   *Monika Banaś*

The comparison reveals a clear proximity between Finland and Sweden in terms of 'power distance', juxtaposed against Russia and Ukraine. While the Nordic countries perceive an unequal distribution of power as undesirable, Russians and Ukrainians consider it an acceptable and, in contemporary contexts, normal condition. This observation holds significance as it presents the criteria dictating the requisite attributes of a leader to gain support from a society predisposed or disinclined to make large-scale sacrifices (indulgence).

Individualism as a cultural trait is relatively high among Swedes and Finns, while it is less pronounced among Russians and Ukrainians. This implies that individuals within the first pair perceive themselves as autonomous, whereas those in the second pair tend to view themselves as subordinate. The dichotomy of individualism versus collectivism reflects the degree to which the social structure either constrains individual freedom or allows individuals to develop and act autonomously, including in economic matters. In societies exhibiting a strong collectivist orientation, such as Russia and Ukraine, the individual is subject to the community, and any challenge to this order is often met with severe criticism, social ostracism and sanctions, or even legal repercussions.

In terms of conflict resolution through dialogue or competition and confrontation, Finland and Ukraine display similarities. This suggests that assertive attitudes, clear statements of intent, and a preference for competition are valued in socialisation contexts such as schools and workplaces within these nations. Russian cultural norms, as evidenced by the cited cases, tend to align with assertive behaviours, potentially contributing to aggressive conduct, including on the international stage, and exemplified by the invasion of Ukraine in February 2022. Conversely, Sweden favours dialogue and extensive negotiations, prioritising conciliatory approaches. The contemporary image of the state differs significantly from the expansive and imperial ambitions associated with Swedish rulers in previous eras (e.g. *Stormaktstiden*). A low masculinity index may account for the preference, until recently, for a neutral status.

The uncertainty avoidance index refers to the strategy employed by users of a given culture or members of a society to moderate or manage the future, which is inherently unpredictable. Uncertainty about the future can be mitigated through the replication of established patterns and maintenance of the status quo. This tendency is observable in Russia and Ukraine, whereas in Sweden and Finland, a different approach prevails. From an early age, individuals in these Nordic countries are encouraged to be autonomous and act independently within the broader community. Therefore, it is not surprising that the Nordic states have changed their stance, abandoning their previous policy of neutrality and non-alignment, in the face of the escalating threat posed by the Russian Federation, indicative of its efforts to re-establish spheres of influence following the dissolution of the USSR.

The long-term orientation index is high for Russia and Ukraine, which indicates a preference in these societies for investing in ventures that bring outcomes in the distant future, often entailing significant sacrifices. Compared

Sweden, Finland and the Russian-Ukrainian war   65

to Western societies, the relatively low standard of living among Russians is the price most of them are prepared to pay, driven by adherence to the ideology spread by the Kremlin. Similarly, in Ukraine's present circumstances, the imperative of defending the nation justifies the readiness of its citizens to make sacrifices.

Towards the end of the conflict?

Vladimir Putin, in an address to the nation in April 2005, said that the dissolution of the USSR in 1991 was the greatest geopolitical catastrophe of the century, leading to the emergence of separatist movements within Russia and leaving tens of millions of Russians outside the Federation ('*Putin Deplores Collapse of USSR*', 2005). These words foreshadowed subsequent actions, yet Western audiences and elites ignored this (Mearsheimer, 2014, p. 78; Telewizja Republika Kalendarz Historyczny, 2013). Putin was perceived as a modern leader guiding the country towards democracy, albeit in accordance with his own agenda and schedule:

> Russia is a country that, at the will of its own people, chose democracy for itself. It set out on this course itself and, observing all generally accepted political norms, will decide for itself how it will ensure that the principles of freedom and democracy are implemented, taking into account its historical, geopolitical and other characteristics.
>
> (President Putin's speech addressed to nation, broadcast by Russia TV, 25 April 2005; source: http://news.bbc.co.uk/2/hi/europe/4481455.stm)

Despite clear declarations of his intention to restore the country's former power, President Putin was accepted and even applauded by the West (CBS News, 2010).

Richard Pipes, a respected expert on Russian history and culture, has consistently advanced the thesis of Russia's immutability despite changes in leadership. The American scholar based this premise on Russian society's deep attachment to authoritarianism and the concept of the patrimonial state, where it is the property of the ruling autocrat, the sole ruler endowed with the exclusive authority to manage its resources, including the human ones, and exercising complete control over information. The centuries-long autocratic rule impeded the development of a culture, including a political culture, that would have been conducive to respect for liberal law and property rights, particularly land ownership, which is the basis of freedom (Pipes, 1999).

Over generations, exposure to this system has led society to view it as natural and the sole option, resisting any attempts – especially external ones – to alter it. Pipes believed that the theory of authoritarian continuity provides a compelling explanation for the Russian Federation and its society. This theory suggests that Western efforts to democratise Russia are inherently futile, not due to differences primarily in culture, but rather in civilisation (Pipes, 2006; Telewizja Republika Kalendarz Historyczny, 2013; Polskie Radio, 2014).

These differences in approach, or more precisely, this misunderstanding of the Russian mindset, regarding value assignment and action, were also highlighted by John Mearsheimer (2014). In his view, by disregarding Russian concerns regarding NATO enlargement and the inclusion of Ukraine within the sphere of Western influence, the United States and the EU acted provocatively towards the Russian Federation. This is because, in its strategy to safeguard its geopolitical interests, Russia perceives Ukraine (and Georgia) as inviolably within its sphere of influence (2014, pp. 79, 82). Russian *Realpolitik*, which involves defending spheres of influence through hard power, clashed with Western 'Liberal Ideas' *Politik*, characterised by democratisation and liberalisation through smart power. This confrontation resulted in dramatic consequences, ultimately leading to war.

If we return to the two questions posed at the beginning of this chapter, at the time of writing this text (August 2023) it has proven challenging to make definitive judgments regarding the termination and resolution of the ongoing war. A multipolar world comprised of diverse civilisations, as underscored by Samuel Huntington, both shapes and is shaped by culture. So it is culture and cultural identities that create civilisations, thereby forming patterns of cohesion, disintegration and conflict (Huntington, 2000, p. 14). Moreover, Braudel's conceptual framework of the grammar of civilisations refers to identifiable laws that regulate the functioning of civilisations as collective mentalities (Braudel, 2006, pp. 55–57). Given this premise, the confrontation between Western and Eastern civilisations, epitomised by the Russian-Ukrainian war, may yet have many 'reveals' and dimensions. Countries and societies situated on the borderline of civilisations, its meeting point, must prepare accordingly. Sweden and Finland have acknowledged this reality. In times when the global order is being reorganised, neutrality and non-alignment prove ineffective, thus abandoning them mitigates the risk of being attacked.

The stabilisation of the region, based on a strong alliance, professional armies and societies' readiness to defend their territories is found alongside the preservation of national cultures and the inherent values they encapsulate. These elements seem to be essential parts of a security strategy for the future.

Another important aspect of this strategy is the feminisation of foreign policy, as highlighted by Ann Linde, quoted earlier (Statement of Government Policy in the Parliamentary Debate on Foreign Affairs, 10 June 2022, p. 8). The participation of women in politics, at both domestic and international levels, across all domains and dimensions and in key positions, is an indispensable shift in the pursuit of peace that is likely to endure for more than two generations.

Sweden, Finland and the Russian-Ukrainian war   67

The tendency towards power-based solutions, including warfare, to resolve conflicts is rooted in the unequal distribution of power, particularly in its limited accessibility to women (Banaś, 2020, pp. 233–256; Regan & Paskeviciute, 2003). Masculinised power structures, especially at decision-making levels, pose a barrier to dialogue and the peaceful pursuit of mutually acceptable resolutions among conflicting parties. As Russian society is characterised by a high power-distribution index which acknowledges power asymmetry, it favours coercive arguments over negotiation, contrasting with the approach prevailing in contemporary Nordic societies. For the latter, the feminisation of politics, including foreign policy, does not imply a lack of decisiveness, as stereotypical assumptions might suggest. Sweden and Finland initiated the accession process to NATO structures during the tenures of female prime ministers, Magdalena Andersson (Sweden) and Sanna Marin (Finland). The enlargement of the North Atlantic Alliance by Finland (2023) and Sweden (2024), which has finally happened, reinforces the argument for including a female perspective in the quest for enduring peace.

Notes

1 NORDEN – a common name for the five Nordic states and three territories with special status and extensive autonomy.
2 The 13 points: (1) Nordic stabilisation task force, (2) Nordic cooperation on surveillance of Icelandic airspace, (3) Nordic maritime monitoring system, (4 Maritime response force, (5) Satellite system for surveillance and communications, (6) Nordic cooperation on Arctic issues, (7) Nordic resource network to protect against cyber attacks, (8) Disaster response unit, (9) War crimes investigation unit, (10) Cooperation between foreign services, (11) Military cooperation on transport, medical services, education, materiel and exercises, (12) Amphibious unit and (13) Nordic declaration of solidarity.

References

Austin, J. (1962). *How to Do Things with Words*. Cambridge University Press.
Banaś, M. (2012a). Nordic federation as a state. In B. Jóźwik & T. Stępniewski (Eds.), *Yearbook of the Institute of East-Central Europe*, 10/6, European economic integration and convergence.. Instytut Europy Środkowo-Wschodniej.
Banaś, M. (2012b). Rewizja polityki bezpieczeństwa państw nordyckich. Wybrane aspekty. In A. Jach & M. Kuryłowicz (Eds.), *Rozpad ZSRR i jego konsekwencje dla Europy i świata* (pp. 333–350). Wydawnictwo Księgarnia Akademicka
Banaś, M. (2020). Kulturowy potencjał femipolityki na przykładzie Irlandii przełomu XX i XXI wieku. In M. Banaś (Ed.), *Kobiety w polityce. Sfera publiczna* (pp. 233–256). Wydawnictwo Księgarnia Akademicka.
Bayer, L. (2023, April 12). 'Annoying sideshow': Hungary frustrates NATO allies. *Politico*. www.politico.eu/article/hungary-nato-sweden-bid-accession-block-democracy-viktor-orban/
Bilginsoy, Z., & Cook, L. (2022, November 3). *NATO chief urges Turkey to endorse Finland, Sweden accession*. AP. https://apnews.com/article/nato-middle-east-turkey-sweden-istanbul-b6e4402dedfd028e6042c3d5b8f6b6e2
Braudel, F. (2006). *Gramatyka cywilizacji*. Oficyna Naukowa.

68 Monika Banaś

Brundtland, A. O. (1966). The nordic balance: Past and present. *Cooperation and Conflict, 1*(4), 30–63.

CBS News. (2010, December 14). Putin sings for Hollywood stars [Video]. *YouTube*. www.youtube.com/watch?v=Y96ju_nOuAc&t=9s

Clark, M. (2020). *Russian Hybrid Warfare*. Institute for the Study of War.

Crow, D., & Jones, M. (2018). Narratives as tools for influencing policy change. *Policy and Politics, 46*(2), 217–234.

Europe's Energy Crisis: Russia Gets Approval to Build Two New Nuclear Reactors in Hungary. (2022, August 27). *Euronews*. www.euronews.com/2022/08/27/hungary-gives-russia-green-light-for-nuclear-reactor-expansion

Gosling, T. (2023, April 14). Hungary's loyalties tested as Russia's war in Ukraine grinds on. *Al Jazeera*. www.aljazeera.com/news/2023/4/14/hungarys-loyalties-tested-as-russias-war-in-ukraine-grinds-on

Haugevik, K., & Sverdrup, U. (Eds.). (2019). *10 Years on: Reassessing the Stoltenberg Report on Nordic Cooperation*. Norwegian Institute of International Affairs, Institute of International Affairs, University of Iceland, Danish Institute for International Studies, Finnish Institute of International Affairs, Swedish Institute of International Affairs.

Hofmann, F. (2022, February 18). Russia's hybrid war against Ukraine. *Deutsche Welle*. www.dw.com/en/russias-hybrid-war-against-ukraine/a-60829873

Hofstede, G., Hofstede, G. J., & Minkov, M. (2010). *Cultures and Organizations: Software of the Mind* (3rd ed.). McGraw Hill Education.

Huntington, S. (2000). *Zderzenie cywilizacji i nowy kształt ładu światowego*. Muza S.A.

Koneczny, F. (2002) [Originally published 1935]. *O wielości cywilizacji*. Wydawnictwo ANTYK.

Mearsheimer, J. (2014). Why the Ukraine crisis is the west's fault: The liberal delusions that provoked Putin. *Foreign Affairs, 93*(5), 77–89.

Ministry of Foreign Affairs of Republic of Türkiye. (2022). *Relations between Türkiye and the Russian Federation*. www.mfa.gov.tr/relations-between-turkey-and-the-russian-federation.en.mfa

Myndigheten för samhällsskydd och beredskap. (2018). *Om krisen eller kriget kommer*. Karlstad.

Nordic Statistic Database. (2023). *The Population of the Nordic Region [Data for 2022]*. www.norden.org/en/information/population-nordic-region

Noreen, E. (1983). The Nordic balance: A security policy concept in theory and practice. *Cooperation and Conflict, 18*(1), 43–56.

North Atlantic Treaty Organization. (2022). *Madrid Summit Declaration Issued by NATO Heads of State and Government Participating in the Meeting of the North Atlantic Council in Madrid 29 June 2022*. www.nato.int/cps/en/natohq/official_texts_196951.htm?selectedLocale=en

North Atlantic Treaty Organization. (2023, March 28). *Relations with Finland*. www.nato.int/cps/en/natohq/topics_49594.htm

Nye, J. S. (2009). Get smart: Combining hard and soft power. *Foreign Affairs, 88*(4), 160–163.

Pamuk, H., & Shalal, A. (2022, June 29). Biden administration throws support behind potential F-16 sale to Turkey. *Reuters*. www.reuters.com/world/biden-administration-throws-support-behind-potential-f-16-sale-turkey-2022-06-29/

Pipes, R. (2006). The past in the present. In P. Desai (Ed.), *Conversations on Russia: Reform from Yeltsin to Putin* (pp. 353–369). Oxford University Press. DOI: 10.1093/acprof:oso/9780195300611.003.0018

Pipes, R. (1999). *Property and Freedom*. Alfred A. Knopf.

Polkinghorne, D. (1988). *Narrative Knowing and the Human Sciences*. Suny Press.

Sweden, Finland and the Russian-Ukrainian war 69

Polletta, F., & Callahan, J. (2017). Deep stories, nostalgia narratives, and fake news: Storytelling in the Trump era. *American Journal of Cultural Sociology, 5*(3), 392–408. DOI: 10.1057/s41290-017-0037-7

Polskie Radio. (2014, November 5). Ryszard Pipes: w Rosji demokracja i prawa człowieka nie są ważne (Radio Poland) [Video interview given by R. Pipes to Polskie Radio]. *YouTube*. www.youtube.com/watch?v=ZV09W3tL2Xw

Putin Deplores Collapse of USSR. (2005, April 25). *BBC*. http://news.bbc.co.uk/2/hi/4480745.stm

Regan, P., & Paskeviciute, A. (2003). Women's access to politics and peaceful states. *Journal of Peace Research, 40*(3), 287–302.

Reuters. (2022, June 29). *Putin: Russia will Respond if NATO Sets Up Infrastructure in Finland, Sweden.* www.reuters.com/world/europe/putin-russia-will-respond-if-nato-sets-up-infrastructure-finland-sweden-2022-06-29/

Reuters. (2023, May 23). *Hungary's Orban: Better Relations with Sweden Needed before NATO Membership.* www.reuters.com/world/europe/hungarys-orban-better-relations-with-sweden-needed-before-nato-membership-2023-05-23/

RFE/RL. (2022). Turkey sets conditions for backing Swedish, Finnish NATO membership. *Radio Free Europe/Radio Liberty.* www.rferl.org/a/turkey-conditions-nato-sweden-finland/31861513.html

Rieker, P. (2006). *Europeization of National Security Identity. The EU and the Changing Security Identities of the Nordic States.* Routledge.

Shenhav, R. (2006). Political narratives and political reality. *International Political Science Review, 27*(3), 245–262. DOI: 10.1177/0192512106064474

Stoltenberg, T. (2009). *Nordic Cooperation on Foreign and Security Policy: Proposals Presented to the Extraordinary Meeting of Nordic Foreign Ministers in Oslo on 9 February 2009.* www.google.com/url?sa=t&source=web&rct=j&opi=89978449&url=www.regjeringen.no/globalassets/upload/ud/vedlegg/nordicreport.pdf&ved=2ahUKEwiwwND9u62FAxWcIhAIHVL7CWAQFnoECA8QAQ&usg=AOvVaw0-BIFp_U4kllm4ycrTGURd

Szakacs, G. (2023, February 24). Hungary PM says more talks needed on Finland, Sweden NATO bids. *Reuters.* www.reuters.com/world/europe/hungary-pm-says-more-talks-needed-finland-sweden-nato-bids-2023-02-24/

Tanis, F. (2022). *Turkey Plays a Tough Balancing Act as It Strengthens Ties with Russia [Talk recording and transcript]* NPR. www.npr.org/2022/12/10/1142099362/turkey-plays-a-tough-balancing-act-as-it-strengthens-ties-with-russia

Telewizja Republika Kalendarz Historyczny. (2013, September 20). Wolne głosy – Gościem Antoniego Trzmiela jest Richard Pipes [Video interview given by R. Pipes to Telewizja Republika]. *YouTube*. www.youtube.com/watch?v=fXa-_2HwGXI

Toksabay, E., & Hayatsever, H. (2023). Turkey set to keep strong Russia ties whoever wins election. *Reuters.* www.reuters.com/world/turkey-set-keep-strong-russia-ties-whoever-wins-election-2023-05-05/

Trilateral Memorandum [Signed by Representatives of Türkiye, Finland and Sweden]. (2022, June 28). www.nato.int/nato_static_fl2014/assets/pdf/2022/6/pdf/220628-trilat-memo.pdf

Turkey Rejects NATO Offer of Trilateral Talks with Sweden and Finland. (2022, June 15). *Financial Times.* www.ft.com/content/ef709c86-aead-4b85-803a-c1b274be85cf

UN Body Condemns Quran Burning in Sweden. (2023, January 23). *Al Jazeera.* www.aljazeera.com/news/2023/1/23/un-body-condemns-quran-burning-in-sweden

Waterhouse, J. (2022, January 21). Do Ukrainians and Russians believe a full-scale war is possible? *BBC.* www.bbc.com/news/world-europe-60090991

Wetterberg, G. (2010). *Förbundsstaten Norden.* Nordish Council of Ministers.

5 The vision of peace à la Putin

Russia's strategic objectives towards the Baltic Sea states in the context of the war in Ukraine

Magdalena Lachowicz and Agnieszka Legucka

'There is no Russia without Ukraine': the ideological sources of Russian aggression against Ukraine

After the dissolution of the USSR, the Russians rediscovered geopolitics (Legucka, 2013). According to Adam Rotfeld, this geopolitical perception of the world was related to the failure of communist ideology and an intellectual inability to find out how Russia could continue to influence foreign relations (Rotfeld, 2004, p. 90). Russia has been predestined by geography to be a global power, and its political and intellectual elites held strong beliefs that without Ukraine Russia would not be able to rule the world and to be an empire (Zhiltsov et al., 2003, p. 15; Brzeziński, 1998, pp. 40–47). The most radical attitude towards Ukraine was demonstrated by Alexander Dugin who argued that as an independent state with some territorial ambitions, it poses an immense threat for the whole of Eurasia, and without solving the Ukrainian problem there is no point in talking about continental geopolitics (Dugin, 1997). For Dugin, the only solution is the 'decomposition' of Ukraine, and its entire territory should be within the sphere of influence of the RF (Dugin, 2004).

The literature mentions a number of ideological foundations for Russian aggression in Ukraine (Götz & Staun, 2022). Some consider it to be a symptom of postcolonial 'lost territory' syndrome (Tolz & Hutchings, 2023), while others see it as a geopolitical building of a 'sphere of influence' or of 'privileged interest', as it was described in 2009 by Dmitry Medvedev ('*Rosyjsko-amerykański reset*', 2009). This allows Russia to present itself as a regional power with global aspirations, within which Ukraine is not a subject of international relations but a territory where the interests of powers clash (Walt, 2022; Mearsheimer, 2022). Thus, in Russian propaganda, Ukraine appears either as a part of Russia or as 'anti-Russia', acting under the influence and on the orders of the West (Legucka & Szczudlik, 2023; Götz & Staun, 2022). Going deeper, Russian politicians (including Vladimir Putin) and researchers highlight Russia's historical right to Ukraine, referring in particular to the origins of the Russian state in Kievan Rus (Bychkov, 2005). This also has an impact on Russians' sense of cultural superiority over

DOI: 10.4324/9781003558040-7

Ukrainians. After the full-scale invasion of Ukraine, researchers point to a specific form of Putin's obsession (Liik, 2022), arguing that the annexation of Crimea in 2014 increased support for the Russian leader, so the future of Ukraine is not only an element of the RF's foreign strategy but also an issue of internal policy, which includes the stability of the authoritarian regime within this state.

The desire of Russian authorities to keep Ukraine in their sphere sometimes bears the hallmarks of a civilising mission. Putin referred to the idea of Slavic unity, writing in his article from 12 July 2021 that Ukrainians are an eternal, inseparable part of the 'triune Russian nation' (*триединый русский народ*). According to Putin, this concept is based on a thousand years of history, language, 'Russian' ethnic identification, shared cultural space and Orthodox religion (Domańska, 2021; Stat'ya Vladimira Putina, 2021). He argued that Ukraine's connections with the Russian state are organic in character, and only through unity with Russia can Ukraine develop; otherwise, it will fall apart. The Kremlin narrative has rejected the right of Ukraine and Belarus to establish sovereign states, suggesting that the common motherland for all of them should be Russia (Stat'ya Vladimira Putina, 2021). Russian historians Kirillov and Kryuchkov maintain that Russia has never attacked anyone, and has reached for military instruments only to defend and protect Russians (Kirillov & Kryuchkov, 2008).

Operational goals of the Russian Federation towards Ukraine after 2014 and after 2022: a comparative perspective

During the press conference on 13 December 2023, President Putin stated that 'peace will come only when we reach our [Russian – A.L.] goals' (*'Pryamaya liniya s Putinym'*, 2023). What differentiates the Russian narrative on the aggression against Ukraine in 2014 from the one in 2022 is the scale of manipulation, disinformation and propaganda regarding the reasons for invasion, although the arguments used are very similar (Bildziukiewicz, 2022; Jones & Wasilewski, 2022). A turning point for the Russian power elite was the Ukrainian 'revolution of dignity' from late 2013 and early 2014, which led to the fleeing of Viktor Yanukovych, the pro-Russian president of Ukraine, and the election of Petro Poroshenko. This also meant that Ukrainian foreign policy took on a pro-Western orientation. The perspective of Ukraine's democratisation was interpreted by Putin as a challenge to the RF's internal policy (the question of maintaining the Putin system) as well as foreign and security policy (an increase in the influence of the EU and the United States in Russia's neighbourhood and a weakening of the RF's position in the Black Sea region) (Ash et al., 2023). Following these events, three international Russian goals became clear, and three supporting narratives of Russia about Ukraine emerged.

1. Russia wants to change the existing international order by weakening the West, in particular the United States (Allan et al., 2021). The ongoing

military conflict with Ukraine is presented as a proxy war of the United States against Russia, for example, by the expansion of NATO towards the east, and the growing international rivalry into which Russia was 'forced' (Bryjka, 2022). Thus, the Russian authorities insist that Western sanctions are not related to aggression against Ukraine but allegedly are only to weaken Russia in the international arena ('*Putin Says Western Sanctions*', 2022). The target of this narrative is mainly Russian society as well as states from the Global South. Hence in the context of the war in Ukraine, the pro-Kremlin media describe Ukrainian authorities as 'Washington's puppets' (Grishin, 2023), thus denying that Ukraine is a subject with agency in deciding about its own future and security. From Putin's point of view, what is at stake is the survival of his authoritarian regime. The authoritarian leader is afraid of the very existence of a democratic superpower, whose values are a foundation of the current international order, and could spread to Russia's neighbours or to Russia itself. According to Robert Person and Michael McFaul, the strengthening of democratic values and practices (such as free elections) in Ukraine is perceived in Russia as a threat to Putin's position in the RF (the spillover effect) (Person & McFaul, 2022).

2. In stopping the pro-Western trajectory of Ukrainian foreign policy, Russia declares that it wants to stop NATO's eastward expansion. With the use of military instruments, the Russian authorities wanted to discourage the West from engaging in the sphere of the RF's 'privileged interests' (Dyner et al., 2023). This purpose was served by the Russo-Georgian war in August 2008 and the annexation of min 2014, while the 2022 invasion was for Russia another reason for manipulation. The Russian authorities maintained that the war against Georgia was an 'operation to enforce peace', while in 2014 they redirected attention to the separatist movements in Donbas and negated Russia's direct participation in the military operations in Crimea. Deciding to start a war against Ukraine, Russia abandoned such masks and officially involved Russian armed forces in the intervention which, however, was not called a 'war' but a 'special military operation'. Under the pretext of demilitarisation and denazification of Ukraine Putin, 2022), Russia has been waging a war of attrition according to the idea that if Ukraine does not want to be in the Russian sphere of influence, its access to NATO and the EU should be blocked. To this aim, Russian propaganda attempts to discourage both the international community and its own citizens from supporting Ukrainians and this is accompanied by efforts to discredit the Ukrainian government, which since 2014 has been described as the 'Kiev/Bandera regime', 'the fascist authorities in Kiev' or 'far-right extremists' (Putin, 2022). Since 2022, portraying Ukrainian as 'Nazis' was also useful for the Russian authorities to mobilise soldiers going to war, among whom the legends of the Great Patriotic War (1941–1945) are deeply held ('*Putin podcherknul skhodstvo*', 2023).

The vision of peace à la Putin 73

3. The increase in pro-Russian influences in Ukraine led to a declaration of its special protection for Russian-speaking people outside RF borders in order to gain influence over Ukrainian internal and foreign policy. The assumptions behind the war in Donbas and the signing of the Minsk agreements (2014 and 2015) were changes in the Ukrainian constitution and federalisation of this state. The allegedly peaceful, negotiation-oriented stance of the Russian authorities was the result of the Kremlin's conviction that including Donbas in Ukraine would offer Russia a special opportunity to destabilise the political life of its neighbour (Koshiw, 2022). However, the RF itself did not respect the obligation to withdraw Russian soldiers and military equipment from the contested territories. Russia usurped the right to oppose Ukrainian regulations, including the law on the national language. From 2014 the Russian propaganda argued that 'genocide' against Russian-speaking population was taking place in Donbas (*'Putin sravnil deystviya'*, 2014). After eight years of conflict and the accompanying propaganda, Russian society was convinced about the need to protect the population of Donbas from the 'Nazis'. This is confirmed by EU StratCom analyses revealing that between February and March 2022 the use of phrases regarding 'genocide' and 'Nazism' in Russian media increased in frequency by 550% and 290%, respectively (Bildziukiewicz, 2022).

The lack of a well-prepared information campaign for the 2022 invasion, as opposed to the one focused on the annexation of Crimea (Fridrichová, 2023), contributed to a public relations disaster. The declared goals of the Russian war in Ukraine evolved with changes at the frontline; narratives were changing and sometimes became mutually exclusive. For example, during the first phase of the Russian offensive (February-April 2022) they spoke about the need to de-Nazify and demilitarise Ukraine. After the first setbacks at the front (April-September 2022) Russian propaganda increased the frequency of messages that Russia is not fighting Ukraine but NATO (the West) on the Ukrainian front. Pro-Russian media presented the so-called special military operation as a clash between two civilisations. Russia focused on convincing Russians to participate in the war effort in defence of their motherland, threatened by the possible victory of the West. Kremlin propaganda argued that in the case of defeat, the perpetrators would be brought to justice ('a second Nuremberg'). In the third phase of the war (from October 2022), the Russian army focused on defending their positions in the occupied territories and building fortifications to stop a Ukrainian counteroffensive. The narrative repeated at that time spoke about victorious Russia. As a result, the attitude of Russian society towards the war changed little, and its citizens, for different reasons, continued to support the state's war effort ('Conflict with Ukraine', 2023). According to the publications of Meduza, even those who initially opposed the aggression, after several months of military operations joined the 'supporters' of war as they could not imagine the possibility of defeat (Meduza, 2023).

Peace initiatives on Russian terms versus the stances of Ukraine and the states supporting it

In Russian the word 'mir' has a double meaning: it denotes both 'peace' (as opposed to 'war') and 'the world'. Thus 'Russkiy mir' (*Русский мир*) does not mean a Russian version of peace, but the 'Russian world' which includes societies that have a civilisational connection to Russia (in terms of language, religion and/or identity). The concept of 'Russkiy mir' is directed at Russian and Russian-speaking minorities (Russkiy Mir Foundation, 2023) and is an ideological base for claiming that Russia has a right to intervene in the matters of other states if in their territories there are residents who culturally identify with Russia.

The Russian authorities claim that they are open to diplomatic talks and declare peaceful attitudes (Faulconbridge, 2022). The Soviet Union acted in a similar way, using peace propaganda when Josef Stalin repressed his own citizens and subjugated Central European states, trying to convince the rest of the world about the need for 'peaceful existence' (Konrat, 2019). As Marek Konrat notes, the false vision of peace shaped by the USSR was based on the erroneous assumption that 'a fair and lasting peace can be created with a country that uses inhuman methods of governance in its own territory' (Konrat, 2019, p. 17).

Similarly, Putin tries to convince the world that Russia began the special military operation in Ukraine in order to prevent a war or to end it (Bloomberg Quicktake, 2023). The peace narrative of the Kremlin is well-received in the country while the declared willingness to partake in dialogue is perceived positively by states not involved in the war in Ukraine. In this way the Russian president convinces the ruling elite of the RF that the isolation of Russia is impossible and Western sanctions are ineffective. Holding talks with the West is supposed to prove that the latter is afraid of Russia and ready to make concessions so as to de-escalate the conflict. In this way, the RF's tendency to continue its aggressive policy is growing, and the belief of the Russian elite in the efficiency of such a policy is strengthening (Menkiszak, 2023). The Russian propaganda machine perversely uses 'peace' slogans to discredit Ukraine and the West's support for it. The Kremlin promotes the narrative that the war could have ended a long time ago if Ukraine was not still receiving 'deadly' weapons. Ukraine is blamed for civilian casualties and war damages ('*MID nazval usloviya*', 2023). The spokesperson of the Russian Ministry of Foreign Affairs, Maria Zakharova, stated that to achieve a 'lasting and fair peace' in Ukraine, the West should stop delivering weapons to Kyiv, and the latter should accept the 'new territorial reality', cease fighting and withdraw its troops from Russian territories ('*MID nazval usloviya*', 2023)

Due to differences in understanding the term 'peace', Russia and Ukraine held only three rounds of negotiations. The parties managed to reach an agreement as to creating humanitarian corridors and POW exchange, but not with regard to ceasing military operations. Russia did not abandon the goals of the so-called special military operation which comprise stopping the expansion of NATO, Ukraine's neutral status and prolonging the activities connected with the denationalisation of this state (Putin, 2022). In May 2022, the talks stopped after Russia's withdrawal from northern Ukraine and the discovery of crimes committed by Russian soldiers against the civilian population in the municipalities of Bucha and Borodyanka located near Kyiv. The Russian minister of foreign affairs summed this up by stating that there is no question of negotiations with Zelenskyy, putting the blame on the Ukrainian side as the one controlled by the West ('*Szef MSZ Rosji*', 2023).

To overcome the Russian threat and close the debate on negotiations with Russia, on 11 October 2022, President Zelenskyy presented a 'peace formula', consisting of a ten-point plan. Ukraine declares that this formula remains the only way to restore 'fair and lasting peace in Ukraine' ('What is Zelenskyy's 10-point peace plan', 2023). It concerns radiological and nuclear security, food and energy security, release of all prisoners and return of deported persons back to Ukraine, implementation of the UN Charter with regard to Ukrainian territorial integrity, withdrawal of Russian troops and the cessation of military operations, justice, environmental protection, preventing conflict escalation and confirmation of the end of the war.

Promotion of Russian 'peace propaganda' in the Baltic region

After the Black Sea, the Baltic region is the second key area from the point of view of Russia's national security and of strengthening its sovereignty (Security Council of the Russian Federation, 2022), and this is caused by the unfavourable strategic situation of Russian seaports in the region (Legucka, 2013). At the same time, this is an area of ongoing rivalry with NATO states (Włodkowska-Bagan, 2013). Russia is convinced that NATO expansion, particularly in the context of the accession of Finland and Sweden, is a challenge for the RF's international position and status as a power. At the same time, the most important countries in Russia's foreign policy are the Baltic states (i.e. former Soviet republics) and Poland due to their influence on the shape of the eastern policy of the EU and NATO. These four states consider Russia's aggressive policy a direct threat to peace, stability and security in the Baltic region (Crowther, 2023). Meanwhile Mikhail Kasyanov, Russia's former prime minister, stated that if Ukraine falls, the Baltic states will be next (Teh, 2022).

Until the outbreak of full-scale war with Ukraine, Russia's relations with the Nordic countries were correct, particularly with regard to fishing and activities in the Arctic. At the same time the RF continued to destabilise the situation by increasing its military capabilities in Kaliningrad, violating the airspace of Baltic states and inciting border crises such as the one with Finland in 2015 (Chmielewski & Tarociński, 2023). This step was to convince Finland to make efforts towards the normalisation of EU-Russia relations and to curb Finland's aspirations regarding cooperation with NATO. Russia attempted to influence the situation in the region through propaganda and disinformation, making use of Russian minorities, who were the main target of such activities, as well as recipients of significant support. Such aid for existing networks takes the forms of organisational help, personal and professional connections, as well as the provision of funds and media strategies for Russian minorities, their organisations and other pro-Russian interest groups in politics and business (Grigas, 2012). In Estonia and Latvia, Russia attempted to pressure the governments to converge with the Russian point of view. An example of such pressure was the situation in 2007 when the Estonian parliament passed the War Graves Protection Act, which allowed the government to relocate Soviet soldiers' graves and the Bronze Soldier monument from the centre of Tallinn. This met with disinformation campaigns, intended to discredit the governments of the Baltic states and their supporters, which ultimately led to protests and a riot during the monument's relocation (Ciziunas, 2008).

All the states in the Baltic region have adopted a clearly negative stance on the war started by Russia and have not been misled by the peace narrative of Russian authorities. Norway and Denmark strengthened their cooperation within NATO, Germany declared reform of the Bundeswehr, while Finland and Sweden decided to abandon neutrality and join NATO. Russian aggression against Ukraine contributed to this change of stance regarding NATO: between January and May 2022, support for abandoning the non-alliance policy grew in Finnish society from 24% to 82%, and in Sweden from 35% to 58% (Legucka, 2022). The subsequent military doctrines of the RF (2000, 2010, 2014, 2015) presented the increase of NATO's military potential, which included military infrastructure moving closer to Russia's borders, as a potential source of military conflict. For Russia, a particularly important change was Finland joining the alliance which led to a doubling of the total length of NATO-Russia borders (from 1300 km to 2600 km), close to the region of St Petersburg (ca. 180 km from the city). On 16 May 2022 Putin reassured Russians that it does not perceive NATO's expansion to include Finland and Sweden as a threat (Yakovenko, 2022). However, Putin's conservative statements about NATO expansion in the Baltic Sea region should be seen as an attempt to reduce the importance of this process for Russia's security in the eyes of its own society.

Together with Latvia, Lithuania and Poland, Estonia closed its borders to Russian tourists with Schengen visas for security reasons (Cabinet of Ministers Republic of Latvia, 2022). These four states continuously argue for toughening EU sanctions against Russia and for applying economic and financial pressure in order to force the RF to stop the war in Ukraine. More than half Lithuanians think that this war poses a threat to their own lives (53%) and the lives of their relatives (63%), while a quarter worry about the risk of becoming refugees (25%). In crisis situations, the trust people put in state and local authorities is crucial. Lithuanians place trust in the

The vision of peace à la Putin   77

Lithuanian Armed Forces (56%) and NATO forces (56%), the Lithuanian Riflemen's Union and the Lithuanian National Defence Volunteer Forces (55%), the police (50%) and Lithuanian and international non-governmental organisations (31% and 42%, respectively) (Vilniaus Universiteto, 2023). Eighty-eight per cent of respondents agreed that Ukraine should become a full member of the EU and NATO, but in a longer perspective (only 46% see Ukraine in NATO within a year). The EU is here associated with climate policy and security during the energy crisis and is trusted by 46% of Lithuanians (Kostiuchenko et al., 2022, p. 10); what is more, as many as 65% think that the Russian invasion of Ukraine and its consequences should accelerate the green transformation (European Investment Bank, 2022).

The societies of the Baltic states also support the fighting in Ukraine. The majority of Estonians agree with the statement that the allies must continue to offer military help to Ukraine (67% in March and June 2023, while only 16% opposed military support for Ukraine and 11% remained neutral). In 2022, positive perception of Ukraine increased in Lithuania (from 62% before the full-scale invasion to 74%) (Kostiuchenko et al., 2022, p. 8). Disinformation activities among the Russian-speaking population are reflected in surveys as while 78% Latvians support Ukraine, only 27% of citizens from Russian-speaking families express support for the Ukrainian state (LETA, 2023). A year after the beginning of Russian military aggression, support for Ukraine decreased significantly among Latvian-speaking and Russian-speaking citizens of Latvia (but so did their assessment of Vladimir Putin[1]). In mixed-language families, a very notable drop in support for Ukraine was recorded from 45% in April 2022 to 32% in April 2023. A similar tendency is also visible with regard to numerous issues; it is more likely that the views of respondents from families using both languages would be closer to those Russian-speaking. Since the Russian invasion of Ukraine, the attitude of Latvians to the Russian-speaking minority in their country has worsened (40% agreed with such a statement in 2022, and 60% in 2023). In Latvian mixed families, in which both languages are used, support for Latvia's membership in NATO[2] and the EU, as well as for sanctions against Russia and accepting Ukrainian refugees, has decreased, while fears related to an ethnic conflict and the rebirth of Nazism in Latvia have grown stronger. The policy of history plays here an important role (LETA, 2023). Latvians also are more likely to perceive Russia as a threat to Europe in every aspect: military, disinformation, cybersecurity, fuelling social or ethnic unrest and influencing elections. With regard to the current war, there is a deep difference of opinion between Latvians and the Russian minority in Latvia with 79% of the former considering Russia as the main culprit. However, according to the Latvian Russians, the responsibility is split between Russia (32%) and the United States (28%). Significant changes have occurred only in the opinions of mixed families whose members are less and less inclined to see Russia as responsible (LETA, 2023).

The war in Ukraine strengthened Latvian nationalism which decreases the potential for influence within the 'Russkiy mir'. The level of patriotism in Latvian society remains high, while the respondents from Latvian-speaking families are increasingly aware of the importance of Latvia as a nation state. Russia's influence in Latvia is decreasing, and so is the sense of belonging to Russia and the number people claiming to be Russian patriots. The popularity of Russian media content controlled by the Latvian state and the trust in it are on the decline. As to another important issue, internal security, views are polarised according to the language used in respondents' families; however, an increased trust in Latvian National Armed Forces among Russian-speaking citizens should be emphasised as a significant positive fact (Berzina, 2023, pp. 5, 21–422).

In Lithuania, a public initiative portal Manabalss.lv began in December 2022 to collect signatures under a motion to recognise the 'Russkiy Mir' foundation as an extremist entity. This step was a requirement as it was necessary to introduce, at the level of an act of parliament, a ban on using the symbols of Nazism and communism as well as a ban on propagating these criminal ideologies as well as the 'Russian world' concept (LRT, 2022). A political problem is posed by the right-wing groups that criticise the Lithuanian political elite for putting 'foreign forces' above 'the will of its citizens' and blame Brussels for 'political and cultural dictatorship'. As regards NATO, they support strengthening military cooperation with the UK and the United States but not with Germany which currently commands the NATO brigade in Lithuania (Ulinskaitė & Garškaitė-Antonowicz, 2023).

A very important issue is the awareness of the real threat posed by Russia. The research shows that more than a half of Lithuanian residents consider the war in Ukraine as a threat to their own lives and the lives of their relatives, but they feel relatively safe and resilient in the context of threat assessment and personal capability to withstand the negative influence of rivalry. Hence, Lithuanians' vision of eliminating dependence on Russia is a long-term one.

Conclusion

Russia uses peace argumentation to improve its image in the eyes of the world and Vladimir Putin's image in the eyes of his own society. This fits the narrative about Ukraine's special role in civilisational relations with Russia as well as Russian arguments about Western threats. Within this 'peace', as understood by the RF, Ukraine is not a subject of international relations but a territory of the clash of the US and Russia. Arguments about the creation of an 'anti-Russia' strengthen the perception of this war in terms of the categories of good and evil, a necessary war in defence of Russia's territory and identity. The goals declared by Russia with regard to Ukraine and their operationalisation in the form of peace proposals are mutually exclusive. Russia does not care about peace in its positive sense, but only as a way to pressure Ukraine and Western states so that they give up fighting and accept Russian interests in the region.

The states of the Baltic region share their response to the peace propaganda promoted by Russia. In particular the three Baltic states have adopted a negative stance with regard to the war, while at the same time they also bear the burden of supporting Ukraine in terms of economic and social costs (Hartwell et al., 2022, p. 9). Hence, reactions in each Baltic state differ. The elites of these states publicly express their scepticism as to the possibility of negotiating with Russia, mostly because compromise is perceived by the Russian authorities as weakness (Hartwell et al., 2022, p. 6). The politicians of the Baltic states hold the opinion that Moscow frequently uses negotiations to ensure its military victory.

Notes

1 In April 2022, 22% Russians in Latvia admitted to liking Russia and Putin's policy, but in 2023, this answer was selected by 16%, while the majority (50%) chose the answer 'I like Russia but I don't like Putin's policy' ('Aptauja: Latvijas iedzīvotāju', 2023).
2 Among Russians in Latvia support for Latvia's membership in NATO increased from 21% to 28%, while mixed families showed a reverse tendency (a drop from 42% to 35%); a decrease was also noted among Latvians (from 81% to 79%).

References

AKIpress News. (2023, December 12). Pryamaya liniya s Putinym. LIVE (polnaya zapis' pryamogo efira) [Прямая линия с Путиным. LIVE (полная запись прямого эфира)] [Video]. *YouTube*. www.youtube.com/watch?v=XziDYRoB4to

Allan, D., Bohr, A., Boulègue, M., Giles, K., Gould-Davies, N., Hanson, P., Lough, J., Lutsevych, O., Mallinson, K., Marin, A., Nixey, J., Noble, B., Petrov, N., Schulmann, E., Sherr, J., Wolczuk, K., & Wood, A. (2021, May 13). Myths and misconceptions in the debate on Russia: How they affect Western policy, and what can be done: A chatham house report. *Chatham House*. www.chathamhouse.org/2021/05/myths-and-misconceptions-debate-russia

Ash, T., Bohr, A., Busol, K., Giles, K., Lough, J., Lutsevych, O., Nixey, J., Sherr, J., Smith, S., & Wolchuk, K. (2023, June 27). How to end Russia's war on Ukraine: Safeguarding Europe's future, and the dangers of a false peace. *Royal Institute of International Affairs*. DOI: 10.55317/9781784135782

Berzina, E. (2023). Latvijas sabiedrības un valsts attiecības Krievijas-Ukrainas kara kontekstā. *DSPC stratēģiskais apskats*, 21–30.

Bildziukiewicz, M. (2022). Rozmowa z Martyną Bildziukiewicz – szefową unijnego zespołu ds. walki z rosyjską dezinformacją (EU East StratCom Task Force) [Countering Russian disinformation: An interview with Martyna Bildziukiewicz – The head of the EU East StratCom task force]. *Sprawy Międzynarodowe*, 2.

Bloomberg Quicktake. (2023, October 9). *Putin Says Russia Did Not Start the War in Ukraine* [Video]. www.youtube.com/shorts/3QycSCZm9M0

Bryjka, F. (2022). Russian disinformation regarding the attack on Ukraine. *PISM Commentary*, 15. www.pism.pl/publications/russian-disinformation-regarding-the-attack-on-ukraine

80 *Magdalena Lachowicz, Agnieszka Legucka*

Brzeziński, Z. (1998). *Wielka Szachownica: główne cele polityki amerykańskiej*. Trans. T. Wyżyński. Politeja.

Bychkov, A. (2005). *Kiyevskaya Rus'. Strana, kotoroy nikogda ne bylo?: legendy i mify [Киевская Русь. Страна, которой никогда не было?: легенды и мифы]*. Izdatelstvo AST.

Cabinet of Ministers, Republic of Latvia. (2022, September 8). *Joint Statement of Estonia, Latvia, Lithuania and Poland*. www.mk.gov.lv/en/article/joint-statement-estonia-latvia-lithuania-and-poland

Chmielewski, B., & Tarociński, J. (2023). The Baltic states and Finland: Fencing themselves off from Russia and Belarus. *Ośrodek Studiów Wschodnich*. www.osw.waw.pl/en/publikacje/osw-commentary/2023-09-15/baltic-states-and-finland-fencing-themselves-russia-and

Ciziunas, P. (2008). Russia and the baltic states: Is Russian imperialism dead? *Comparative Strategy*, 27, 287–307. DOI: 10.1080/01495930802185692

Conflict with Ukraine: Assessments for September 2023. (2023, November 17). *Levada-Center*. www.levada.ru/en/2023/11/17/conflict-with-ukraine-assessments-for-september-2023/

Crowther, G. A. (2023). The Baltic Sea region at an inflection point. *PRISM*, 10(2). https://ndupress.ndu.edu/Media/News/News-Article-View/Article/3323873/the-baltic-sea-region-at-an-inflection-point/

Domańska, M. (2021). Putin's article 'on the historical unity of Russians and Ukrainians': An OSW analysis. *Ośrodek Studiów Wschodnich*. www.osw.waw.pl/en/publikacje/analyses/2021-07-13/putins-article-historical-unity-russians-and-ukrainians

Dugin, A. (1997). *Osnovy geopolitiki. Geopoliticheskoe budushchee Rossii [Основы геополитики: геополитическое будущее России]*. Arktogeja.

Dugin, A. (2004). *Yevraziyskaya missiya Nursultana Nazarbayeva [Евразийская миссия Нурсултана Назарбаева]*. ROF 'Evrazija'.

Dyner, A. M, Legucka, A., & Lorenz, W. (2023, February 2). *The Impact of the War in Ukraine on the Political Stability of Russia, „Strategic File", PISM*. https://www.pism.pl/publications/the-impact-of-the-war-in-ukraine-on-the-political-stability-of-russia#

European Investment Bank. (2022, October 27). *Two-Thirds of Lithuanians Say the War in Ukraine and High Energy Prices Should Accelerate the Green Transition*. www.eib.org/en/press/all/2022-434-two-thirds-of-lithuanians-say-the-war-in-ukraine-and-high-energy-prices-should-accelerate-the-green-transition

Faulconbridge, G. (2022, December 25). Putin says Russia ready to negotiate over Ukraine, Kyiv says Moscow doesn't want talks. *Reuters*. www.reuters.com/world/europe/putin-says-russia-ready-negotiate-over-ukraine-2022-12-25/

Fridrichová, K. (2023). Mugged by reality: Russia's strategic narratives and the war in Ukraine. *Defense & Security Analysis*, 39(3), 281–295. DOI: 10.1080/14751798.2023.2201018

Götz, V., & Staun, J. (2022). Why Russia attacked Ukraine: Strategic culture and radicalized narratives. *Contemporary Security Policy*, 43(3), 482–497. DOI: 10.1080/13523260.2022.2082633

Grigas, A. (2012). Legacies, coercion and soft power: Russian influence in the baltic states [Briefing paper]. *Chatham House*. www.academia.edu/3120427/Legacies_Coercion_and_Soft_Power_Russian_Influence_in_the_Baltic_States

Grishin, A. (2023, June 5). Vzbesivshayasya marionetka Zelenskiy vyshel iz-pod kontrolya: Kiyev vydal glavnuyu strategicheskuyu tsel' Zapada [Взбесившаяся марионетка Зеленский вышел из-под контроля: Киев выдал главную стратегическую цель Запада]. *Komsomolskaya Pravda*. www.kp.ru/daily/27511/4773480/

Hartwell, L., Rakštytė, A., Ryng, J., & Selga, E. K. (2022). Winter is coming: The Baltics and the Russia-Ukraine war: Implications and policy recommendations [Report]. *LSE Ideas*. www.lse.ac.uk/ideas/publications/reports/Baltics

The vision of peace à la Putin 81

Jones, S. G., & Wasielewski, P. G. (2022, January 13). Russia's possible invasion of Ukraine [A CSIS brief]. *Center for Strategic and International Studies.* www.csis.org/analysis/russias-possible-invasion-ukraine

Konrat, M. (2019). Jałta – fałszywa wizja pokoju światowego. In S. Łukasiewicz (Ed.), *Jałta. Rzeczywistość – Mit i pamięć* (pp. 15–48). Instytut Pamięci Narodowej.

Kostiuchenko, T, Gerasymczuk, S., & Koval-Honchar, M. (2022). *Peace and Security Ukraine and Central Europe: Attitudes and Perceptions.* Friedrich Eber Stiftung.

Koshiw, I. (2022, February 4). Everyone is talking about Minsk but what does it mean for Ukraine? *OpenDemocracy.* www.opendemocracy.net/en/odr/russia-ukraine-what-are-the-minsk-agreements/

Kirillov, B. B., & Kryuchkov, Y. N. (2008). Vliyanie voyny na razvitie i mezhdunarodnoe znachenie Rossii. *Voen'naya Mysl'* (Vol. 2). Krasnaja zvezda.

Legucka, A. (2013). *Geopolityczne uwarunkowania i konsekwencje konfliktów zbrojnych na obszarze poradzieckim.* Difin.

Legucka, A. (2022). Russia on NATO enlargement to Sweden and Finland. *Polski Instytut Spraw Międzynarodowych.* www.pism.pl/publications/russia-on-nato-enlargement-to-sweden-and-finland

Legucka, A., & Szczudlik, J. (2023). Breaking down Russian and Chinese disinformation and propaganda about the war in Ukraine. *PISM Strategic File, 123*(2). www.pism.pl/publications/breaking-down-russian-and-chinese-disinformation-and-propaganda-about-the-war-in-ukraine

LETA. (2023, July 13). *Aptauja: Latvijas iedzīvotāju vidū saglabājas atšķirīgi vērtējumi par Krievijas karu Ukrainā.* Available at: https://www.aprinkis.lv/index.php/sabiedriba/dzive-un-ticiba/43959-aptauja-latvijas-iedzivotaju-vidu-saglabajas-atskirigi-vertejumi-par-krievijas-karu-ukraina [access: 17.12. 2023].

Liik, K. (2022, February 25). War of obsession: Why Putin is risking Russia's future. *European Council on Foreign Relations.* https://ecfr.eu/article/war-of-obsession-why-putin-is-risking-russias-future/

LRT. (2022, November 17). *Survey Shows Growing Hostility towards Local Russian Speakers in Lithuania.* www.lrt.lt/en/news-in-english/19/1823775/survey-shows-growing-hostility-towards-local-russian-speakers-in-lithuania

Mearsheimer, J. J. (2022). Why the west is principally responsible for the Ukrainian crisis. *The Economist.* www.economist.com/by-invitation/2022/03/11/john-mearsheimer-on-why-the-west-is-principally-responsible-for-the-ukrainian-crisis

Meduza. (2023). *Eto voyna tol'ko Putina ili vsekh rossiyan? Vozmozhno, ni to ni drugoye [Это война только Путина или всех россиян? Возможно, ни то ни другое].* https://meduza.io/feature/2023/07/21/eto-voyna-putina-ili-vseh-rossiyan-ni-to-ni-drugoe

Menkiszak, M. (2023). Winning the war with Russia. The West's counter-strategy towards Moscow. *Point of View OSW,* 89. www.osw.waw.pl/en/publikacje/point-view/2023-04-26/winning-war-russia

MID nazval usloviya "ustoychivogo i spravedlivogo" mira na Ukraine [*МИД назвал условия "устойчивого и справедливого" мира на Украине*] (2023, December 9). *RBC.* www.rbc.ru/politics/09/12/2023/657482d09a7947a7686f57aa

Person, R., & McFaul, M. (2022, April). What Putin fears most. *Journal of Democracy, 33*(2), 18–27. www.journalofdemocracy.org/articles/what-putin-fears-most/ [Access: 10.12.2023].

Putin, V. (2022). *Address by the President of the Russian Federation.* http://en.kremlin.ru/events/president/news/67843

Putin podcherknul skhodstvo sovremennykh ukrainskikh natsionalistov s fashistami [*Путин подчеркнул сходство современных украинских националистов с фашистами*]. (2023, February 2). *TASS.* https://tass.ru/obschestvo/16950935

Putin Says Western Sanctions Are Akin to Declaration of War. (2022, March 5). *Reuters.* www.reuters.com/world/europe/putin-says-western-sanctions-are-akin-declaration-war-2022-03-05/

82 Magdalena Lachowicz, Agnieszka Legucka

Putin sravnil deystviya ukrainskoy armii s fashistskoy [Путин сравнил действия украинской армии с фашистской]. (2014). *BBC News Russkaya Sluzhba*. www.bbc.com/russian/russia/2014/08/140829_putin_seliger_ukraine_russia

Republic of Estonia, Ministry of Foreign Affairs. (2023). *Estonia's Aid to Ukraine*. https://vm.ee/en/estonias-aid-ukraine

Rosyjsko-amerykański reset różny w oczach obu stron. (2009, March 30). *Wprost*. www.wprost.pl/przeglad-prasy/157389/rosyjsko-amerykanski-reset-rozny-w-oczach-obu-stron.html

Rotfeld, A. (2004). Bezpieczeństwo międzynarodowe czasu przemian. In K. Gorlach, M. Niezgoda & Z. Seręga (Eds.), *Władza, naród, tożsamość, Studia dedykowane Profesorowi Hieronimowi Kubiakowi* (pp. 89–100). Wydawnictwo Uniwersytetu Jagiellońskiego.

Russkiy Mir Foundation. (2023, June 28). *Russian MFA Criticized Russophobic Policy in the Baltics*. https://russkiymir.ru/en/news/315089/

Security Council of the Russian Federation. (2022). *Morskaya doktrina Rossiyskoy Federatsii [Морская доктрина Российской Федерации]*. www.scrf.gov.ru/security/military/document34/

Stat'ya Vladimira Putina. (2021, July 12). *Ob istoricheskom yedinstve russkikh i ukraintsev [Статья Владимира Путина "Об историческом единстве русских и украинцев"]*. Prezident Rossii. kremlin.ru

Szef MSZ Rosji zgłasza gotowość do negocjacji z Zachodem ws. Ukrainy. (2023, January 18). *Rzeczpospolita*. www.rp.pl/konflikty-zbrojne/art37797481-szef-msz-rosji-zglasza-gotowosc-do-negocjacji-z-zachodem-ws-ukrainy

Teh, C. (2022, June 14). Former Russian PM says the Baltic states 'will be next' if Ukraine loses its war against Russia. *Business Insider*. www.businessinsider.com/ex-russian-pm-says-baltic-states-next-if-ukraine-loses-2022-6?IR=T

Tolz, V., & Hutchings, S. (2023). Truth with a Z: Disinformation, war in Ukraine, and Russia's contradictory discourse of imperial identity. *Post-Soviet Affairs*, *39*(5), 347–365. DOI: 10.1080/1060586X.2023.2202581

Ulinskaitė, J., & Garškaitė-Antonowicz, R. (2023). The populist far right in Lithuania during Russia's war against Ukraine. In G. Ivaldi & E. Zankina (Eds.), *The Impacts of the Russian Invasion of Ukraine on Right-wing Populism in Europe* (pp. 1–12). European Center for Populism Studies (ECPS). DOI: 10.55271/rp0024

Vilniaus Universiteto. (2023). *Įvyko apskritojo stalo diskusija „Bendruomenės ir visuomenės atsparumas karo Ukrainoje kontekste*. https://naujienos.vu.lt/ivyko-apskritojo-stalo-diskusija-bendruomenes-ir-visuomenes-atsparumas-karo-ukrainoje-kontekste/

Walt, S. M. (2022). Liberal illusions caused the Ukraine crisis. *Foreign Policy*. https://foreignpolicy.com/2022/01/19/ukraine-russia-nato-crisis-liberal-illusions/

What is Zelenskyy's 10-Point Peace Plan? (2023, August 11). *Russia's War in Ukraine*. https://war.ukraine.ua/faq/zelenskyys-10-point-peace-plan/

Włodkowska-Bagan, A. (2013). *Rywalizacja mocarstw na obszarze poradzieckim*. Difin.

Yakovenko, Y. (2022, May 16). Putin zayavil ob otsutstvii ugrozy dlya RF iz-za vstupleniya Finlyandii i Shvetsii v NATO [Путин заявил об отсутствии угрозы для РФ из-за вступления Финляндии и Швеции в НАТО]. *Izvestia*. https://iz.ru/1335121/2022-05-16/putin-zaiavil-ob-otsutstvii-ugrozy-dlia-rf-iz-za-vstupleniia-finliandii-i-shvetcii-v-nato

Zhiltsov, S. S., Zonn, I. S., & Ushkov, A. M. (2003). Geopolitika kaspiiskogo regiona. *Mezhdunarodnije otnoshenija*.

6 The role of states and international organisations in bringing war crimes to account in the context of the Russian-Ukrainian war

From documenting crimes to trying war criminals

Agnieszka Florczak, Anna Jach and Joanna Rosłon-Żmuda

Categorisation of international crimes committed against the state and people of Ukraine after 24 February 2022

When analysing the phenomenon of war, achieving a comprehensive and satisfactory description proves impossible. This challenge is particularly salient in the context of categorising the international crimes committed by Russia since the onset of the so-called special military operation (SMO, Russian: *специальная военная операция, сво*). The legal basis informing the realisation of this objective will draw on international laws 'applied by international criminal tribunals, which address individual criminal responsibility for crimes of international law in the international arena and the proceedings related to such crimes' (Hofmański & Kuczyńska, 2020, p. 17).

Genocide

Under the UN Convention on the Prevention and Punishment of the Crime of Genocide (CPPCG or the Genocide Convention), ratified by the UN General Assembly on 9 December 1948 in Paris, the acts perpetrated by the Russian aggressor against the Ukrainian state and its people do not unequivocally fulfil the definitional criteria of genocide. The *Verkhovna Rada* of Ukraine officially recognised the actions of the RF during its armed aggression against Ukraine as Ukrainian genocide on 14 April 2022 ('*Rada vyznala*', 2022), as did several other states: Poland ('The Sejm Has Condemned', 2022), Lithuania ('*Litwa uznaje*', 2022), Estonia ('*Estonia uznaje*', 2022), Latvia ('*Sejm Łotwy*', 2022), Canada ('*Kanadyjscy parlamentarzyści*', 2022), Czechia ('*Czeski Senat*', 2022) and Ireland ('*Irlandzki Senat*', 2022). However, in March 2023, the UN Human Rights Council (HRC) declared that it found no evidence that Russia was perpetrating genocide in Ukraine ('UN Commission

DOI: 10.4324/9781003558040-8

Fails', 2023; HRC, 2023). Nonetheless, this does not imply an absence of crimes bearing the hallmarks of genocide.

The international community, while issuing political declarations condemning the aggression itself, highlighted a series of mass atrocities perpetrated by Russian forces. These include intentional killings, mutilation of corpses, forced relocation of Ukrainian children to Russia, as well as instances of torture and rape committed by Russian soldiers. This stance mirrors that of the Ukrainian authorities who have classified the actions of the RF as genocide based on several factors:

1. Mass atrocities committed by Russian troops in temporarily occupied territories
2. Systematic instances of premeditated killings targeting civilians
3. Mass deportations of civilian populations
4. Relocation of Ukrainian migrant children into the education system of the RF
5. Seizure and deliberate destruction of economic infrastructure
6. Systematic actions by the RF aimed at the gradual destruction of the Ukrainian people ('*Rada vyznala*', 2022)

These assumptions are in themselves a basis for asserting that the Russian aggressor deliberately and systematically sanctions the deployment of exceedingly brutal methods against Ukrainian citizens, encompassing the civilian population, the nation of Ukrainians, as well as the state itself. While these actions constitute severe violations under international criminal law, they do not meet the legal criteria to be classified as acts of genocide.

The actions carried out by Russian soldiers can be traced back to a directive formulated by Timofey Sergeytsev, a prominent Kremlin ideologue and propagandist, as early as 2014 (Sergeytsev, 2014). This directive outlined a plan for the 'Final Solution of the Ukrainian Question' (*Окончательное решение украинского вопроса*) through de-Ukrainisation, debanderisation,[1] de-Europeanisation, *de-ukranasification*, demilitarisation, decriminalisation, decolonisation and decommunisation (commonly referred to as '8xD') (Jach, 2023, pp. 139–151).

Crimes against humanity

This category of international crime encompasses mass crimes perpetrated against civilians, meeting the criteria of extensive, systematic and indiscriminate actions. These crimes include acts such as murder, torture, enslavement, rape and forced displacement of individuals.

An example of an international crime falling within this category is unquestionably the Bucha massacre, committed in March 2022 in the village of Bucha by the land forces of the Russian Federation. It is estimated that this massacre resulted in the murder of over 400 unarmed Ukrainian civilians (Andreikovets, 2022; Sly, 2022), although this figure has yet to be verified by the UN which is currently investigating the case. The Bucha war crime stands as a testament

The role of states and international organisations 85

to the actions of the Russian aggressor against the civilian population, where mass killings were carried out in the occupied regions of Ukraine, including Bucha, Hostomel, Borodyanka and Irpin ('Rada Recognizes', 2022).

War crimes

In the context of war crimes, the Law of Armed Conflict or International Humanitarian Law (IHL) applies; it aims to mitigate human suffering and limit the scale of destruction. While delving into the intricacies of IHL is beyond the scope of this discussion, it is noteworthy that it upholds principles such as humanitarianism, distinction, military necessity and proportionality. These principles guide the determination of permissible methods and means during combat and identify acceptable targets for attack (Marcinko, 2014, pp. 23–57). As Stanislaw Waszczykowski concludes, 'The norms and principles outlined are a standard, enabling the conduct of warfare while parties adhere to appropriately established limits to minimise suffering for both combatants and civilians' (Waszczykowski, 2022).

The Rome Statute delineates a comprehensive list of war crimes, comprising 50 distinct laws, which encompass:

1. strikes against civilian infrastructure
2. attacks on civilian populations
3. use of prohibited or restricted methods of warfare
4. perfidy

Table 6.1 provides a summary of the most salient war crimes perpetrated by Russian soldiers against Ukrainians after 24 February 2022.

Table 6.1 Catalogue of war crimes committed in Ukraine by Russian troops after 24 February 2022

War crime	Examples
Strikes against civilian infrastructure	Missile strikes and city bombings, among them attacks on residential buildings (Collins et al., 2022), schools (including kindergartens, secondary schools and universities) ('Six Million Children', 2022), shopping centres, sports facilities, cultural facilities (Piechowska, 2022) including museums, theatres (300 people), places of religious worship (Biesecker et al., 2022) and hospitals (*'Ukraina. Ataki na szpitale'*, 2022).
Attacks on civilian population	Premeditated murder ('Russian troops', 2022), torture (Pyrih, 2022), kidnapping/forced deportation (Hryn'ko, 2022; *'Wojska rosyjskie "wykradają"'*, 2022), hostage/unlawful imprisonment (Tuysuz & Qiblawi, 2022), looting (UGC, 2022), rape (Taylor, 2022), forced military service (*'Prymusova mobilizatsiya v ORDLO'*, 2022)

(Continued)

86 Agnieszka Florczak, Anna Jach and Joanna Rosłon-Żmuda

Table 6.1 (Continued)

War crime	Examples
Use of prohibited or restricted methods of warfare	Cluster munitions (Cluster Munition Monitor, 2022; Higgins, 2022), thermobaric weapons ('TOS-1', 2022; *'Brytyjskie Ministerstwo Obrony'*, 2022), phosphorus weapons (Hambling, 2022; p.mal, 2022) and anti-personnel mines (Waszczykowski, 2021; 'Ukraine: Russia', 2022)
Perfidy – military ruses	A common means of achieving advantage which may involve camouflage, ambush or disinformation about troop movements. However, if the attempt to mislead the opponent exploits their good faith, this constitutes the prohibited act of perfidy. Examples include false use of the white flag, feigning protected status, unlawful use of international protective signs (Żeligowski, 2014, pp. 267–302), the use of Ukrainian uniforms and civilian clothing by Russian soldiers to approach Ukrainian outposts covertly, the use of cars with OSCE symbols by Russian soldiers ('War Crimes in the Wake', 2022; 'War Crimes, Indiscriminate Attacks', 2023), abandoned Russian medical vehicles marked with red cross symbols carrying ammunition (Nazarkevych, 2022).

Source: Authors based on Waszczykowski, S. (2022). Rosyjskie zbrodnie wojenne podczas agresji na Ukrainę w 2022 roku. https://ine.org.pl/rosyjskie-zbrodnie-wojenne-podczas-agresji-na-ukraine-w-2022-roku/

Crime of aggression

On 24 February 2022, the armed forces of the RF perpetrated a crime of aggression against the sovereignty, territorial integrity and political independence of Ukraine, contravening the principles enshrined in the UN charter. All five acts defined in paragraph 8 bis of the Rome Statute have been documented in the context of Russian aggression.

Efforts by the Baltic Sea states to obtain evidence and document international crimes committed in Ukraine

On 2 March 2022, the UN General Assembly passed a resolution that unequivocally condemned Russia's invasion of Ukraine, deeming it a breach of article 2(4) of the UN Charter. The resolution demanded the immediate withdrawal of Russian troops from Ukrainian territory (UN GA, 2022a). Additionally, it urged states to document Ukrainian crimes and losses. Subsequently, in a resolution adopted by the General Assembly on 14 November 2022 (UN GA, 2022b), the UN reaffirmed that the RF must be held accountable for its violations of international law. Furthermore, it asserted that Russia should face the legal consequences for all its actions contrary to international law. The resolution recommended that member states collaborate with Ukraine to

The role of states and international organisations 87

establish an international register documenting damage, evidence and claims arising from the actions of the RF.

Since the first days of the war, Russian destructive action on Ukrainian territory has been documented by Ukrainian institutions and organisations cooperating with judicial representatives from other countries and international bodies. The same procedures have been launched by the Baltic Sea states alongside the actions of Ukrainian authorities. The gathering of evidence by state institutions frequently occurs within investigations instigated by competent national authorities. Hence, these matters pertaining to investigation and documentation will be addressed collectively.

Poland was the first country among the Baltic Sea states to commence an investigation into the Moscow-induced aggression, based on article 117 § 1 of the Polish Criminal Code, which stipulates penalties of up to and including life imprisonment ('*Działania Ministerstwa Sprawiedliwości*', 2022). This investigation pertains to acts of aggression against the sovereignty and territorial integrity of Ukraine, war crimes as well as crimes against peace and humanity. The primary objective of the Polish investigation is to gather and safeguard evidence from witnesses and victims, a process that commenced on 28 February 2022 by a decree of the National Prosecutor's Office (*Prokuratura Krajowa*, 2023). From March 2022 to mid-February 2023, Polish investigators collected numerous photographs and recordings and interviewed over 1,700 witnesses (Mikowski, 2023).

On 3 March 2022, the Prosecutor General's Office of Lithuania initiated proceedings concerning crimes against humanity and the war crimes perpetrated during the Russian aggression in Ukraine, in accordance with the Criminal Code of Lithuania. Specifically, these proceedings are guided by article 100 (prohibition of treatment contrary to international law), 110 (initiation of aggression against a state) and 111 (commission or conduct of prohibited acts of war) (*Lietuvos Respublikos baudžiamasis kodeksas*, 2000). Alongside the collection and documentation of testimonies from those compelled to flee Ukraine to other European countries as a result of the war, the Lithuanian Ministry of Justice requested the Prosecutor General's Office to initiate proceedings against Russian President Vladimir Putin and the authoritarian Belarusian leader Alexander Lukashenko in connection with the war in Ukraine ('*Litwa: wszczęto postępowanie*', 2022; *Lietuvos Respublikos baudžiamasis kodeksas*, 2000). It is noteworthy that under the bilateral memorandum of cooperation signed on 3 March 2022 between Lithuania and Ukraine, Lithuanian investigators are actively involved in the inquiry conducted on Ukrainian territory ('*Litewski zespół śledczy*', 2022).

The Latvian State Security Service commenced criminal proceedings against Russia on 15 March 2022 under three provisions of the Criminal Code of Latvia. Specifically, Articles 71.2, 72 and 74, which relate respectively to crimes against humanity, crimes against peace, and war crimes (*Krimināllikums, Laidiens*: 08.07.1998., No. 199/200). Upon crossing the border of the Republic of Latvia, refugees from Ukraine are informed by

88 Agnieszka Florczak, Anna Jach and Joanna Rosłon-Żmuda

Latvian Border Guard officers of the opportunity to provide testimony and are given a special information card prepared for this purpose by the state security service, available in Ukrainian, Russian, Latvian and English. By February 2023, 92 individuals had provided testimony. Information is shared with the International Criminal Court (ICC) or with other member states of the Joint Investigation Group (Libeka, 2023).

Investigators from the Federal Republic of Germany, operating under the Code of Crimes against International Law (*Völkerstrafgesetzbuch*, VStGB), enacted in Germany in 2002, are actively engaged in the collection of evidence pertaining to international crimes committed in Ukraine. This legal framework enables Germany to prosecute, charge and convict perpetrators of international crimes, including:

(a) genocide, war crimes and crimes against humanity, even concerning crimes committed abroad and having no connection with Germany (§§ 6–12 Part 2 of the Code of Crimes against International Law (VStGB, 2002));

(b) crimes of aggression §13 of the Code of Crimes against International Law (VStGB) (*Bundesgesetzblatt Jahrgang*, 2016, Teil I Nr. 6), (VStGB, 2002);

(c) incitement to aggression § 80a of the German Criminal Code (*Strafgesetzbuch*, StGB) (StGB, 2021).

In March 2022, Peter Frank, Germany's federal prosecutor, initiated a comprehensive structural investigation ('*Generalbundesanwalt ermittelt*', 2022), aimed at gathering evidence without specifying individual suspects. By March 2023, 74 witnesses of war crimes and crimes against humanity in Ukraine had been interviewed as part of this effort. However, no specific suspects were identified at that point ('*Niemcy: Szef policji kryminalnej*', 2023).

Finland also collects testimonies of war crimes from witnesses or victims of Russian aggression against Ukraine. Any Ukrainian resident in Finland who is a witness or victim of a crime can provide testimony or evidence at a police station. Subsequently, this information is relayed to the Finnish National Bureau of Investigation (NBI) headquarters in Vantaa, which documents testimonies from refugees and conducts investigations into suspected war crimes in Ukraine. As of July 2023, only 50 individuals had been interviewed ('Finland's NBI interviewing witnesses', 2023), primarily consisting of witnesses to crimes.

In early April 2022, the Swedish Public Prosecutor's Office disclosed the presence of suspected war crimes in Ukraine and subsequently initiated an investigation into the matter ('*Svensk förundersökning inledd*', 2022). The prosecution of international crimes under Swedish law is governed by the Swedish Parliament Act on punishment for certain international crimes (*Lag 2014: 406 om straff för vissa internationella brott*) and Article 6 of Chapter 22 of the Swedish Criminal Code (*Brottsbalk (1962:700)*).

The role of states and international organisations   89

Procedures for gathering evidence of crimes from Ukrainian victims and witnesses have also been established by Danish authorities. Through the Danish Peace and Stabilisation Fund scheduled for 2022–2025, the Danish government is supporting Ukraine's endeavours to effectively obtain testimonies from victims and eyewitnesses of Russian crimes, document the information collected, and enhance Kiev's defence capabilities. Additionally, Denmark has assigned civilian experts to collaborate with the EU Advisory Mission to Ukraine (MFA of Denmark, 2023).

Similarly, the Estonian Prosecutor's Office has commenced evidence collection efforts. Estonia has also extended political and practical assistance to ICC investigations ('*Ukrainas toime pandavate*', 2022).

International cooperation of states in documenting international crimes committed in Ukraine after 24 February 2022

As mentioned earlier, the Baltic Sea states, with the exception of Russia, are actively engaged in efforts to document international crimes committed by Russia. They act both individually and through institutionalised channels of international collaboration. The basis for this lies in the shared membership of all Baltic Sea states, including Russia, in the UN and the Organization for Security and Co-operation in Europe (OSCE). On the other hand, the RF was excluded from the Council of Europe (CoE) on 16 March 2022 (Committee of Ministers, 2022) and suspended from the Council of Baltic Sea States (Declaration by the Ministers of Foreign Affairs, 2022), eventually withdrawing from it on 17 May 2022.

The initial actions within international organisations, of which the Baltic Sea states are members, to record the crimes committed by the RF on Ukrainian territory, were initiated as early as 2014. An example is the establishment of the UN Human Rights Monitoring Mission in Ukraine (HRMMU), tasked primarily with observing and reporting human rights violations and facilitating accountability measures (Office of the High Commissioner for Human Rights, 2023). Since 24 February 2022, the mission has been primarily engaged in documenting human rights infringements and breaches of humanitarian law by the conflicting parties.

The entity engaged in the process of documenting international crimes since the conflict's onset is the Human Rights Council (HRC).[2] On 4 March 2022, the council established the UN Independent International Commission of Inquiry on Ukraine (HRC, 2022) to probe all alleged violations of human rights, IHL and related crimes within the context of the aggression committed by the RF. The Baltic Sea states, which were members of the HRC at the time (excluding Russia), voted in favour of the resolution. The commission is presently collating testimonies from witnesses, survivors and their relatives regarding the transfer and deportation of children, violations or abuses in detention facilities, and the adverse repercussions of attacks on civilian infrastructure.[3]

One of the key institutions actively engaged in not only documenting but also adjudicating international crimes in Ukraine is the International Criminal Court (ICC). The Office of the Prosecutor (OTP) is tasked with investigating situations falling under the court's jurisdiction, conducting investigations and undertaking pre-trial proceedings against individuals suspected of committing international crimes. In accordance with Article 54 of the ICC Statute (Rome Statute of the ICC, 1998), the OTP's responsibilities encompass, among others, the collection and evaluation of all pertinent information and evidence, summoning and interviewing suspects, witnesses and victims, as well as cooperating with states and international organisations. It is noteworthy that the OTP has been amassing information and evidence on international crimes in Ukraine for over eight years deploying teams of investigators and forensic experts to assist the Ukrainian authorities in documenting crimes ('ICC Prosecutor Karim A.A. Khan QC', 2022). The evidence compiled by the ICC has facilitated, as will be discussed next, the commencement of investigations into alleged war crimes as well as crimes against humanity committed in Ukraine.

Another active organisation operating within Ukrainian territory is the OSCE.[4]

In March 2022, 45 out of the 57 OSCE member states, including all Baltic Sea states, supported the UK's proposal to activate the Moscow Mechanism[5] and dispatch an expert mission to Ukraine. This initiative did not gain support from Belarus, the Central Asian states or Russia, which refused to cooperate ('*OBWE wysyła misję do Ukrainy*', 2022). The mission's objective is to 'establish the facts and circumstances surrounding potential instances of war crimes and crimes against humanity, including deliberate and indiscriminate attacks on civilians and civilian infrastructure' ('*OBWE wysyła misję do Ukrainy*', 2022). The specialised expert mission released its inaugural report on 13 April 2022 and within it, experts confirmed numerous breaches of IHL, human rights violations and the perpetration of crimes by the RF which can be classified as war crimes and crimes against humanity (Kolarz, 2022, p. 2).

Reports presented by the Office for Democratic Institutions and Human Rights (ODIHR), an institution of the OSCE, serve as additional tools for holding perpetrators of crimes committed in Ukraine accountable. The most recent report, delivered on 17 July 2023, outlined allegations of arbitrary detentions and enforced disappearances of civilians residing in areas occupied by the RF. It detailed instances of summary executions, torture and the deployment of prohibited weapons such as cluster munitions, and thermobaric and phosphorus weapons in densely populated regions. Witnesses interviewed provided accounts of various forms of sexual violence perpetrated by the Russian armed forces. Additionally, the report documented instances of mistreatment of prisoners of war by both sides of the conflict. ODIHR has also amassed evidence of forced displacement of civilians, including children, by Russian authorities into and from the occupied territories of Ukraine (ODIHR, 2023).

The role of states and international organisations   91

The necessity to document the crimes resulting from the RF's invasion of Ukraine has been consistently emphasised by the main institutions of the EU, namely the European Commission (EC), the European Council and the European Parliament (EP). EU initiatives have progressed along dual pathways: strengthening and broadening the competencies of existing bodies, while also establishing new specialised institutions. Key achievements include:

- The special agreement between the EU and the ICC, concluded back in 2006, sets out the conditions for cooperation and assistance between the EU and the court (Agreement between the ICC and the EU on cooperation and assistance, 2006).
- The EU Advisory Mission (EUAM) Ukraine established on 1 December 2014 (Council Decision 2014/486/CFSP, 2014) has been offering assistance to Ukrainian authorities since April 2022, following the change to their mandate to facilitate the investigation and prosecution of international crimes linked to Russian aggression against Ukraine (Council Decision (CFSP) 2022/638, 2022).
- The activities of the EU Agency for Criminal Justice Cooperation (Eurojust), which hosts the secretariats of the European Judicial Network (EJN), the Network of National Experts on Joint Investigation Teams (JITs Network) and the Network for investigation and prosecution of genocide, crimes against humanity and war crimes (Genocide Network), and other institutions established in recent months to document crimes committed in Ukraine.
- The establishment on 25 March 2022 by Poland, Lithuania and Ukraine of a JIT to collect evidence and investigate war crimes and crimes against humanity with the support of Eurojust and the participation of the ICC OTP. The team currently consists of Lithuania, Latvia, Estonia, Slovakia, Poland and Romania.
- The start of the Core International Crimes Evidence Database (CICED) located within Eurojust on 23 February 2023. The database was created to protect, store and analyse evidence of crimes committed in Ukraine (CICED, 2023).
- The launch in July 2023, within and with the support of Eurojust, of the International Centre for Prosecution of the Crime of Aggression (ICPA), which aims to support and improve the investigation of crimes of aggression.

In July 2022, a conference held in The Hague concerning the coordination of state actions to address crimes committed in Ukraine by the RF ('Accountability for Ukraine – Enhancing coordination of action to deliver justice') resolved to establish a *Dialogue Group on Accountability for Ukraine ('the Dialogue Group')*. Its primary objective is to achieve coherence, efficiency and effectiveness among various actors in documenting and prosecuting those responsible for crimes committed in Ukraine (Ukraine Accountability Conference: a step towards justice, 2022).

The CoE[6] has taken a resolute stance against Russian military aggression in Ukraine. As early as 16 March 2022, through a decision by the Committee of Ministers of the CoE, the RF was expelled from the organisation (Resolution CM/Res(2022)2, 2022). Within the resolutions passed by the Parliamentary Assembly of the CoE, there is strong condemnation of the Russia's aggression against Ukraine. Support for Ukraine's sovereignty, independence and territorial integrity, alongside the need to hold accountable those responsible for the crimes perpetrated during this conflict, is also expressed.[7]

In terms of documenting Russian international crimes, the most important initiatives by the CoE include the establishment of the *Register of Damage Caused by the Aggression of the RF against Ukraine*. This decision was made during the 4th CoE summit of member state leaders held on 16–17 May 2023 in Reykjavík (Reykjavík Declaration, 2023). The establishment of this register aims, on the one hand, to aid the post-war rebuilding of Ukraine following devastation, and on the other, to facilitate the prosecution and trial of those responsible for international crimes (Committee of Ministers, 2023). A declaration to this effect was signed by the leaders of 40 countries, including all Baltic Sea states. The registry is scheduled to collect information over the next three years.

Action by international judicial bodies to hold perpetrators of crimes committed in Ukraine after 24 February 2022 accountable: chances of bringing perpetrators to justice

It is challenging to imagine any Russian-Ukrainian peace process without holding perpetrators accountable for international crimes since 2014, when Russia committed, among other atrocities, the crime of aggression against independent Ukraine. Since that time, Ukraine has presented significant determination in using international judicial mechanisms to uphold rights effectively and prosecute those responsible for international crimes committed within its borders. Ukraine has access to permanent courts operating within the UN (the International Court of Justice – ICJ) and the CoE (the European Court of Human Rights, ECHR), as well as the Permanent Court of Arbitration (PCA) and the (ICC). Furthermore, there have been proposals, as discussed later, to establish an ad hoc tribunal dedicated to trying crimes of aggression. These tribunals possess the authority to adjudicate disputes between states (such as the ICJ, ECHR and PCA) and to prosecute and sanction individuals for the most severe breaches of international law, including crimes against humanity, genocide, crimes against peace and war crimes (ICC).

Even prior to the outbreak of full-scale war in 2022, a number of proceedings had been initiated against the RF before the European Court of Human Rights (Zaręba, 2022, p. 2), the Permanent Court of Arbitration (PCA) (Dispute Concerning Coastal State Rights in the Black Sea, Sea of Azov and Kerch Strait (Ukraine v. the Russian Federation, case no. 2017–06);

The role of states and international organisations   93

Dispute Concerning the Detention of Ukrainian Naval Vessels and Servicemen (Ukraine v. the Russian Federation; case no. 2019–28) and before the ICJ[8] (Diec et al., 2023).

One of the key international judicial institutions competent to try international crimes is the ICC. Presently, neither the RF nor Ukraine is a party to the Rome Statute. However, according to article 12(3), a non-party state can confer jurisdiction on the court by issuing a declaration to the ICC Registrar thereby recognising the court's authority over the crime in question. Ukraine has exercised this option twice, initially in 2014 (*Posol'stvo Ukrayiny*, 2014) and subsequently in 2015. In the second declaration, Ukraine consented to the ICC's jurisdiction to identify, prosecute and try all crimes committed on Ukrainian territory since 20 February 2014 (Minister of Foreign Affairs of Ukraine, 2015). Ukraine's submission to the ICC's jurisdiction empowered the court to prosecute war crimes, crimes against humanity and genocide committed on Ukrainian territory without time limitation.

Following the ICC Prosecutor's decision in 2014, where it was deemed likely that war crimes and crimes against humanity had been committed, which led to the opening of a preliminary examination ('The Prosecutor of the ICC', 2014), the OTP announced on 28 February 2022 that there was a reasonable basis to suspect that crimes outlined in the Rome Statute had occurred on Ukrainian territory, indicating an intention to commence proceedings under article 15(3) of the statute. Concurrently, an appeal was made to the parties to the ICC statute to request an investigation ('Statement of ICC Prosecutor, Karim A.A. Khan QC', 2022a), as Ukraine, not being a party to it is unable to refer a complaint to the ICC, but such a referral can be made by other states. Lithuania was the first to report the situation in Ukraine to the ICC on 1 March 2022, followed by 38 others on 2 March (currently totalling 43, including all Baltic Sea states). This facilitated the launch of an investigation into the situation in Ukraine by the OTP. In a communication dated 2 March 2022, Prosecutor Karim A. A. Khan QC announced that the investigation would encompass events from 21 November 2013 onwards,[9] addressing war crimes, crimes against humanity and acts of genocide committed on any part of Ukrainian territory by any individual ('Statement of ICC Prosecutor, Karim A.A. Khan QC', 2022b). The ICC has also intensified its efforts to document these crimes, deploying the largest investigative team in its history to Ukraine.

On 17 March 2023, the Pre-Trial Chamber II of the ICC issued two arrest warrants ('Statement by Prosecutor Karim A. A. Khan KC', 2023). The first warrant pertained to Russian President Vladimir Putin, while the second concerned Maria Lvova-Belova, Commissioner for Children's Rights in the Office of the President of the RF. The ICC Prosecutor's directives stemmed from incidents involving unaccompanied Ukrainian children being sent to Russia, where they were granted Russian citizenship and placed in Russian families or orphanages. Both the Russian President and the children's ombudsman are held criminally liable for the illegal deportation and transfer of Ukrainian children from the occupied areas of Ukraine to the RF ('Statement by Prosecutor Karim A. A. Khan KC', 2023). Ukraine estimates that approximately 16,000 children fall under this category of war crime (Zaręba, 2023, p. 1). Once apprehended, the highest-ranking military and political leaders of the RF subject to the arrest warrants must be surrendered to the tribunal; failure to do so would impede their trial before it.

In addition to activities aimed at the prosecution and adjudication of international crimes – namely, war crimes, crimes against humanity and genocide – the ICC holds jurisdiction over the crime of aggression. This authority was conferred following the amendment of the Rome Statute during the 2010 Kampala Conference, which introduced the definition of the crime of aggression and delineated the procedural steps in the event of suspicion of such a crime. The statute confines accountability for the crime to individuals holding positions of effective control over the political or military actions of the state or those directing them (Article 8 bis of Rome Statute, 1998; Kittichaisaree, 2001, p. 223). An act of aggression, by its inherent nature, gravity and magnitude, must clearly violate the UN Charter.

There is indisputable evidence that Russia perpetrated an act of aggression against Ukraine in 2014. Despite the clear breach of the foundational tenets of the UN Charter, the Security Council, impeded by Russia's veto power as a permanent member, failed to pass a resolution acknowledging this fact. Instead, the act of aggression was condemned by the UN General Assembly (UN GA, 2022a). A critical stance towards Russia's actions was also articulated by the HRC (HRC, 2022). Apart from condemning the act of aggression, it underscored states' obligation to prosecute and extradite individuals responsible for committing or ordering serious violations of international human rights treaties.

The exercise of jurisdiction by the ICC over this category of crime appears unfeasible presently, for two primary reasons:

1. The IC's jurisdiction can only extend to individuals from states that are signatories to the Rome Statute and the Kampala Amendments, and that have not made reservations to exclude the ICC's authority to prosecute crimes of aggression (Kuczyńska, 2022, p. 14). However, Russia, the aggressor state, has not ratified the statute.
2. Recognition of an act of aggression must be established by a UN Security Council resolution, and it is incumbent upon the Security Council to refer the case to the ICC. The RF's status as a permanent member of the Security Council renders this procedure unattainable.

The limitations of the ICC in prosecuting crimes of aggression have prompted initiatives regarding the establishment of a new tribunal to address Russia's crimes of aggression against Ukraine. This proposal gained endorsement from the Ukrainian government and received approval within the EU forum. Specifically, it gained support from the EC (Leyen,

2023), the European Council (European Council Conclusions, 15 December 2022, point 8) and the EP (point 12 of the resolution on the fight against impunity for war crimes in Ukraine (European Parliament, 2022); see also European Parliament, 2023). According to the EP, the functions of a prospective tribunal should adhere to the norms and principles outlined in the Rome Statute governing the ICC (point 3 of the resolution). Moreover, the concept of establishing a tribunal to address crimes of aggression gained support in the Parliamentary Assembly of the CoE (Parliamentary Assembly, 2022a).[10]

Despite strong backing from the CoE and the EU, the prospects for establishing a special tribunal to prosecute the crime of aggression against Ukraine remain rather uncertain. Achieving this would necessitate a considerable consensus within the international community to enable, for instance, the negotiation of a special agreement outlining the framework for the tribunal's operations. Presently, there is a lack of clarity regarding the tribunal's composition and jurisdiction. Moreover, its success would largely hinge on the ability to apprehend and extradite the top Russian officials accountable for the act of aggression. However, this appears challenging without a change in leadership within the RF and the full cooperation of relevant states.

Conclusion

The issue of Russian international crimes in Ukraine after 24 February 2022, as discussed in this chapter, focuses not only on the documentation process but also on the prosecution of war criminals and subsequent reparations, which stands as one of the key subjects concerning the RF invasion of Ukraine. Indeed, it could be argued that the new balance of international power, not only within the region but globally, hinges upon documentation, prosecution and reparation. The initiatives undertaken by individual countries as well as groups of states and international organisations to establish facts, gather evidence, identify perpetrators and hold them accountable for breaches of international law, position the conflict in Ukraine as arguably the most extensively documented war in history. This, in turn, significantly enhances the capacity of states and the international community to hold the perpetrators of crimes responsible. Moreover, the complementary relationship between national criminal justice systems and the ICC has led to numerous investigations being initiated in individual states, including those in the Baltic Sea region, based on the principle of universal jurisdiction. Concurrently, it is important for the international community to possess, to some extent, the capability to hold perpetrators of international crimes committed in Ukraine accountable, primarily through the ICC and its ongoing proceedings.

In practice, the conflict in Ukraine exposes the shortcomings and gaps within the international criminal justice system, evident in the failure to hold

96 Agnieszka Florczak, Anna Jach and Joanna Rosłon-Żmuda

Russia accountable for the crime of aggression. In response, the international community seeks alternative solutions, one of which could entail establishing a tribunal with jurisdiction limited only to adjudicating the crime of aggression. Such an institution could be established through:

- an international agreement open to all interested states, and
- an agreement between Ukraine and an international organisation, such as the UN, or more plausibly, a regional organisation like the CoE or the EU.

Nevertheless, it is anticipated that both the legal proceedings within existing national and international courts and the establishment of a new tribunal to address the crime of aggression will be a lengthy process.

Notes

1 Word coined from the name of Stepan Bandera (1909–1959), highly controversial leader of far-right militant wing of the Organisation of Ukrainian Nationalists (OUN-B), who collaborated during World War II with Germans in order to establish independent Ukraine (see, e.g. Szumiło, 2021).
2 It is a subsidiary body of the General Assembly established in 2006, replacing the Commission on Human Rights. The council is composed of 47 countries. Currently (as of 19 August 2023), of the Baltic Sea states, three are members of the council: Finland, Germany and Lithuania. Until the end of 2022, this body also included Poland, which was elected for a term from 2020 to 2022.
3 For more on the commission's activities, see the websites: www.ohchr.org/en/hr-bodies/hrc/iicihr-ukraine/index, www.ohchr.org/en/hr-bodies/hrc/iicihr-ukraine/call-for-submission. Compare also the first report published by the commission, *Report of the Independent International Commission of Inquiry on Ukraine*, United Nations, General Assembly, 18 October 2022, A/77/533. https://documents-dds-ny.un.org/doc/UNDOC/GEN/N22/637/72/PDF/N2263772.pdf?OpenElement
4 The OSCE was established on 1 January 1995 from the transformation of the Conference on Security and Cooperation in Europe (CSCE) into an organisation. It currently comprises 57 states.
5 The Moscow Mechanism, established in the OSCE in 1991, applies when one participating state determines that a threat to the realisation of provisions within the human dimension of the OSCE has emerged in another state. In such a situation, the initiating state may, with the support of at least nine other states, send a mission of rapporteurs or experts to the country violating fundamental rights and freedoms.
6 An organisation established in 1949, currently comprising 46 states, with the protection of human rights as one of its most important objectives.
7 See, for example, Parliamentary Assembly, 2022
8 Information on ongoing proceedings can be found at pca-cpa.org/en/cases/229/ and www.icj-cij.org/case/166
9 On the basis of the first declaration made in April 2014, the government of Ukraine accepted the ICC's jurisdiction over alleged crimes committed on Ukrainian territory since 21 November 2013.
10 One hundred and sixteen representatives voted in favour of the resolution, no one voted against, one representative from Türkiye abstained (Parliamentary Assembly, 2022b).

References

Agreement between the International Criminal Court and the European Union on cooperation and assistance. *Official Journal of the European Union* L 115/50. Publications Office of the EU (europa.eu). 28.4.2006.

Andreikovets, K. (2022, August 8). At least 458 Ukrainians died in the Bucha community as a result of the actions of the Russians. *Babel*. https://babel.ua/en/news/82626-at-least-458-ukrainians-died-in-the-bucha-community-as-a-result-of-the-actions-of-the-russians

Biesecker, M., Kinetz, E., & Dupuy, B. (2022, March 25). *War Crimes Watch: Russia's Onslaught on Ukrainian Hospitals*. The Associated Press. https://apnews.com/article/russia-ukraine-war-crimes-tracker-b39137c3a96eef06f4ba1793fd694542

Brottsbalk. (1962:700). www.riksdagen.se/sv/dokument-och-lagar/dokument/svensk-forfattningssamling/brottsbalk-1962700_sfs-1962-700/

Brytyjskie ministerstwo obrony: Rosja potwierdza użycie broni termobarycznej. (2022, March 9). *Polska Agencja Prasowa*. www.pap.pl/aktualnosci/news%2C1109770%2Cbrytyjskie-ministerstwo-obrony-rosja-potwierdza-uzycie-broni

Bundesgesetzblatt Jahrgang 2016 Teil I Nr. 65, ausgegeben zu Bonn am 28. Dezember 2016. (2016). www.enorm.bund.de/SharedDocs/Gesetzgebungsverfahren/DE/Aenderung_Voelkerstrafgesetzbuch.html

Cluster Munition Monitor 2022. (2022). www.the-monitor.org/media/3348257/Cluster-Munition-Monitor-2022-Web_HR.pdf

Collins, K., Ivory, D., Huang, J., Queen, C. S., Higgins, L., Ruderman, J., White, K., Wong, B. G., & Gates, G. (2022, April 1). Russia's attacks on civilian targets have obliterated everyday life in Ukraine. *The San Juan Daily Star*. www.sanjuandailystar.com/post/russia-s-attacks-on-civilian-targets-have-obliterated-everyday-life-in-ukraine

Committee of Ministers. (2022). *Resolution CM/Res(2022)2 on the Cessation of the Membership of the Russian Federation to the Council of Europe (Adopted by the Committee of Ministers on 16 March 2022 at the 1428ter meeting of the Ministers' Deputies)*. https://search.coe.int/cm/Pages/result_details.aspx?ObjectID=09000016 80a5da51

Committee of Ministers. (2023). *Resolution CM/Res(2023)3 Establishing the Enlarged Partial Agreement on the Register of Damage Caused by the Aggression of the Russian Federation Against Ukraine (Adopted by the Committee of Ministers on 12 May 2023 at the 1466th Meeting of the Ministers' Deputies)*. https://search.coe.int/cm/Pages/result_details.aspx?ObjectID=0900001680ab2595

Core International Crimes Evidence Database (CICED). (2023, December 11). *Eurojust*. www.eurojust.europa.eu/publication/core-international-crimes-evidence-database-ciced

Council Decision 2014/486/CFSP of 22 July 2014 on the European Union Advisory Mission for Civilian Security Sector Reform Ukraine (EUAM Ukraine). *Official Journal of the European Union* L 217/42. 23.7.2014, 42–47.

Council Decision (CFSP) 2022/638 of 13 April 2022 amending Decision 2014/486/CFSP on the European Union Advisory Mission for Civilian Security Sector Reform Ukraine (EUAM Ukraine). *Official Journal of the European Union* L 117, 19.4.2022, 38–39.

Czeski Senat uznał zbrodnie Rosji na Ukrainie za ludobójstwo. (2022, May 11). *Rzeczpospolita*. www.rp.pl/konflikty-zbrojne/art36275871-czeski-senat-uznal-zbrodnie-rosji-na-ukrainie-za-ludobojstwo

Declaration by the Ministers of Foreign Affairs of Denmark, Estonia, Finland, Germany, Iceland, Latvia, Lithuania, Norway, Poland and Sweden and the High Representative of the European Union for Foreign Affairs and Security Policy on the participation by the Russian Federation and Belarus in the work of the Council of

98   Agnieszka Florczak, Anna Jach and Joanna Rosłon-Żmuda

the Baltic Sea States 3 March 2022. (2022, March 3). https://cbss.org/wp-content/uploads/2022/03/220303-final-draft-declaration-cbss-minus-russia.pdf

Diec, J., Jach, A., & Pachucki-Włosek, K. (Eds.). (2023). *Inwazja Rosji na Ukrainę 2022*. Wydawnictwo Księgarnia Akademicka. DOI: https://doi.org/10.12797/9788381388719

Dispute Concerning Coastal State Rights in the Black Sea, Sea of Azov, and Kerch Strait (Ukraine v. the Russian Federation), case no. 2017–06. https://pca-cpa.org/en/cases/149/

Dispute Concerning the Detention of Ukrainian Naval Vessels and Servicemen (Ukraine v. the Russian Federation), case no. 2019–28. https://pca-cpa.org/en/cases/229/

Działania Ministerstwa Sprawiedliwości i polskiej prokuratury wobec wojny na Ukrainie. (2022, March 1). *Serwis Rzeczpospolitej Polskiej*. www.gov.pl/web/sprawiedliwosc/dzialania-ministerstwa-sprawiedliwosci-i-polskiej-prokuratury-wobec-wojny-na-ukrainie

Estonia uznaje działania Rosji na Ukrainie za ludobójstwo. (2022, April 21). *Rzeczpospolita*. www.rp.pl/polityka/art36118711-estonia-uznaje-dzialania-rosji-na-ukrainie-za-ludobojstwo

European Council Conclusions. (2022, December 2022). – Konkluzje. Bruksela. *EUCO 34/22, CO EUR 29 CONCL 7*. www.consilium.europa.eu/media/60885/2022-12-15-euco-conclusions-pl.pdf

European Parliament. (2022, May 19). *European Parliament Resolution of 19 May 2022 on the Fight against Impunity for War Crimes in Ukraine (2022/2655(RSP)*. *Official Journal of the European Union* C 479, 16.12.2022, 68–74.

European Parliament. (2023). The establishment of a tribunal on the crime of aggression against Ukraine. *European Parliament Resolution of 19 January 2023 on the Establishment of a Tribunal on the Crime of Aggression against Ukraine (2022/3017(RSP)) (2023/C 214/10)*. EU OJ C214/109. 16.6.2023.

Finland's NBI Interviewing Witnesses, Victims of Suspected War Crimes in Ukraine. (2023, July 18). *Yle*. https://yle.fi/a/74-20041466

Generalbundesanwalt ermittelt wegen Verdachts auf russische Kriegsverbrechen. (2022, March 8). *Der Spiegel*. www.spiegel.de/politik/deutschland/ukraine-generalbundesanwalt-ermittelt-wegen-verdacht-auf-russische-kriegsverbrechen-a-20b9eb86-3c2d-4487-a411-cbe1ae458022

Hambling, D. (2022, March 25). 'White phosphorus' claimed to be used In Ukraine may really be Russian Napalm weapon. *Forbes*. www.forbes.com/sites/davidhambling/2022/03/25/white-phosphorus-may-really-be-soviet-napalm-weapon/?sh=76251f01e6ae

Higgins, E. (2022, March 11). These are the cluster munitions documented by Ukrainian civilians. *Bellingcat*. www.bellingcat.com/news/rest-of-world/2022/03/11/these-are-the-cluster-munitions-documented-by-ukrainian-civilians/

Hofmański, P., & Kuczyńska, H. (2020). *Międzynarodowe prawo karne*. Wolters Kluwer.

Hryn'ko, O. (2022). Rosiys'ki viys'kovi vykraly mis'koho holovu Beryslava na Khersonshchyni [Гринько О. (2022). Російські військові викрали міського голову Берислава на Херсонщині]. *Zaxid.net*. https://zaxid.net/rosiyski_viyskovi_vikrali_miskogo_golovu_berislava_na_hersonshhini_n1539113

Human Rights Council. (2022, March 4). *Resolution Adopted by the Human Rights Council on 4 March 2022: Situation of Human Rights in Ukraine Stemming from the Russian Aggression*. A/HRC/RES/49/1. https://documents-dds-ny.un.org/doc/UNDOC/GEN/G22/277/44/PDF/G2227744.pdf?OpenElement

Human Rights Council. (2023, March 16). *Press Conference*. https://media.un.org/en/asset/k1c/k1cqpqyep9

The role of states and international organisations 99

ICC Prosecutor Karim A.A. Khan QC announces deployment of forensics and investigative team to Ukraine, welcomes strong cooperation with the Government of the Netherlands. (2022, May 17). *International Criminal Court*. www.icc-cpi.int/news/icc-prosecutor-karim-aa-khan-qc-announces-deployment-forensics-and-investigative-team-ukraine

Independent International Commission of Inquiry on Ukraine – Note by the Secretary-General. A/77/533. (2022, October 18). *United Nations*. www.ohchr.org/en/documents/reports/a77533-independent-international-commission-inquiry-ukraine-note-secretary

Irlandzki Senat: działania Rosji w Ukrainie to ludobójstwo. (2022, June 2). *ONET Wiadomości*. https://wiadomosci.onet.pl/swiat/irlandzki-senat-dzialania-rosji-w-ukrainie-to-ludobojstwo/t2wch41

Jach, A. (2023). W stronę "ostatecznego rozwiązania kwestii ukraińskiej". Rosyjski projekt inwazji. In J. Diec, A. Jach & K. Pachucki-Włosek (Eds.), *Inwazja Rosji na Ukrainę 2022. Źródła, przebieg, konsekwencje* (pp. 115–172). Wydawnictwo Księgarnia Akademicka. DOI: 10.12797/9788381388719.05

Kanadyjscy parlamentarzyści uznali działania Rosji w Ukrainie za ludobójstwo. (2022, April 28). *Gazeta Prawna*. www.gazetaprawna.pl/wiadomosci/swiat/artykuly/8409747,kanada-parlament-rosja-ludobojstwo-w-ukrainie.html

Kittichaisaree, K. (2001). *International Criminal Law*. Oxford University Press.

Kolarz, S. (2022, September 16). Unijne wsparcie ukraińskiego wymiaru sprawiedliwości wobec wojny. *Polski Instytut Spraw Międzynarodowych*. www.pism.pl/publikacje/unijne-wsparcie-ukrainskiego-wymiaru-sprawiedliwosci-wobec-wojny

Krimināllikums, Laidiens: 08.07.1998., Nr. 199/200, Latvijas Vēstnesis. www.vestnesis.lv/ta/id/88966

Kuczyńska, H. (2022). Odpowiedzialność przed Międzynarodowym Trybunałem Karnym za zbrodnie prawa międzynarodowego popełnione w czasie konfliktu w Ukrainie. *Palestra 4/2022*. https://palestra.pl/pl/czasopismo/wydanie/4-2022/artykul/odpowiedzialnosc-przed-miedzynarodowym-trybunalem-karnym-za-zbrodnie-popełnione-w-czasie-konfliktu-w-ukrainie

Lag (2014:406) om straff för vissa internationella brott. (2014). www.riksdagen.se/sv/dokument-och-lagar/dokument/svensk-forfattningssamling/lag-2014406-om-straff-for-folkmord-brott-mot_sfs-2014-406/

Libeka, M. (2023, February 17). "Lielākā daļa Ukrainas kara bēgļu nevēlas liecināt. Viņi baidās . . ." Saruna ar prokurori Evitu Šibu. *LA.LV*. www.la.lv/par-kara-noziegumiem-noilgums-neiestajas

Lietuvos Respublikos baudžiamasis kodeksas (Žin., 2000, Nr. 89–2741). (2000). www.infolex.lt/ta/66150#

Litewski zespół śledczy na Ukrainie pomoże w badaniu zbrodni wojennych. (2022, May 5). *TVP Wilno*. https://wilno.tvp.pl/60007244/litewski-zespol-sledczy-na-ukrainie-pomoze-w-badaniu-zbrodni-wojennych

Litwa uznaje wojnę na Ukrainie za ludobójstwo, a Rosję za państwo terrorystyczne. (2022, May 10). *Rzeczpospolita*. www.rp.pl/konflikty-zbrojne/art36261881-litwa-uznaje-wojne-na-ukrainie-za-ludobojstwo-a-rosje-za-panstwo-terrorystyczne

Litwa: wszczęto postępowanie ws. zbrodni wojennych na Ukrainie. (2022, July 3). *DW.com*. www.dw.com/pl/haga-ruszy%C5%82o-centrum-%C5%9Bcigania-zbrodni-przeciwko-ukrainie/a-66105548

Marcinko, M. (2014). Główne założenia międzynarodowego prawa humanitarnego konfliktów zbrojnych. In Z. Falkowski & M. Marcinko (Eds.), *Międzynarodowe Prawo Humanitarne Konfliktów Zbrojnych* (pp. 23–57). Wojskowe Centrum Edukacji Obywatelskiej.

Mikowski, M. (2023, February 24). Polska prokuratura zbiera dowody na rosyjskie zbrodnie wojenne. Zapoznaje się z nimi Trybunał w Hadze. *Gazeta Prawna*. www.

gazetaprawna.pl/wiadomosci/swiat/artykuly/8667373,polska-prokuratura-dowody-rosyjskie-zbrodnie-wojenne-trybunal-w-hadze.html

Minister of Foreign Affairs of Ukraine. (2015, September 8). *Letter to ICC Registrar.* www.icc-cpi.int/sites/default/files/iccdocs/other/Ukraine_Art_12-3_declaration_08092015.pdf#search=ukraine

Ministry of Foreign Affairs of Denmark (MFA of Denmark). (2023). *Danish Support for Ukraine.* https://um.dk/en/foreign-policy/danish-support-for-ukraine

Nazarkevych, V. (2022). Okupanty vozyat' snaryady avtomobilyamy z chervonym khrestom [Назаркевич В. (2022). Окупанти возять снаряди автомобілями з червоним хрестом]. *ArmiaInform.* https://armyinform.com.ua/2022/03/03/okupanty-vozyat-snaryady-avtomobilyamy-z-chervonym-hrestom/

Niemcy: Szef policji kryminalnej. Chcemy postawić przed sądem sprawców zbrodni wojennych Rosji na Ukrainie. (2023). *wnp.pl.* www.wnp.pl/parlamentarny/wydarzenia/niemcy-szef-policji-kryminalnej-chcemy-postawic-przed-sadem-sprawcow-zbrodni-wojennych-rosji-na-ukrainie,592915.html

OBWE wysyła misję do Ukrainy, aby zbadać doniesienia o zbrodniach wojennych. (2022, March 3). *Radio Zet.* https://wiadomosci.radiozet.pl/swiat/OBWE-wysyla-misje-do-Ukrainy-aby-zbadac-doniesienia-o-zbrodniach-wojennych

Office for Democratic Institutions and Human Rights. (2023, July 17). Third interim report on reported violations of international humanitarian law and international human rights law in Ukraine. *OSCE.* www.osce.org/odihr/548629

Office of the High Commissioner for Human Rights. (2023, July 12). *UN Human Rights in Ukraine.* www.ohchr.org/en/countries/ukraine/our-presence

Parliamentary Assembly. (2022a, April 28). Resolution 2436. *The Russian Federation's Aggression against Ukraine: Ensuring Accountability for Serious Violations of International Humanitarian Law and Other International Crimes.* https://pace.coe.int/en/files/30024/html

Parliamentary Assembly. (2022b, April 28). Vote on Recommendation – Doc. 15510: The Russian Federation's aggression against Ukraine: Ensuring accountability for serious violations of international humanitarian law and other international crimes. *Assembly's Voting Results.* https://pace.coe.int/en/votes/38931

Piechowska, M. (2022, March 14). Rosyjska agresja na Ukrainę a zagrożenie dla dziedzictwa kulturowego. *Polski Instytut Spraw Międzynarodowych.* www.pism.pl/publikacje/rosyjska-agresja-na-ukraine-a-zagrozenie-dla-dziedzictwa-kulturowego

p.mal. (2022, March 24). Zełenski: Rosjanie użyli na Ukrainie bomb fosforowych. *Rzeczpospolita.* www.rp.pl/konflikty-zbrojne/art35934911-zelenski-rosjanie-uzyli-na-ukrainie-bomb-fosforowych

Posol'stvo Ukrayiny [Посольство України]. No. 61219/35-673-384. (2014, April 9). *Letter to ICC Registrar.* www.icc-cpi.int/sites/default/files/itemsDocuments/997/declarationRecognitionJuristiction09-04-2014.pdf

Prokuratura Krajowa. (2023, February 24). *Briefing w sprawie śledztwa dotyczącego napaści Rosji na Ukrainę.* www.gov.pl/web/prokuratura-krajowa/briefing-w-sprawie-sledztwa-dotyczacego-napasci-rosji-na-ukraine

The Prosecutor of the International Criminal Court, Fatou Bensouda, Opens a Preliminary Examination in Ukraine [Press Release]. (2014, April 25). *International Criminal Court.* www.icc-cpi.int/news/prosecutor-international-criminal-court-fatou-bensouda-opens-preliminary-examination-in-ukraine

Prymusova mobilizatsiya v ORDLO: sered "pryzovnykiv" – studenty i 65+ sered "pryzovnykiw" – studenty i 65+ [Примусова мобілізація в ОРДЛО: серед "призовників" – студенти і 65+]. (2022, March 23). *Ukrinform.* www.ukrinform.ua/rubric-ato/3435802-primusova-mobilizacia-v-ordlo-sered-prizovnikiv-studenti-i-65.html

Pyrih, W. (2022). V odnomu z harazhiv Trostyantsya znayshly zakatovanoho rosiyanamy cholovika [Пиріг В. (2022). В одному з гаражів Тростянця знайшли закатованого росіянами чоловіка]. *Zaxid.net*. https://zaxid.net/v_odnomu_z_trosty anetskih_garazhiv_znayshli_zakatovanogo_rosiyanami_cholovika_n1539714

Rada recognizes Russian army's actions in Ukraine as genocide of Ukrainian people. (2022, April 4). *Interfax-Ukraine*. https://interfax.com.ua/news/general/824182.html

Rada vyznala diyi viys'k Rosiyi v Ukrayini henotsydom ukrayins'koho narodu [Рада визнала дії військ Росії в Україні геноцидом українського народу]. (2022, April 14). *Radio Svoboda*. www.radiosvoboda.org/a/news-rada-vyznala-diyi-viysk-henotsydom/31803585.html

Reykjavík Declaration – United around Our Values. (2023, May 16–17). Reykjavík summit 16–17 May 2023. 4th summit of heads of state and government of the CoE. *Council of Europe*. https://rm.coe.int/4th-summit-of-heads-of-state-and-government-of-the-council-of-europe/1680ab40c1

Rome Statute of the International Criminal Court. (1998). U.N. DOC. AJCONF. 183/9, 1998; Done at Rome on 17 July 1998, in force on 1 July 2002, United Nations, Treaty Series, vol. 2187, No. 38544, Depositary: Secretary-General of the United Nations. http://treaties.un.or

Russian Troops Shoot Civilian with Hands Up – German Media Evidence. (2022). *Ukrinform*. www.ukrinform.net/rubric-ato/3430915-russian-troops-shoot-civilian-with-hands-up-german-media-evidence.html

The Sejm Has Condemned the Russian Genocide in Ukraine. "No One Who Values Freedom, Human Rights and Dignity, the Rules of Democracy and the Foundations of Civilization has the Right to be Indifferent to the Tragedy of the Ukrainians". (2022, April 8). *Sejm Rzeczpospolitej Polskiej*. www.sejm.gov.pl/sejm9.nsf/komunikat.xsp?documentId=F1C8C323BBE5152BC125881D007641CA

Sejm Łotwy: Rosja dokonuje na Ukrainie ludobójstwa. (2022, April 21). *Forsal.pl*. https://forsal.pl/swiat/aktualnosci/artykuly/8405018,sejm-lotwy-rosja-dokonuje-na-ukrainie-ludobojstwa.html

Sergeytsev, T. (2014). Chto Rossyya dolzhna sdelat' s Ukraynoy [Что Россия должна сделать с Украиной, РИА Новости]. *RIA Novosti*. https://archive.ph/FoMBp

Six Million Children Trapped in Ukraine Face Grave Danger as Attacks on Schools and Hospitals Soar. (2022, March 21). *Save the Children*. www.savethechildren.net/news/six-million-children-trapped-ukraine-face-grave-danger-attacks-schools-and-hospitals-soar

Sly, L. (2022, August 8). *Accounting of Bodies in Bucha Nears Completion*. https://web.archive.org/web/20220809120452/www.washingtonpost.com/world/2022/08/08/ukraine-bucha-bodies/

Statement by Prosecutor Karim A. A. Khan KC on the Issuance of Arrest Warrants against President Vladimir Putin and Ms Maria Lvova-Belova. (2023, March 17). *International Criminal Court*. www.icc-cpi.int/news/statement-prosecutor-karim-khan-kc-issuance-arrest-warrants-against-president-vladimir-putin

Statement of ICC Prosecutor, Karim A.A. Khan QC, on the Situation in Ukraine: "I Have Decided to Proceed with Opening an Investigation". (2022a, February 28). *International Criminal Court*. www.icc-cpi.int/news/statement-icc-prosecutor-karim-aa-khan-qc-situation-ukraine-i-have-decided-proceed-opening

Statement of ICC Prosecutor, Karim A.A. Khan QC, on the Situation in Ukraine: Receipt of Referrals from 39 States Parties and the Opening of an Investigation. (2022b, March 2). *International Criminal Court*. www.icc-cpi.int/news/statement-icc-prosecutor-karim-aa-khan-qc-situation-ukraine-receipt-referrals-39-states

Strafgesetzbuch (StGB). (2021). www.gesetze-im-internet.de/englisch_stgb/index.html

Svensk förundersökning inledd om misstänkta krigsbrott i Ukraina. (2022, April 5). *Åklagarmyndigheten*. www.aklagare.se/nyheter-press/pressmeddelanden/2022/april/svensk-forundersokning-inledd-om-misstankta-krigsbrott-i-ukraina/

Szumiło, M. (2021). Stepan Bandera – przywódca Organizacji Ukraińskich Nacjonalistów. *Przystanek Historia*. https://przystanekhistoria.pl/pa2/tematy/ukraina/80245,Stepan-Bandera-przywodca-Organizacji-Ukrainskich-Nacjonalistow.html

Taylor, H. (2022, March 27). Russian soldiers raping and sexually assaulting women, says Ukraine MP. *The Guardian*. www.theguardian.com/world/2022/mar/27/russian-soldiers-raping-and-sexually-assaulting-women-says-ukraine-mp

TOS-1 czyli broń termobaryczna na linii frontu rosyjskiej agresji w Ukrainie. (2022, March 3). *Defence24*. https://defence24.pl/technologie/tos-1-czyli-bron-termobaryczna-na-linii-frontu-rosyjskiej-agresji-w-ukrainie

Tuysuz, G., & Qiblawi, T. (2022). Russian forces seize control of Chernobyl nuclear plant and hold staff hostage: Ukrainian officials. *CNN*. https://edition.cnn.com/2022/02/24/europe/ukraine-chernobyl-russia-intl/index.html

UGC. (2022, March 2). 'Hungry' Russian soldiers loot Ukrainian shops. *Radio Free Europe/Radio Liberty*. www.rferl.org/a/russian-soldiers-loot-ukraine/31732450.html

Ukraina. Ataki na szpitale a zbrodnie wojenne. (2022, April 7). *DW*. www.dw.com/pl/ukraina-ataki-na-szpitale-a-zbrodnie-wojenne/a-61392421

Ukrainas toime pandavate sõjakuritegude uurimisel teevad koostööd 41 riiki. (2022, March 25). *EKEI*. www.ekei.ee/et/uudised/ukrainas-toime-pandavate-sojakuritegude-uurimisel-teevad-koostood-41-riiki

Ukraine Accountability Conference: A Step Towards Justice. (2022, July 14). *Government of the Netherlands*. www.government.nl/ministries/ministry-of-foreign-affairs/news/2022/07/14/ukraine-accountability-conference

Ukraine: Russia uses banned antipersonnel landmines. (2022, March 29). *Human Rights Watch*. www.hrw.org/news/2022/03/29/ukraine-russia-uses-banned-antipersonnel-landmines

UN Commission Fails to Find Evidence of Russia's Genocide in Ukraine. (2023, March 16). *Yahoo!News*. https://news.yahoo.com/un-commission-fails-evidence-russias-160057021.html

United Nations General Assembly. (2022a, March 2). Resolution adopted by the general assembly on 2 March 2022, ES-11/1. *Aggression against Ukraine A/RES/ES-11/1*. https://documents-dds-ny.un.org/doc/UNDOC/GEN/N22/293/36/PDF/N2229336.pdf?OpenElement

United Nations General Assembly. (2022b, November 14). Resolution adopted by the general assembly on 14 November 2022. *Furtherance of Remedy and Reparation for Aggression against Ukraine A/ES-11/L.6*. www.securitycouncilreport.org/atf/cf/%7B65BFCF9B-6D27-4E9C-8CD3-CF6E4FF96FF9%7D/a_res_es_11_5.pdf

Völkerstrafgesetzbuch (VStGB). (2002). www.gesetze-im-internet.de/vstgb/BJNR225410002.html

von der Leyen, U. (2023, November 30). *Statement by President von der Leyen on Russian Accountability and the Use of Russian Frozen Assets*. https://ec.europa.eu/commission/presscorner/detail/pl/statement_22_7307

War Crimes, Indiscriminate Attacks on Infrastructure, Systematic and Widespread Torture Show Disregard for Civilians, Says UN Commission of Inquiry on Ukraine. (2023, March 16). *Human Rights Office on the High Commissioner*. www.ohchr.org/en/press-releases/2023/03/war-crimes-indiscriminate-attacks-infrastructure-systematic-and-widespread

War Crimes in the Wake of Russia's Military Onslaught on Ukraine. (2022, February 27). *International Partnership for Human Rights*. www.iphronline.org/war-crimes-in-the-wake-of-russia-s-military-onslaught-on-ukraine.html

Waszczykowski, S. (2021, November 17). Miny przeciwpiechotne – podwójna broń separatystów z Donbasu. *Instytut Nowej Europy*. https://ine.org.pl/miny-przeciwpiechotne-podwojna-bron-separatystow-z-donbasu/

The role of states and international organisations   103

Waszczykowski, S. (2022, April 6). Rosyjskie zbrodnie wojenne podczas agresji na Ukrainę w 2022 roku. *Instytut Nowej Europy.* https://ine.org.pl/rosyjskie-zbrodnie-wojenne-podczas-agresji-na-ukraine-w-2022-roku/

Wojska rosyjskie 'wykradają' mieszkańców Mariupola. To nielegalne deportacje. (2022, March 20). *Forsal.pl.* https://forsal.pl/swiat/ukraina/artykuly/8383003,wojska-rosyjskie-wykradaja-mieszkancow-mariupola.html

Zaręba, S. (2022, June). Walka o sprawiedliwość. Kroki prawne Ukrainy w obronie przed rosyjską agresją. *PISM Policy Paper, 3*(211).

Zaręba, S. (2023, March 20). *Władimir Putin objęty nakazem aresztowania przez Międzynarodowy Trybunał Karny. Polski Instytut Spraw Międzynarodowych.* https://pism.pl/publikacje/wladimir-putin-objety-nakazem-aresztowania-przez-miedzynarodowy-trybunal-karny

Żeligowski, M. (2014). Zakazane i dozwolone metody prowadzenia działań zbrojnych w świetle MPHKZ. In Z. Falkowski & M. Marcinko (Eds), *Międzynarodowe Prawo Humanitarne Konfliktów Zbrojnych* (pp. 267–302). Wojskowe Centrum Edukacji Obywatelskiej.

Part II

Social activism in Baltic Sea states

7 Societies of the Baltic Sea states in the face of security issues

Piotr Sula, Kamil Błaszczyński and Michał Kuś

Introduction

One of the key dimensions of national security research is public perception of the issue. This is because the sense of security, or its lack, among citizens influences both their opinions and the attitudes and actions of the political elites of individual states. The authors believe that this problem acquires significant importance in the situation in which the Baltic Sea states currently find themselves in view of the ongoing Russian-Ukrainian war. Hence, the subject of this chapter will be the results of security-related public opinion polls conducted there in the period before and after the outbreak of the war.

The representative version of democracy presupposes a need for the public to legitimise those in power through cyclical and competitive general elections. However, it can be assumed that, in the era of the spread of opinion polls, the process of legitimisation is taking place on a continuous basis and not just cyclically. Empirical confirmation of this is provided by all the changes in political strategies and decisions made by democratic governments under the influence of public opinion. The sensitivity of rulers to polls is more intense when parliamentary or presidential elections are imminent. However, the formulation that the voice of public opinion is always an important guidepost for those in power seems somewhat risky. As Dalton (2014, p. 2) rightly points out, societies are not homogeneous and hence the use of the term 'public opinion' can be considered controversial. Notwithstanding these doubts however, the authors accept that survey results, by showing the distribution of opinions on a given topic occurring in society, are an important determinant of the decisions taken by those in power. The explanation for this mechanism is quite simple – within the framework of public opinion research, some sort of majority is always revealed, even if it is only relative in nature. Hence, the doubts raised by Dalton are thought to be irrelevant in the context of this study.

When considering the role of public opinion, it is worth making a few more observations. Firstly, the majority opinion of the public is subject to change. Secondly, it sometimes takes longer for those in power to react to these changes. Thirdly, changes in public opinion can take a radical turn in

DOI: 10.4324/9781003558040-10

the face of unforeseen events or threats. It was precisely the societies of the Baltic Sea states that found themselves in such a threatening situation following the outbreak of full-scale war in Ukraine. It is noteworthy, however, that the Baltic states (Lithuania, Latvia and Estonia) are much more threatened by Russia than, for example, Germany. Consequently, the sense of threat felt by those societies is much more justified than the fears of the German public for whom the vision of aggression from Russia is purely theoretical.

Given that Russia's invasion of Ukraine has profoundly changed perceptions of the importance of security in the Baltic Sea region, the authors decided that this chapter would present the opinions of the societies of the region before and after the outbreak of full-scale conflict in Ukraine. The aim is to characterise the social determinants of decisions made at the level of the political elites. However, it is worth bearing in mind that public opinion is evolving, which, in addition to its heterogeneity or the lack of will on the part of politicians, constitutes an additional complication in the process of mapping public preferences in political space (Wlezien & Soroka, 2012, p. 55). Sometimes, too, those in power may not be interested in responding to public opinion, for instance when they expect changes in dominant opinions which could result in poll losses and gains for the opposition (Mader et al., 2024, p. 17).

This chapter used data from Round 10 of the European Social Survey (Sikt – Norwegian Agency for Shared Services in Education and Research, 2023), as well as results from the Eurobarometer (European Union, 2022) and the SiE survey on solidarity in Europe (Hemerijck et al., 2023). In the context of the issue addressed, the work that emerged from the Volkswagen Foundation-funded project 'European Common Defence and Shared Security in an Age of Brexit and Trump' is extremely important (Mader, 2024; Mader et al., 2023, 2024). The base (Mader, 2023) used in these articles was not selected for this chapter as the authors wanted to refer to opinion surveys not only from before the war in Ukraine, but also more recent ones conducted after the war broke out. The aforementioned research, on the other hand, was carried out in 2020, while the surveys referred to by Mader (2024), although conducted after Russia's aggression against Ukraine, did not include the opinions of respondents from Denmark, Lithuania and Latvia.

The attitude of the societies of the Baltic Sea states to the problem of security is explained by means of an analysis of their opinions in relation to four issues:

- the importance they attribute to living in a secure environment,
- opinions on the importance of war for the internal security of the EU,
- their sense of security in the context of available military defence capabilities, and
- an assessment of the adequacy of defence expenditure.

The issues mentioned will be analysed in the order presented earlier. The first question is important, in the authors' view, as it shows the respondents'

Societies of the Baltic Sea states 109

attitudes to security in a situation 'undisturbed' by a full-scale war. The following questions were posed after Russia's invasion of Ukraine and this context probably strongly influenced respondents' opinions.

The attitudes to security included in this study (from the importance attributed to living in a secure environment to an assessment of the financial involvement of the state in strengthening security) form a relatively broad picture of societies' attitudes to security. The authors recognise that there are numerous research findings available on specific demands for increased feelings of security (e.g. the extent of NATO involvement). However, the four issues taken up are considered to be the variables most relevant to understand the needs of societies in the Baltic Sea states in this regard.

Functioning in a secure environment

In line with the assumptions made in the Introduction, the characterisation of the opinions of the societies of the Baltic Sea states begins with a presentation of those collected in the European Social Survey before the outbreak of the full-scale Russian-Ukrainian war in 2022 (Table 7.1).

The first question (how important is to live in a safe environment?) shows that the issue of safety was an important value for the majority of respondents. However, it is noticeable that there are some differences between the responses in different countries.

Firstly, those who consider living in a safe environment to be 'very important' or 'important' accounted for more than 70% of all respondents in Poland, more than 60% in the Baltic states, between 50 and 57% in Denmark, Finland and Germany, and just under 40% in Sweden. At the same time, 10% of respondents in Denmark, 14% in Germany and 20% in Sweden declared that it was 'completely unimportant' or 'not important' whether they lived in a safe environment. However, Denmark, Germany and Sweden also had the highest number of extreme opinions (the standard deviation was 1.24 in Denmark and 1.36 in Germany and Sweden).

From the European Social Survey, the authors further selected a question on the importance respondents attached to the fact that the government is strong and provides security. The highest number of respondents expressing the opinion that this is 'very important' or 'important' was found in Latvia (over 70%). Slightly lower proportions were identified for Poland (around 70%), and Estonia, Lithuania and Denmark (over 60%). The lowest proportions were recorded in Finland (about 60%), Germany (51%) and Sweden where only just over 47% of respondents gave such answers. At the same time, in Germany (11%) and Sweden (12%), the largest number of respondents declared that it was 'completely unimportant' or 'unimportant' whether the state was strong and provided security. The highest percentage of extreme answers was found among respondents in Finland, Germany and Sweden (in the first case, the standard deviation was 1.26 and in the other two 1.27).

Table 7.1 Opinions on safety and security in the Baltic Sea states – descriptive statistics (European Social Survey 10th Round)

Questions	Country	N	Proportions (%)						M	SD
			1	2	3	4	5	6		
Important to live in secure and	Denmark	2,310	1.5%	8.5%	12.3%	21.2%	39.0%	17.6%	4.40	1.24
safe surroundings[a]	Germany	1,534	2.3%	11.7%	14.9%	20.5%	31.8%	18.8%	4.24	1.36
Scale:	Estonia	3,436	0.9%	7.2%	10.5%	19.3%	44.3%	17.7%	4.52	1.17
6-Very much like me,	Finland	3,263	1.9%	5.8%	11.0%	25.5%	37.8%	18.0%	4.45	1.19
5-Like me,	Lithuania	3,309	0.9%	5.1%	12.1%	17.7%	34.5%	29.7%	4.69	1.21
4-Somewhat like me	Latvia	885	1.6%	4.9%	7.9%	18.6%	40.5%	26.6%	4.71	1.17
3-A little like me	Poland	1,437	0.6%	3.9%	8.0%	15.0%	41.4%	31.1%	4.86	1.10
2-Not like me	Sweden	1,495	2.8%	17.3%	18.1%	22.2%	28.4%	11.2%	3.90	1.36
1-Not like me at all	Total	1,7776	1.5%	7.6%	11.8%	20.4%	37.7%	21.1%	4.48	1.24
Important that government is	Denmark	2,310	1.1%	5.3%	9.6%	18.5%	41.6%	24.0%	4.66	1.16
strong and ensures safety[b]	Germany	1,534	1.8%	9.4%	14.7%	22.8%	34.4%	16.9%	4.29	1.27
Scale:	Estonia	3,436	1.0%	7.3%	9.5%	20.3%	45.5%	16.4%	4.51	1.15
6-Very much like me,	Finland	3,263	2.5%	6.0%	10.0%	22.2%	35.7%	23.7%	4.54	1.26
5-Like me,	Lithuania	3,309	1.0%	4.8%	12.9%	18.3%	32.5%	30.4%	4.68	1.22
4-Somewhat like me	Latvia	885	1.0%	2.9%	6.0%	15.6%	36.7%	37.7%	4.97	1.10
3-A little like me	Poland	1,437	1.3%	4.7%	8.4%	16.6%	42.0%	27.1%	4.74	1.16
2-Not like me	Sweden	1,495	2.1%	10.0%	16.7%	23.8%	33.0%	14.4%	4.19	1.27
1-Not like me at all										
	Total	17,776	1.5%	6.3%	11.0%	20.0%	38.0%	23.2%	4.56	1.22

[a] ESS10 data base code – impsafe
[b] ESS10 data base code – ipstrgv

Societies of the Baltic Sea states 111

It is not the authors' ambition within the scope of this chapter to provide a detailed interpretation of all the results discussed. The complexity of the phenomena described would have to include the analysis of many variables, and this would simply be beyond the scope of this study. The aim is to present the social background to the political processes. Undoubtedly, however, the differences between the Baltic states and Poland and the other countries deserve to be highlighted.

Interpretation of opinions on the importance of security in the environment and the role of the state in ensuring security seems difficult in the context of the presented data for yet another reason. As mentioned, data collection in the 10th round of the European Social Survey ended just before Russia's invasion of Ukraine in 2022. This means that the interview period coincided with the last phase of the COVID-19 pandemic. This fact may have distorted respondents' perceptions of security issues. Indeed, as another study (Jung & Krüger, 2022, p. 238) shows, the need for security was mentioned by only 3.6% of respondents, while social contacts were mentioned by as many as 47.7%.

Citizens facing the probability of war

The outbreak of a full-scale war between Russia and Ukraine in February 2022 has placed the citizens of the countries analysed in a new situation an active high-intensity armed conflict in the immediate vicinity of the Baltic Sea region. Although Ukraine borders only one country in the region (Poland), Russia shares a border with as many as five of the eight countries analysed (Poland, Lithuania, Latvia, Estonia and Finland). Belarus, which borders Poland, Lithuania and Latvia, is also an additional factor in the increased threat, being a base for Russian military operations.

Regardless of whether or not they have a border with Ukraine, Russia or Belarus, the outbreak of this conflict brought closer the prospect of an armed conflict in which the states and their societies would be directly involved. Such a prospect was particularly imminent in the first phase of the Russian-Ukrainian war, when it seemed likely that Russia would be quickly victorious and would take full control of Ukraine, either directly or by the establishment of a puppet government in Kiev, implementing in full policies imposed by the Russian authorities.

This was therefore a significant change in the perception of the Russian-Ukrainian conflict which had, after all, been going on since 2014, but which until then had been perceived in most countries in the region and by their citizens as an event that was of course significant, but which did not translate into an imminent threat of armed conflict on their own territory or even involving just their own country.

The scale of the perceived threat from this is very well illustrated by the results of the Eurobarometer survey (European Union, 2022) conducted in spring 2022 (April–May), entitled 'Key challenges of our times – the EU in

112　*Piotr Sula, Kamil Błaszczyński and Michał Kuś*

Table 7.2 Opinions on challenges to the internal security of the EU in the Baltic Sea states

(In your opinion, how important are the following challenges to the internal security of the EU? – War in the EU's neighbourhood – descriptive statistics? (Eurobarometer 97.3/2022).)

Country	Proportions (%)				M	SD
	1	2	3	4		
Denmark	0.9%	2.4%	21.2%	75.6%	3.71	0.55
Germany	1.5%	2.8%	25.7%	70.0%	3.64	0.61
Estonia	1.5%	6.3%	31.0%	61.2%	3.52	0.68
Finland	0.6%	1.4%	14.1%	83.9%	3.81	0.46
Latvia	0.2%	1.2%	18.6%	79.9%	3.78	0.45
Lithuania	1.7%	3.9%	19.2%	75.2%	3.68	0.63
Poland	0.5%	2.7%	28.7%	68.1%	3.64	0.56
Sweden	0.5%	4.7%	29.5%	65.3%	3.60	0.60
Total	1.0%	3.2%	23.7%	72.2%	3.67	0.58

Note: Measuring scale: 4 – Very important, 3 – Fairly important, 2 – Not very important, 1 – Not at all important.

2022'. Of particular interest in this context are the respondents' answers to question 1.5 ('In your opinion, how important are the following challenges to the internal security of the EU? War in the EU's neighbourhood'), which are presented in Table 7.2.

It can be noted that in all eight countries surveyed, the number of respondents answering that war in the EU's immediate environment is a 'very important' or 'fairly important' challenge to EU security (which should also be interpreted as stating that this war is a challenge to their own country's security) was over 90%, in five out of the eight reaching above 95%. The highest rates in this respect were recorded in Latvia (98.5%) and Finland (98%), who also recorded the highest percentage of 'very important' responses (79.9% in Latvia and 83.9% in Finland).

Interestingly, the fact of having a border with Russia did not prove to be a factor that automatically and unambiguously increased the percentage of 'very important' or 'fairly important' responses. While such an effect was observed in Latvia and Finland, Lithuania and especially Estonia (92.2%), had fewer 'very important' or 'fairly important' responses than countries such as Denmark, Sweden and Germany without a border with Russia. The lower figure for Estonia, compared to other countries, may be potentially linked to the presence of a significant proportion of its population being of Russian origin – although this effect was not present in neighbouring Latvia, which also has a large Russian minority (perhaps differences in survey sample selection and representation are at play here).

By far, however, the citizens of at least some of the Baltic Sea states in the study 'Key challenges of our times – the EU in 2022' (European Commission,

Societies of the Baltic Sea states 113

2022) turned out to be those who to the greatest extent (EU-wide) believe that the war in Ukraine poses a threat to their national security. In question 6.2 ('Please tell to what extent you agree or disagree with each of the following statements. The invasion in Ukraine is a threat to the security of (OUR COUNTRY)'), the sum of 'totally agree' and 'tend to agree' responses was highest in Poland (94%), Lithuania (91%) and Sweden (88%), with an EU-wide average of 77%. However, this was not a feeling observed across the region at the time, as Latvia, Estonia and Denmark, for example, had rates below the EU-wide average.

Sense of security and defence capabilities

Feelings of insecurity may increase or decrease, depending on how strong a sense of support individuals feel from their group. When the individual perceives the available resources, the quality of the organisation and proficiency in dealing with threats to their group as sufficient, their sense of security will be high. Individuals will have the belief that, in a crisis situation, their social and institutional environment will respond adequately to the situation and thus support them. In contrast, if individuals perceive their social environment as ineffective, unprepared or vulnerable to attack, their sense of threat will be very high and their degree of trust in people as well as institutions will be shaken.

One of the pillars of defence within a country is its armed forces which have the appropriate personnel and equipment to provide security effectively. Citizens' faith in their own armed forces is an important factor in building their sense of security, as the army is symbolically associated with the strength of the state. Contemporary governments use them as part of building a vision of state stability, and among empirical examples we have both democratic (U.S. imperialism) and non-democratic (Russian and Chinese imperialism) models.

In light of the external threat hypothesis, the most recent events in the form of the armed conflict in the Donbas, Russia's unlawful annexation of Crimea, and the war in Ukraine have revealed that diplomacy and peace treaties are not sufficient tools to protect against Russia's aggressive policy. Thus, confidence in the defensive capabilities of the armed forces of these states, and the sense of security that flows from this, appears to be increasingly crucial.

Based on GESIS data (Hemerijck et al., 2023) covering the years 2018–2021 (so after the unlawful annexation of Crimea and the war in Donbas in 2014, but before the full-scale armed conflict between Russia and Ukraine in 2022), and a sample from six Baltic Sea states (n=29767), we can conclude that a very small proportion (6.5%) of respondents indicated that they feel very secure in terms of military defence capabilities (see Table 7.3). Interestingly, the average value has not changed significantly over the four years in question and a majority of citizens of the countries surveyed felt some degree of security (39.8%). In contrast, there was also a significant proportion who were unable to assess whether they felt secure or not in terms of military defence capabilities (12.7%).

114 *Piotr Sula, Kamil Błaszczyński and Michał Kuś*

Table 7.3 How secure or insecure do you feel about military defence?
Baltic Sea states – descriptive statistics (SiE survey on solidarity in Europe trendfile (2018–2023))

	Country	N	Proportions (%)				
			Don't know	Very insecure	Fairly insecure	Fairly secure	Very secure
2018	Denmark	1,030	17.1%	5.1%	19.9%	48.3%	9.5%
	Finland	981	16.0%	6.6%	32.1%	39.9%	5.4%
	Germany	1,017	12.6%	16.7%	36.2%	29.3%	5.2%
	Lithuania	738	6.1%	14.6%	26.6%	45.3%	7.5%
	Poland	956	9.3%	17.9%	37.4%	31.3%	4.1%
	Sweden	1,019	11.6%	23.4%	33.7%	28.1%	3.3%
	Total	5,741	12.4%	14.0%	31.1%	36.7%	5.8%
2019	Denmark	1,002	19.3%	3.0%	16.2%	52.5%	9.1%
	Finland	1,001	17.7%	6.9%	31.4%	39.3%	4.8%
	Germany	1,014	13.6%	19.6%	31.8%	29.5%	5.5%
	Lithuania	761	8.3%	9.7%	23.5%	49.8%	8.7%
	Poland	784	7.7%	18.1%	36.0%	32.7%	5.6%
	Sweden	1,000	12.6%	16.3%	36.0%	31.9%	3.2%
	Total	5,562	13.6%	12.2%	29.1%	39.1%	6.1%
2020	Denmark	2,014	15.4%	2.8%	15.6%	55.6%	10.6%
	Finland	1,005	13.6%	8.2%	28.7%	42.2%	7.4%
	Germany	2,053	15.0%	13.8%	31.8%	34.2%	5.2%
	Lithuania	1,013	7.2%	11.2%	27.2%	45.9%	8.5%
	Poland	1,012	7.7%	16.6%	34.2%	35.5%	6.0%
	Sweden	2,004	8.7%	18.0%	37.6%	32.1%	3.7%
	Total	9,101	11.9%	11.7%	28.9%	40.8%	6.7%
2021	Denmark	2,141	16.8%	2.8%	14.3%	56.1%	10.0%
	Finland	1,026	13.7%	6.9%	28.9%	43.3%	7.1%
	Germany	2,138	15.0%	17.6%	29.5%	33.1%	4.8%
	Lithuania	1,011	6.7%	10.5%	27.7%	45.3%	9.8%
	Poland	1,006	12.7%	15.6%	32.9%	32.1%	6.7%
	Sweden	2,041	9.9%	13.6%	37.0%	35.1%	4.4%
	Total	9,363	13.0%	11.2%	27.8%	41.1%	6.9%
Total	Denmark	6,187	16.8%	3.2%	16.0%	54.1%	10.0%
	Finland	4,013	15.3%	7.2%	30.3%	41.2%	6.2%
	Germany	6,222	14.4%	16.6%	31.7%	32.3%	5.1%
	Lithuania	3,523	7.1%	11.4%	26.4%	46.4%	8.7%
	Poland	3,758	9.4%	17.0%	35.0%	32.9%	5.6%
	Sweden	6,064	10.2%	17.1%	36.5%	32.4%	3.8%
	Total	29,767	12.7%	12.1%	29.0%	39.8%	6.5%

Several characteristic trends are discernible in cross-country comparisons. The first is the relatively strong sense of security of the Danes, Finns and Lithuanians in contrast to the Germans, Poles and Swedes, who reported the weakest sense. The Lithuanians were the most decisive in their assessment, while the Danes, Finns and Germans were the least decisive.

The observed trends seem to suggest that countries that are smallest in area or least populous (i.e. Denmark, Finland and Lithuania) are characterised by a stronger sense of security in terms of military defence than larger countries. Such a result can be explained from the perspectives of social homogeneity theory (Simon & Pettigrew, 1990) and social cohesion theory (Fonseca et al., 2019). According to these, it can be assumed that smaller communities can create more efficient and centralised methods of governance and problem-solving, and build stronger bonds between members of their community. These in turn foster greater trust, action and mutual support. It can thus be concluded that Danes, Finns and Lithuanians have a stronger sense of security in the context of military defence capabilities, as they feel a stronger bond with the individuals who represent these services and feel that they are supported by them.

Analysing this result critically, we can also conclude that the difficult geopolitical situation (neighbourhood with Russia in the case of Finland and Lithuania) and strong economic ties with neighbouring countries (Denmark) create a favourable ground for romanticising one's own military potential in order to maintain individual psychological stability (e.g. from collective fear or panic) as well as structural social stability (e.g. protests or riots). Larger or more populous countries (Sweden, Poland and Germany) may be characterised by a stronger decentralisation of power and anonymity, resulting in weaker social ties, a lower willingness to sacrifice, low social trust and more differentiated threat perceptions. It is worth noting that a special case in this respect, in terms of the results obtained, is Finland, which has a relatively vast territory (larger than Poland), although its population (5.5 million inhabitants) is similar to Denmark (5.9 million).

Sense of security and defence spending

Just as important as the sense of security is the sense of legitimacy of the costs incurred by citizens to maintain or develop their country's defence capabilities. The military potential of modern states is largely based on the use of budgetary funds for modernisation, rearmament and the maintenance of adequate personnel. The legitimacy of government action depends on the satisfaction of its citizens – the taxpayers. Failure to meet the basic need for security can be an incentive to discredit those in power or even to change decision-makers, as they are then perceived as incompetent and thus unworthy of trust and further support. Consequently, a government's ineffectiveness in the management of defence funding may be grounds for breaking the social contract on the part of citizens and for disobedience which will usually manifest itself in the form of protest and demands for the resignation of the government concerned.

Based on data from GESIS (Hemerijck et al., 2023) covering the period from 2018 to 2023 and the opinions of respondents from the six Baltic Sea states (n = 42,438), we can conclude that a majority of respondents (38%) rate defence spending as adequate, while just under 30% (29.2%) indicated that it is too low (Table 7.4). A noticeable number (14.6%) indicated that

116 Piotr Sula, Kamil Błaszczyński and Michał Kuś

Table 7.4 Do you think your country currently spends too little on defence, too much on defence or about the right amount?

Baltic Sea states – descriptive statistics (SiE survey on solidarity in Europe trendfile (2018–2023))

Year	Country	N	Proportions (%)			
			Don't know	*Too much*	*Right amount*	*Too little*
2018	Denmark	1,030	20.2 %	24.5 %	35.6 %	19.7 %
	Finland	981	18.5 %	12.8 %	47.9 %	20.8 %
	Germany	1,017	19.1 %	20.6 %	23.7 %	36.6 %
	Lithuania	738	11.1 %	33.6 %	39.7 %	15.6 %
	Poland	956	17.2 %	16.4 %	35.8 %	30.6 %
	Sweden	1,019	22.4 %	10.6 %	19.4 %	47.6 %
	Total	5,741	18.4 %	19.2 %	33.3 %	29.1 %
2020	Denmark	2,014	21.7 %	13.6 %	46.6 %	18.1 %
	Finland	1,005	18.3 %	14.6 %	54.3 %	12.7 %
	Germany	2,053	21.3 %	18.5 %	31.2 %	29.0 %
	Lithuania	1,013	14.1 %	34.1 %	40.9 %	11.0 %
	Poland	1,012	21.4 %	16.3 %	36.1 %	26.2 %
	Sweden	2,004	18.3 %	9.8 %	28.1 %	43.8 %
	Total	9,101	19.6 %	16.5 %	38.1 %	25.7 %
2021	Denmark	2,141	20.7 %	13.6 %	48.4 %	17.2 %
	Finland	1,026	18.6 %	10.8 %	55.3 %	15.3 %
	Germany	2,138	21.8 %	18.0 %	30.6 %	29.6 %
	Lithuania	1,011	14.1 %	27.5 %	46.1 %	12.3 %
	Poland	1,006	22.8 %	11.1 %	36.8 %	29.3 %
	Sweden	2,041	19.5 %	10.2 %	33.1 %	37.2 %
	Total	9,363	20.0 %	14.8 %	40.3 %	25.0 %
2022	Denmark	2,039	17.0 %	9.1 %	37.7 %	36.3 %
	Finland	1,013	12.7 %	5.5 %	60.5 %	21.2 %
	Germany	2,000	15.2 %	17.3 %	28.1 %	39.5 %
	Lithuania	1,023	14.7 %	17.3 %	47.3 %	20.7 %
	Poland	1,068	22.0 %	6.0 %	36.7 %	35.3 %
	Sweden	2,005	14.7 %	7.9 %	24.8 %	52.7 %
	Total	9,148	15.9 %	10.8 %	36.2 %	37.1 %
2023	Denmark	2,020	17.3 %	13.3 %	38.3 %	31.1 %
	Finland	1,005	12.0 %	9.0 %	69.5 %	9.6 %
	Germany	2,014	17.9 %	19.1 %	27.1 %	36.0 %
	Lithuania	1,000	14.5 %	15.9 %	43.6 %	26.0 %
	Poland	1,045	22.9 %	12.3 %	45.1 %	19.7 %
	Sweden	2,001	18.0 %	8.8 %	37.0 %	36.1 %
	Total	9,085	17.3 %	13.3 %	40.3 %	29.0 %
Total	Denmark	9,244	19.3 %	13.7 %	42.0 %	24.9 %
	Finland	5,030	16.0 %	10.5 %	57.5 %	15.9 %
	Germany	9,222	19.1 %	18.5 %	28.6 %	33.8 %
	Lithuania	4,785	13.9 %	25.2 %	43.7 %	17.2 %
	Poland	5,087	21.3 %	12.3 %	38.1 %	28.2 %
	Sweden	9,070	18.2 %	9.3 %	29.5 %	43.0 %
	Total	42,438	18.3 %	14.6 %	38.0 %	29.2 %

Societies of the Baltic Sea states 117

expenditure was too high, while almost one in five (18.3%) were unable to give a clear opinion on the matter.

The highest figures confirming the adequacy of expenditure were recorded in Denmark, Lithuania and especially Finland (57.5%), while in Sweden (43%) too little investment in defence was reported. The feeling of spending too much was reported most strongly in Lithuania (25.2%). In most countries, the proportions of undecided citizens were relatively similar, with the notable exception of Lithuania, where the figure was much lower (13.9%).

In Denmark, the number of people expressing the opinion that defence spending was too low increased significantly from 2022 and 2023 and similar sentiments were also noticed in Lithuania. In Finland and Poland, between 2022 and 2023, the number of people considering this too low decreased significantly and the number assessing it as adequate for the current situation increased. In Sweden, the number perceiving this expenditure as too low initially increased significantly in 2022, but quickly declined in 2023. The most stable opinions were seen in Germany, where the proportions of those who were relatively satisfied and those who were dissatisfied (both from the perspective of too low or too high expenditure) were relatively stable.

Based on the data, we can conclude that the turning point in changes to opinions on defence spending was in 2022–2023. Finns and Poles were the most satisfied with defence spending policy while changes for the worse were recorded among Danish and Lithuanian citizens. Swedes equally manifest satisfaction with current spending and dissatisfaction that it is even too low. A special case in this analysis is that of German citizens, on whom (presumably) the current war in Ukraine, in view of their own defence investments, did not seem to make an impression. Such attitudes can be explained using Construal-Level Theory of Psychological Distance (CLT) by Trope and Liberman (2010), whose authors conclude that the level of fear decreases with the temporal and spatial perspective of the threat experience. Apart from Denmark, Germany is geographically the most distant country from the current armed conflict between Russia and Ukraine. German citizens can be confident that this conflict will not spread to their country in the near future and will not directly threaten their health and general well-being. Germany is a country with a large population, highly industrialised, with a developed arms sector and a strong geopolitical position. These factors generate a very different perspective than, for example, for the Danes, whose country is relatively small and not as strong as Germany. These differences may cause the average Dane to feel much more threatened by the political situation in Eastern Europe than the average German.

An alternative explanation could be media theory (Altheide, 2017) which assumes that the media intentionally filters and either 'heats up' or 'cools down' public sentiment. A media narrative that builds up a strong threat results in Lithuanian and Danish citizens feeling a growing dissatisfaction with the level of defence spending incurred, considering it to be far from

118 *Piotr Sula, Kamil Błaszczyński and Michał Kuś*

sufficient. By contrast, a narrative that shows the government's effectiveness will result in citizens in Finland and Poland feeling satisfied with the level of defence spending. In Germany, by the same token, we may be dealing with a media narrative in which the immediate threat from Russia is presented as unrealistic, so that the average German does not feel compelled to revise his or her views. Ultimately, it is also possible to assume that the German media does not use narratives that could cause radicalisation in this regard, presenting the topic of the war in Ukraine dispassionately and thus creating a certain psychological comfort in the audience.

Conclusion

The data presented here may suggest that security issues have certainly become an important part of the public agenda (McCombs & Shaw, 1972) in the Baltic Sea states over recent years. This is primarily related to the escalation of the Russian-Ukrainian conflict, following the full-scale Russian invasion of Ukraine in February 2022, and its multifaceted consequences for the international order (exacerbation of Russia-NATO relations, including the prospect of a 'new Cold War'; a wave of refugees from Ukraine; the economic consequences of the war in the form of, for example, a food crisis in the Middle East and Africa; and others). This is a consequence of both the scale and nature of these events and the particular attention given to them by the mass media in the countries concerned.

Indeed, there is no doubt that at particular moments, especially in the first half of 2022, the topic of the conflict in Ukraine dominated the media agenda in Europe, thus translating into the interest of citizens in this issue and the importance attached to it. This observation is particularly true for the Baltic Sea states which, due to their immediate borders with Ukraine and Russia, are most tangibly confronted with this reality (with examples such as the reception of war refugees or examples of violations of the airspace of these countries by aircraft and missiles belonging to the parties to the conflict). In these countries, to an extent, the war in Ukraine has intensified discussions on security, leading in some dimensions to an increase in the number of people considering scenarios that include the possibility of armed conflict on their territory, which we can see as an expression of a decreasing sense of security, even if, at the same time, respondents believe that their countries are well prepared for such a circumstance. The persistence of this trend may be confirmed by the results of the Ipsos global survey 'What Worries the World' from March 2024. In the question on armed conflict between states, the three Baltic Sea countries represented in the survey ranked 2nd (Poland, 34%), 3rd (Germany, 26%) and 5th (Sweden, 16%) in terms of the number of respondents fearing the outbreak of war (out of 29 countries surveyed from around the world), overtaken only by Israel (45%) (Ipsos, 2024, p. 20).

A separate issue is the translation of the opinions of the citizens of the Baltic Sea states into decisions taken at the political level. It remains an open question, for example, whether the entry of Finland and Sweden into NATO is the result of an initiative by the political elite or of public pressure on these elites to renounce non-participation in the alliance.

There is also a certain problem in obtaining data comparing the opinions of citizens from the Baltic Sea countries from before and after the outbreak of the Russian-Ukrainian war, as some of the surveys were only conducted either in the period before February 2022 or only after February 2022. In this chapter, for example, the data from Round 10 of the European Social Survey was used. In doing so, it is important to note that the data for this survey was collected entirely before the start of Russia's full-scale invasion of Ukraine. Only the next version of this survey will therefore bring knowledge of the depth of change brought about by the war.

Bibliography

Altheide, D. L. (2017). Media and fear: After terrorism. *Sociologia Della Comunicazione, 54*(2), 19–39. DOI: 10.3280/SC2017-054003

Dalton, R. J. (2014). *Citizen Politics: Public Opinion and Political Parties in Advanced Industrial Democracies* (6th ed.). SAGE Publications.

European Union. (2022). *Special Eurobatometer 526: Key Challenges of Our Times – the EU in 2022.* DOI: 10.2775/934228

Fonseca, X., Lukosch, S., & Brazier, F. (2019). Social cohesion revisited: A new definition and how to characterize it. *Innovation: The European Journal of Social Science Research, 32*(2), 231–253. DOI: 10.1080/13511610.2018.1497480

Hemerijck, A., Genschel, P., Cicchi, L., Stolle, D., Russo, L., & Nasr, M. (2023). *SiE Survey on Solidarity in Europe Trendfile (2018–2023).* https://search.gesis.org/research_data/SDN-10.7802-2647?doi=10.7802/2647

Ipsos. (2024). *What Wories the World?* www.ipsos.com/sites/default/files/ct/news/documents/2024-04/Global-Report-What-Worries-the-World-March-2024.pdf?fbclid=IwAR2fuWO97ygpJfrr_cgxWS7_CXv_GLcsgs5Myp9ToVxxSKNVp-MjLEc3Jkz0_aem_ASd-IXCJq-9tKft5LPJ8PgMmM7raWytmTSHvV1pvv2R8Qt-bOmY8mUGHLHkP4dE5SqkDM1VksewWzb_2OvXowIILJ

Jung, S., & Krüger, T. H. C. (2022). How the COVID-19 pandemic divides society: Towards a better understanding of differences between supporters and opponents of the COVID-19 pandemic lockdown in Germany. *Journal of Psychiatric Research, 155*, 232–240. DOI: 10.1016/J.JPSYCHIRES.2022.09.001

Mader, M. (2023). Reproduction files for: "International threats and support for European security and defence integration: Evidence from 25 countries". *Harvard Dataverse.* DOI: 10.7910/DVN/7OY1CI

Mader, M. (2024). Increased support for collective defence in times of threat: European public opinion before and after Russia's invasion of Ukraine. *Policy Studies.* DOI: 10.1080/01442872.2024.2302441

Mader, M., Gavras, K., Hofmann, S. C., Reifler, J., Schoen, H., & Thomson, C. (2023). International threats and support for European security and defence integration: Evidence from 25 countries. *European Journal of Political Research.* DOI: 10.1111/1475-6765.12605

Mader, M., Neubert, M., Münchow, F., Hofmann, S. C., Schoen, H., & Gavras, K. (2024). Crumbling in the face of cost? How cost considerations affect public support for European security and defence cooperation. *European Union Politics.* DOI: 10.1177/14651165241236777

McCombs, M. E., & Shaw, D. L. (1972). The agenda-setting function of mass media. *The Public Opinion Quarterly, 36*(2), 176–187.

Sikt – Norwegian Agency for Shared Services in Education and Research. (2023). ESS round 10: European social survey round 10 data (2020): Data file edition 3.0. In European Social Survey (Ed.), *ESS Round 8 Documentation Report Appendix A6 ed. 1.1-Classifications and Coding Standards, ESS8–2016.* European Social Survey Data Archive NSD – Norwegian Centre for Research Data, Norway – Data Archive and distributor of ESS data for ESS ERIC. DOI: 10.21338/NSD-ESS10-2020

Simon, B., & Pettigrew, T. F. (1990). Social identity and perceived group homogeneity: Evidence for the ingroup homogeneity effect. *European Journal of Social Psychology, 20*(4), 269–286. DOI: 10.1002/ejsp.2420200402

Trope, Y., & Liberman, N. (2010). Construal-level theory of psychological distance. *Psychological Review, 117*(2), 440. DOI: 10.1037/A0018963

Wlezien, C., & Soroka, S., N. (2012). Political institutions and the opinion–policy link. *West European Politics, 35*(6), 1407–1432. DOI: 10.1080/01402382.2012.713752

8 Social activism for peace models in the Nordic and Baltic Sea states

Magdalena Lachowicz

Introduction

The largest anti-war movement, through a series of mass rallies and protest marches, was born in the early 2000s in opposition to the Iraq war. On 15–16 February 2003, millions of people demonstrated in the streets on all continents in a movement that was global and transnational, based on solidarity and creating a community that identified with the idea of peace. It united traditional anti-war movements, networks of opponents of 'another Vietnam war', the anti-nuclear movement, pacifists and ordinary citizens. An efficient modus operandi emerged and campaigns allowed activists to build coalitions faster and to mobilise larger protests in less time. Many opponents of war attempted to turn those protests into political activity, and after the invasion of Iraq worked on withdrawing the forces through legislative lobbying and election campaigns (Cortright, 2023, pp. 3–4). Although the war in Ukraine did give rise to a mass protest, it did not create a uniform mass anti-war movement on such a scale, nor did it unite politicians across the world. Instead it revealed political divisions and those makers of state policies who were guided primarily by particular interests being unmasked (which, however, did not translate into a lack of support among their societies). Activists, intellectual elites, experts and politicians have debated the shape of peace, forcing reflection on what in particular is behind this and what consequences will it have for the world. To analyse social activism for peace in the Baltic region, let us determine first which areas of civic engagement it concerns.

In the 2022 document *Sustainable Peace Manifesto Never Again 2.0*, representatives of Ukraine and other nations presented the Ukrainian vision of peace as an idea involving its inclusion in the European world of democracy, based on the rule of law in Ukraine and a democratic transformation in Russia. They emphasise that in order to protect Ukraine and the world against new waves of aggression, the anti-war coalition would have to create conditions leading to deep internal changes in Russia which would ensure lasting peace. Russia must adapt its constitutional system, social structure and political systems to contemporary standards. Disproving the concept of 'Russkiy mir' ('Russian world') will be a chance for a further transformation

DOI: 10.4324/9781003558040-11

of social consciousness that will power its decolonisation. The process of what the manifesto authors call 'derashization' must begin by overcoming the imperial historical memory. The Ukrainian intellectual elite, including representatives of Ukrainian civic society, paint a vision of a new world order to eliminate present threats to global security within the framework of international law. They warn, however, that peace cannot be achieved at the cost of justice, nor justice at the cost of peace. To ensure sustainable international security, justice and peace must be achieved at the same time. Securing a lasting peace must involve not only addressing Russia's responsibility for the war but also ensuring Ukraine's membership of the EU and NATO; overcoming stereotypes and Russian anti-Ukraine lobbying in Western politics; decolonisation of Russia and overcoming Russian totalitarianism; overcoming a view of the past which includes the decolonisation of Russian history and information policy; disarmament of the Russian Federation; and changing the global energy balance to a resource-based approach to the economy (Sustainable Peace Manifesto, 2022, pp. 1–2). Mykola Riabchuk writes that the only way to bring about peace in Ukraine is to help Ukraine win the war, but he points out that what may become the greatest obstacle in this context, besides the West's belief in the force of Russian narrative and the cult of Russian cultural supremacy, is Ukraine war fatigue in the West. This risk is connected with the global nuclear threat and high economic costs.

At the same time, Riabchuk sees people working for peace as characterised by a low awareness of the Eastern European context, including knowledge of Russia and Ukraine. The classical models for restoring peace have no application in this case as war is not waged for territory but above all for status and identity. In Ukraine, Russia fights against the 'collective West' and for a new world order where might is right, and brutality and nuclear blackmail are instruments of a global empire. The perpetuated stereotypes still make it difficult to understand this war, to understand it in the categories of colonialism, as a Russian neo-imperial conquest and a Ukrainian struggle for national liberation. Therefore peace negotiations based on a compromise over the issues of freedom, justice and dignity are impossible. Two problems are essential here: the violation of international law by Russia and the genocidal war in Ukraine, and an international debate that should focus only on their consequences for Russia (Riabchuk, 2023, pp. 1–6).

What remains to be seen is the question of the solidarity of activists from the Baltic region states with the Ukrainian stance. The important factors are the content of peace projects and their territorial scope. Due to the short time perspective, we have not been able to assess the impact of the process and its outcomes on the societies of states in the region. Not only are regional cooperation and local initiatives important but also the potential of social capital as well as the origins and practices of activism in individual states. A particular aspect of this region is that for each crisis there is a corresponding social movement. Anti-globalist, anti-waste/pro-environment and anti-migration, all these are considered to be social movements that organise themselves to impact organisational models, principles and routines (Mjøset, 2018, p. 119). The present models are based on the experiences of activists from states such as Nordic-format, welfare and the democracies in the new EU members, that is, the former Soviet Baltic republics.

According to the thoughts of the Ukrainian idealists mentioned, a lasting peace will be ensured by pro-ecology initiatives, green energy implementations (including small nuclear reactors) and energy diversification of Europe, including the Baltic region states. These projects should be considered as an active stabilising factor because it is necessary to not only fully exclude Russia from direct trade with energy carriers at the international level, introduce control mechanisms and unify the buyers but also improve the public programmes of energy education so that the non-monetary costs of energy and the importance of reasonable consumption are widely understood (Sustainable Peace Manifesto, 2022, pp. 19–20). In this area, grassroots initiatives and social activists play a great role.

Another area of peace activity is the issue of opposing Russian supremacy in historical thought and diminish the attractiveness of the Russian approach to analysing the Eastern European context, promoted as well by representatives of leading 'Anglo-Saxon' and other global academic units and think tanks. Riabchuk calls this phenomenon the 'toxic charm of imperial knowledge' and blames the RF for appropriating the history of Kyivan Rus in order to create a global imagination regarding imperial Russia (Riabchuk, 2023, p. 4). A part of fighting for peace is opposing the legitimation of Russian empire through a narrative about its history and high culture. The attractiveness of 'Russkiy mir' for the world should be counteracted in part by social education providing reliable knowledge about Ukraine.

Social activism and its forms

One form of civic engagement is citizen activity within social movements. According to Tilly and Tarrow (2015), a social movement is a permanent campaign for submitting claims, using repeated claim-advertising performances based on the organisations, networks, traditions and solidarity that uphold such activities. The author assumes that the foundation of social movement continuity is in group identity and ideologies, while following the approach of McCarthy and Zald by taking into the account the factor of micro-mobilisation contexts and frame adjustment in the process of symbolic mediation supporting the engagement of individuals (Diani, 1992, p. 7). What becomes important is the tradition of the movement and the historical model of activisation characteristic of particular societies. A variety of social actors are engaged in the process of social peace activism; not only in projects with a formalised format and continuous activities based on convictions and ideology but also in spontaneous protest movements understood as a reaction to national political events, global emotions and critical moments during conflicts. The group identity of activists is defined both internally, in relation to a broader movement (global, regional, political or ideological), and externally by opponents and observers or more broadly by society. Activists usually represent an entire multi-generational spectrum. In the Baltic region, we can distinguish movements operating at the systemic level and those pursuing other kinds of group activity (spontaneous, motivated actions on the internet and street demonstrations). What is important is the continuity, scope, dimension and length of anti-war campaigns. Organisations consider systemic use of European, regional or Nordic instruments to implement their long-term projects. These social movements do not represent any specific interests but of course, their interaction networks facilitate the formulation of demands, promotion of mobilising campaigns and the development and spreading of collective beliefs and identities (Diani, p. 15). Protests and protesters differ depending on issues and nationality; the majority are recruited through formal or informal networks (Giugni & Grasso, 2019, pp. XII-XIII). Let us consider the motivations, social characteristics and values that draw citizens to social and political engagement in seeking solutions for peace, that is, for justice and human rights as well as economic and energy security. What are the politics of protest and the activism of social movements today? What are their main characteristics? To what extent can street citizens be perceived as a driving force powering the social and political changes in the Baltic region (Giugni & Grasso, 2019, p. 1)?

According to Human Rights Careers, there are 13 important types of activism: marches, sit-ins and die-ins (where protesters lie down and stop moving, simulating death), walkouts, vigils and memorials (changing symbolic space), rallies and speeches, petition and letter writing, boycotts (an economic impact on the target), strikes, voting activism, social media activism, street art, 'craftivism' (protest-related crafting arts) and mutual aid (Human Rights Careers, 2023). All these formats have been combined by organisations and initiative groups of the peace movement in the Baltic region. Demonstrations and rallies are a natural social reaction to policies that threaten or violate public interest and are the main way of attracting media attention to the issue of peace. They also help build activists' solidarity and engagement, however, anti-war movements also tend to attract fringe left-wing groups, which may cause divisions (Cortright, 2023, pp. 32–33).

Bill Moyer's 'Movement Action Plan' defines stages and advocacy roles in social movements. For a social change to take effect, activists and movements must take on four different roles as: citizen, rebel, change agent and reformer. Each of these has different goals and needs, requires different skills and styles, and there are effective and ineffective ways of playing them (Moyer, 1987). Social activists must be perceived by society as responsible citizens, which also depends on the tradition and political culture of social movements in a particular country (Giugni & Grasso, 2019, p. 3).

In the Baltic region the author has determined the following key areas of peace-oriented social activism in the period of the escalation of the Russo-Ukrainian war: education for peace (change agents); projects aimed at increasing security; activism for strengthening social consciousness of the threat and countering Russian influence in the region; social activities for peaceful/conflict-free coexistence in society (considering the influx of Ukrainian refugees and Russian migrants); and activities aimed at development aid for Ukraine. What remains outside the scope of analysis are responsibility and human rights (discussed in other chapters of this book). Activism in the discussed areas follows models of peace activities focused on counteracting internal social conflicts, ensuring global peace and increasing security (issues related to nuclear weapons, climate, energy), raising social awareness, and changing the perception of Ukraine in the world (civic education), as well as consolidation of pro-peace and human rights activist groups. This part of the analysis omits the peace movement in Germany, discussed in a separate chapter.

Peace activities for countering internal social conflicts

The pro-peace function of activism is implemented through development assistance for Ukraine and Ukrainians implemented within the framework of structural and systemic change. These projects are not mere interventions but focus on future social change in Ukraine. The objectives of many projects in this area include combating war trauma (post-traumatic stress disorder, PTSD) while providing psychological and economic support. A unique systemic model has been implemented in Sweden, based on the experience of the creators of developmental aid programmes, Swedish institutions and social activists. Besides increasing humanitarian and military support for Ukraine, funding for civilian crisis management as well as support for reform and reconstruction were ensured. On 17 July 2023, the Swedish government presented a new aid strategy, focused on cooperation in reconstruction and reforms; with a total assistance figure of SEK 6 billion it is the largest bilateral proposal in the history of Sweden. Swedish assistance for Ukraine has a long-term character, covering the period of 2023–2027, and its general aim is the integration of Ukraine with the EU. The assistance is provided for the territory of Ukraine as well as for migrants and refugees in Sweden, and within a coalition of international and trans-border cooperation for lasting peace. Sweden is here a unique example of the implementation of a model based on the long-term experience of traditional actors in the peace movement, and on cooperation between organisations and government agencies. Implementation of mechanisms for building civic society can be observed in Ukraine as the main objective of the programme is a stronger, more effective and sustainable civic society, developed due to increased technological, organisational and adaptive capabilities of non-governmental organisations. Institutional support is directed towards significant transformations in the structures of management and financial control, anti-corruption and public procurement policies, which constitute a solid foundation for organisational transparency and sustainable long-term development for the Ukrainian third

126 *Magdalena Lachowicz*

sector. Swedish partners in Ukraine include such entities as the Reanimation Package of Reforms Civic Coalition, Think Tanks Development Initiative, Gurt Resource Centre for NGOs, Centre UA CSO, International Renaissance Foundation and the Centre for Democracy and Rule of Law (Embassy of Sweden, 2023).

The Polish programme 'Support for Ukraine' by the Education for Democracy Foundation (*Fundacja Edukacja dla Demokracji*, FED) is directed at Polish non-governmental organisations aiding the Ukrainian civilian population and war refugees residing in Poland. The programme promotes cooperation with Ukrainian entities and consolidates/coordinates the activities of Polish NGOs for Ukraine (e.g. with other institutions/groups); such activities are mostly focused on refugees from Ukraine as well as on initiatives undertaken on its territory (FED, 2023).

This process takes a similar course in the other states of the Baltic region. It is recognised that citizen involvement in matters of developmental aid, including public and national security issues, can be nurtured, supported and directed equally by state entities, NGOs and volunteer movements. Activists from the states of the Baltic region share their experiences and Ukrainians demonstrate the ability to rapidly create various forms of inter-sectoral, local and regional cooperation, strengthened by professional contact networks and based on enthusiasm, flexibility, horizontal communication and good practices in assessing community needs (Teperik, 2023, p. 19).

Activities for global peace and increased security: nuclear issues, climate and energy security

The Swedish peace movement has been running activities consolidating partners in the region under the banner of the 'spirit of Stockholm 1972' (i.e. of the 1972 United Nations Conference on the Human Environment in Stockholm). During an international debate, the 2022 report *Environment of Peace* by the Stockholm International Peace Research Institute (SIPRI), an independent international institute focusing on conflicts, armaments, weapon control and disarmament, formulated three theses fundamental for the crisis caused by the war in Ukraine. The report emphasises the urgent need to predict and manage growing threats resulting from interconnected security and environmental crises. It concludes that without a radical change in actions concerning all aspects of environmental degradation, such as limiting greenhouse gas emissions and pollution as well as stopping the decline of species and ecosystems, the challenge to security will become more serious. We need to learn from examples of collective actions undertaken by governments, civic society, local communities and multi-national groups which successfully deal with dangerous situations. It is necessary to learn and exchange good practices (Stockholm International Peace Research Institute (SIPRI), 2022, p. 3).

It should be remembered that in 2021 the UN Human Rights Council formally recognised healthy environment as a fundamental human right, and

Social activism for peace models 127

that the environment in the areas of military operations is exposed to dynamic degradation. A significant recommendation in the report is to finance peace, not risk. This means meeting international financial obligations, ensuring that funds will reach the most vulnerable communities, ending the subsidisation of conflicts, as well as ensuring a fair and peaceful transformation (assessment and dealing with possible negative effects of pro-environmental activities prior to their implementation, for example, in the face of a crisis involving population dislocation due to conflict) (SIPRI, 2022, pp. 5–7).

During the 2023 annual Stockholm Forum on Peace and Development organised by SIPRI, emphasis was put on the role of innovation, multi-layered solutions, diaspora and so-called regional geopolitics, understood as close cooperation (also cooperation within the Baltic region, such as that modelled on the Life and Peace Institute in Uppsala). Solutions must be based on experience; besides the full-scale war in Ukraine, armed conflicts are taking place in 55 other countries. The restoration of Ukraine is not the only challenge; it should also be considered the ways in which means for ecological transformation can be included in investments in the war-to-peace transition (SIPRI, 2023). What is more, the European approach to security should be verified, particularly with regard to nuclear deterrence. According to Tytti Erästö, Europeans should avoid excesses of nuclear armaments so as to avoid the escalation characteristic of a dynamic arms race and promote long-term solutions for challenges related to the security of the continent (SIPRI, 2023a).

The Finns draw on their experiences from running programmes for Afghanistan and the Western Balkans (Peace and Development in Finland's Country Programme in Afghanistan, and Peace and Development in Finland's Development Cooperation). Also the confrontation between peace and justice is replaced with increasing frequency by an approach that emphasises coordination, staging, complementarity and management based on human rights, not on results. In the case of informal dialogue, it is necessary to build and maintain trust and the will to engage in the peace process among all key subjects, including entities that do not support human rights; the priority is to strengthen inclusivity, provide examples of sustainable, human rights-based solutions and support capabilities (Development Policy Committee, 2023). Major changes have also taken place in Lithuania, Latvia and Estonia, formerly part of USSR territory. Due to the awareness of the realistic geopolitical threats now widespread in society as well as the high level of trust in common safeguards and security assurances, the societies of the Baltic states are currently perceived as more resilient at a national level (Teperik, 2023), and it is such resilience that enables societies and countries to survive upheavals without resorting to conflict.

However, the war in Ukraine demonstrates that increased resilience does not eliminate the causes and risks of such dangers as the threat of poverty and hunger (the grain crisis), risks related to nuclear, hydropower and water infrastructure (the destruction of Kakhovka Dam), environmental and

128 Magdalena Lachowicz

demographic crises (displacement of population, depopulation of Ukraine). These are the challenges for future pro-ecological movements.

Education activities by change agents for increasing social awareness and changing the perception of Ukraine in the world

An interesting case in this area is Denmark, where social activism for peace focuses on education. Representatives here include change agents from the Association of Folk High Schools who promote active humanism, especially among the younger generation through a number of educational, intervention and information projects for Ukraine, refugees and peace. The leaders of the movement also call for a united academic movement for Ukraine and peace. Schoolchildren and students initiate dozens of actions, including symbolic ones such as singing '*En lærke letted*', a 1945 Danish song about freedom (Højskolerne, n.d.). In opposition to 'Russkiy mir', an objection was expressed also by the National Church of Denmark and an associated social movement. On the day when the war broke out, solidarity was symbolically demonstrated by peace and intercession services and pilgrimages; Danish bishops declared pro-Ukrainian and pro-peace stances, while the church and church aid organisations actively participated in actions for Ukrainian refugees (Dylander, 2022).

At the same time, one in five Danish citizens thought in 2022 that Denmark had acted too hastily and should strive to adopt a neutral role in the conflict between Russia and Ukraine. Only one in 12 was a fully convinced neutralist (Andersen et al., 2022, p. 18). Neutrality can be rooted in pacifism, which as a rule considers war to be a crime; it can also result from an unwillingness to involve little Denmark in the conflicts of great politics (Andersen et al., 2022, p. 19). Trust in NATO is greater than in all other Danish and international institutions and organisations (Andersen et al., 2022, p. 20). In 2023 more Danes (54%) perceived the United States as an ally than in 2021 (35%) but at the same time, a large percentage think that Europe should be able to defend itself instead of relying on the US (66% in 2021 and 73% in 2023) (Tænketanken EUROPA, 2023a). The residents of Denmark have been worried by the threat from Russia, which they blame that country for the war, while demonstrating low support for peace talks (Andersen et al., 2022, pp. 20, 29). A report from the Danish police intelligence (*Politiets Efterretningstjeneste*, PET) concludes that Russian intelligence services, as well as Chinese ones, continue to be the greatest threat to Denmark (PET, 2023a, 2023b).

What seems interesting in this context is the study conducted by Think Tank EUROPA together with the European Council on Foreign Relations.[1] The survey demonstrated that after a year of the conflict in Ukraine, the Danes have stable attitude to the war and scenarios for its ending, as well as to a change in world order resulting from the war. Danish society is among those most clearly anti-Russian and conservative. A year after the outbreak of the war, 48% thought that it should end only when Ukraine regains all the lost territories even if the price is going to be a prolonged conflict and more casualties. As a society, Danes accept higher energy prices resulting from limited deliveries of Russian gas, oil and coal; they are also in favour of NATO, with as many as 52% perceiving the US as an ally. The new world order has features of cold-war logic, dividing the world into two blocs, the United States and China. Danes realise the threat to Europe posed by Russia, considering the threat of nuclear war to be high (37% see this as the greatest threat, and 16% as second most serious) (Ash et al., 2023, pp. 1–16; Tænketanken EUROPA, 2023). Twenty-six per cent of Danes think that Denmark should not maintain relations with Russia after a possible peace agreement with Ukraine, 9% envision close cooperation in the future and 50% would accept limited relations in certain areas. In this aspect Denmark is close to the stances of Sweden and Poland, while according to a survey from June 2023, some Germans want closer cooperation (Tænketanken EUROPA, 2023a). This suggests that after the war the EU may find it difficult to reach a consensus regarding Russia.

Transnational activities consolidating the peace activist community

Coalitions and platforms for cooperation instil solidarity and strengthen peace initiatives through uniting forces and building a horizontal network of exchange. Engagement in civil resistance, humanitarian aid and voluntary movement can significantly consolidate a nation and increase its operational resilience through the formation of activist communities and organisations. However, before mobilisation, active members of civic society and relevant non-governmental organisations should be fully prepared, professionally trained and equipped with sufficient resources to be effective resilience subjects in crisis management (Teperik, 2023, p. 11). Pro-peace organisations are dynamically consolidating and cooperating in broad geopolitical (the EU and/ or beyond), interdisciplinary and transnational dimensions. Social organisations of pro-peace activists cooperate both in practical matters (social activities) and in providing analyses, consultations and expertise, uniting social organisations with very different profiles (e.g. gender, environmental, Catholic/church, left-wing) through horizontal networks. An example of such trans-national peace initiatives is the European Peacebuilding Liaison Office (EPLO), established in 2001 and uniting 50 organisations from 17 European countries (NGOs, NGO networks and advisory teams). Its members from the countries of the Baltic region include the Berghof Foundation, the Centre for Feminist Foreign Policy, CSSP – Berlin Center for Integrative Mediation, the Platform Peaceful Conflict Transformation (PZKB) (Germany), CMI – Martti Ahtisaari Peace Foundation, SaferGlobe, Wider Security Network (WISE) (Finland), Conducive Space for Peace (CSP) (Denmark), the Kvinna till Kvinna Foundation and the Life and Peace Institute (LPI) (Sweden). The network assiduously works in the consulting area on good practice exchange and activity consolidation (project co-development). Such initiatives make NGOs professional, increase their public impact through the use of new information channels with wider reach, represent their members (e.g. defending them) and provide mutual help (supporting each other through training, organisational help etc.). The primary goal is the coordination and monitoring of members' activities as well as influencing the shape of public policies in terms of peace building.

It is important to build permanent horizontal networks concerning human potential (recruitment and professionalisation of volunteers, training, improving competencies). An example here is the Danish project 'Young Diplomats for Peace and Dialogue in Ukraine and Georgia', run by the Crossing Borders organisation in 2016–2018. The goal of the project was for the participants to acquire skills in conflict management, advocacy and diplomatic dialogue so that they would be able to help in developing a peace-building culture. The project participants supported the development of the Coalition for the Protection of the Rights of Persons with Disabilities due to Intellectual Disabilities, uniting over a hundred local partners from all regions of Ukraine, and the Peace Engineer programme within the Dignity Space in Ukraine (the Dignity Space programme, focusing on education for peace building, is financed by the German Ministry of Foreign Affairs) (Alternative Og ADP, Crossing Borders Projects, n.d., https://crossingborders.dk/).

The process of building horizontal contacts and so-called intervention initiatives can be seen. Sharing good practices takes place at local, national, regional and global levels, and is focused on obtaining knowledge from the experiences of other areas with similar characteristics. An example of such an initiative reaching beyond the closest neighbourhood is the ALF Lithuanian Network, which gathers 45 civil society organisations. The network's goal is to expand opportunities for creating contact networks, building trust and establishing connections between members through increased engagement, participation and institutional support from and for members, and to provide a platform for those who would like to establish cooperation with partners from the entire Mediterranean region in order to work for an open and tolerant society based on democratic principles Through its initiatives, the ALF network participates in joint international projects with partners from Egypt, Jordan, Tunisia, Morocco, Portugal, Italy, Ireland, Greece, Denmark, Latvia and Czechia. This is a model for local, regional and international/global cooperation with an intensifying exchange of information in diverse formats, from anti-war congresses to cooperation networks and platforms for the protection of activist rights. A similar project, which operates in Poland as well, is the Rotary International network with over 1.4 million members gathered in 34,000 clubs in 200 countries all over the world. One of their programmes is the Rotary Peace Fellowships, awarding grants to increase local leaders' competences in conflict mediation; another involved providing health care for Ukrainians in Poland (Radziszewski, 2023; Rotary, n.d.; Wcisła, 2022).

Instead of conclusion: instruments for the stable financing of social activism for peace and human rights

The states of the Baltic region have different experiences that form the foundation of their activities in human rights protection, so their models of social activism differ as well. Yet the goal remains the same: a civil society as a power working for security by focusing on people. What is important here are instruments for providing stable funding for a horizontal network of cooperation between activists from all Baltic region countries and Ukraine (refugees, Ukrainian citizens remaining in their home country as well as entities that launch initiatives and cooperate in the area of human rights protection in the region).

The European mechanism 'Interreg Baltic Sea Region', part of European territorial cooperation policy, offers a stable instrument for social actors (governments, local governments, public entities and NGOs) in the area of economic, social and territorial development within the EU while providing a framework for trans-border work in the Baltic region.

In 2014, Sweden launched a Regional Strategy for Cooperation with Eastern Europe, the Western Balkans and Türkiye, of which the most significant recipient is Ukraine. Sweden's stance on international collaboration and assistance has its roots in the evolution of Swedish society based on the one hand on the country's involvement in international human rights systems, and on the other on a specific form of scepticism towards constitutionalism, judicial control and the rule of law in internal politics (similar to other Nordic countries). The myth of being the 'global Samaritan' has been attached to Sweden due to the extremely broad scope of its development assistance system, actively promoted since 1960s (Schaffer, 2020). Ukraine and its activists have become one of its beneficiaries as well: since 1995, Sweden has been continuously engaged there, for example, in projects aiming at strengthening democracy and respect for human rights as well as climate action. The entities involved in the collaboration included the Nordic Environment Finance Cooperation (NEFCO), Swedish Association of Local Authorities and Regions (SALAR) and the Estonian e-Governance Academy (Embassy of Sweden, 2023).

Sweden also makes use of its development agency Swedish International Development Cooperation Agency (SIDA), which remains the main instrument for the country's engagement in humanitarian aid and human rights protection. Humanitarian aid is delivered through collaborative horizontal networks. Its main partners have included the Council of Europe, Docudays UA International Human Rights Documentary Film Festival, the Centre for Democracy and Rule of Law, and the Center for Civil Liberties. The question is how the potential of this good practice is used today (Government Offices of Sweden, 2023).

Sweden took significant steps to increase support for the Donetsk and Lugansk regions, experiencing multidimensional crises, and to coordinate

132 *Magdalena Lachowicz*

assistance efforts more closely. The list of main partners includes the UN Development Programme, World Bank, the Office of the UN High Commissioner for Human Rights, the Office of the UN High Commissioner for Refugees (UNHCR), the International Federation of Red Cross and Red Crescent Societies, the OSCE Special Monitoring Mission to Ukraine, International Committee of the Red Cross, the Danish Refugee Council, the Norwegian Refugee Council, Danish Demining Group (DDG), the World Food Programme (WFP), the Ukrainian Red Cross Society, UN Ukraine Humanitarian Fund, Save the Children, UNICEF, the Swedish Civil Contingencies Agency (MSB), Action Against Hunger and the International Rescue Committee. Support was ensured for inclusive economic development, gender equality, environment and energy, democracy and human rights, free and independent media, civil society, decentralisation and public administration reform, as well as peace building in Ukraine. Sweden chooses tried and tested UN distribution channels such as the UN Population Fund and the International Organisation for Migration (Embassy of Sweden, 2023; Government Offices of Sweden, 2023). The effectiveness of aid is ensured by the collaboration of large international entities, characterised by an extensive, well-established network of flow monitoring and impeccable opinion. This network unites entities from the Baltic region in common activities.

A response modelled on SIDA and the development aid template was adopted by Lithuania. Official Development Assistance (ODA) is financial and humanitarian aid for developing countries and territories, financed from the budgets of central and local authorities as well as their subordinate institutions. The Development Cooperation and Democracy Promotion Programme (DCDPP) is an instrument of ODA, financed from targeted budget funds allocated from the Ministry of Foreign Affairs. Lithuania has actively engaged itself in bilateral and multilateral efforts aimed at preventing the global consequences of the war waged under Russia's leadership. In 2022 Lithuania concluded system reforms, enabling the launching of the Development Cooperation and Humanitarian Aid Fund. Concepts have been developed for 11 projects in areas of innovation, digitalisation, education, environmental protection, building administrative capacity and fighting disinformation, all addressed to the EU Eastern Partnership countries. The fund accepted 16 bilateral regional projects with direct financing and national co-financing, to be launched from 2023 in Ukraine, Moldova, Georgia, Armenia, Belarus, Uzbekistan, Palestine and Iraq. Since 2022, Lithuania has been providing full support and aid for Ukraine (humanitarian and financial, related to population protection and assisting refugees), and has implemented projects in education, infrastructure reconstruction and freedom of the media (Lithuanian Development Cooperation, 2023).

An analogous mechanism operates in the Nordic instrument of support, the Programme for NGO Cooperation (Nordic Council of Ministers (NCM), 2021b), which supports the development of a strong and dynamic civil society in the Baltic region and helps increase the potential of NGOs in the Baltic

Social activism for peace models 133

region countries through sharing experiences and knowledge with Nordic partners. It follows the model of network cooperation in the priority areas of knowledge transfer for mutual benefits in different sectors. Since 2022, Ukrainian NGOs operating in Nordic and Baltic states can be included as additional partners. The projects should reflect the strategic priorities included in the Nordic Council of Ministers' Vision 2030, that is to promote the green transformation of societies and strive for carbon neutrality and a sustainable, circular and biology-based economy; promote ecological growth in the Nordic region based on knowledge, innovations, mobility and digital integration; promote an integrative, equal and interconnected region with shared values, and strengthened cultural exchange and well-being. Significantly, the priorities of the programme include a particular profile for projects focused on support for NGOs working towards individual protection, public security and crisis management capabilities (including volunteering); support for NGOs working on integration initiatives targeted at Ukrainian refugees; and support for NGOs working on integration and educational initiatives for Russian-speaking minorities in the region. The main beneficiaries are to be children and young people (NCM, 2021a, 2021b). The council also runs dedicated programmes focused on the third sector of the Baltic countries, supporting Ukrainian refugees (NCM, 2021c) and Ukraine's civil officers (NCM, 2023). This last one is significant as it promotes the social and transformative potential of the future Ukrainian society.

Social activism is initiated through entities of global importance. In recent years, UNHCR has intensified its presence in Estonia, Latvia and Lithuania, employing staff in each of these countries. It cooperates closely not only with the government and local authorities but also with civil society, and there are UNHCR offices in Tallinn, Riga and Vilnius. In 2023 Estonia, Latvia and Lithuania are covered by the Regional Refugee Response Plan (United Nations High Commissioner for Refugees (UNHCR), 2023a). Interestingly, the plan does not have funds at its disposal but rather serves as a fund-gathering platform, providing the financial frame required for funding activities planned by different partners, including NGOs, and enabling all the participating partners to gather funds independently (UNHCR, 2023a, 2023b).

The potential of cooperation instruments in the Baltic region has grown due to the conclusion of the agreement between the Nordic Council and the Baltic assembly for 2022–2023 (25 April 2022, parliamentary level). The Nordic and Baltic countries agreed on a common strategy for supporting Ukraine and ensuring peace and stability in the region. The agreement points out that Russia's activities threaten peace and stability in Ukraine as well as in the Nordic-Baltic region. The agreement covers nine areas which both organisations consider priorities for 2022–2023. Cooperation was strengthened in the field of foreign policy and security, including cybersecurity, as well as fake news and the propaganda spread by authoritarian regimes. The priorities include promoting democratic values, supporting secure energy supplies in the region, cooperation in preventing climate change, a circular economy

134 *Magdalena Lachowicz*

and drawing conclusion from the COVID-19 pandemic in order to be better prepared for the next crisis. Systemic solutions provide an impulse that strengthens activisation mechanisms in the non-profit sector. The agreement provides a stable foundation for the future strengthening of mechanisms and creating social projects focused on building peace in the region of Denmark, Norway, Sweden, Finland, Estonia, Latvia and Lithuania.

Note

1 The survey was made on a sample of 14,439 respondents between 3 and 24 February 2023.

References

Alternative Og ADP, Crossing Borders Projects. (n.d.). *Vejen Til Fred GÅR Genem Dyplomatu og Dialog*. https://crossingborders.dk/
Andersen, J., Andersen, J. G., & Hede, A. (2022). Danskerne og krigen i Ukraine. *Trygbedsmåling* (pp. 1–27). TrygFonden.
Ash, T. G., Krastev, I., & Leonard, M. (2023, February). United West, divided from the rest: Global public opinion one year into Russia's war on Ukraine. *European Council on Foreign Relations*. https://thinkeuropa.dk/files/media/document/Garton%20Ash%20Krastev%20Leonard%20ECFR%20report.pdf
Cortright, D. (2023). *A Peaceful Superpower: Lessons from the World's Largest Antiwar Movement*. NYU Press.
Development Policy Committee. (2023). *A Human Rights-Based Approach to Finnish Development Policy: Tense Times Demand a More Ambitious Direction*. www.kehityspoliittinentoimikunta.fi/wp-content/uploads/sites/27/2023/04/a-human-rights-based-approach-to-finnish-development-policy-1.pdf
Diani, M. (1992). The concept of social movement. *The Sociological Review, 40*(1). DOI: 10.1111/j.1467-954X.1992.tb02943.x
Dylander, V. (2022, February 24). Efter krigsudbrud: Biskopper opfordrer præster til at sætte fokus på fred. *Kirke.dk*. www.kirke.dk/efter-krigsudbrud-biskopper-opfordrer-praester-til-saette-fokus-paa-fred
Embassy of Sweden. (2023). *Swedish Reform Cooperation with Ukraine*. www.swedenabroad.se/en/about-sweden-non-swedish-citizens/ukraine/development-and-aid/reform-cooperation-with-ukraine/
Fundacja Edukacja dla Demokracji. (2023). *Wspieramy Ukrainę*. https://fed.org.pl/wspieramy-ukraine/
Giugni, M., & Grasso, M. (2019). *Street Citizens. In Street Citizens: Protest Politics and Social Movement Activism in the Age of Globalization*. Cambridge University Press.
Government Offices of Sweden. (2023a, 16 August). *Sveriges stöd till Ukraina*. www.regeringen.se/globalassets/regeringen/dokument/utrikesdepartementet/faktablad-stod-till-ukraina/faktablad-sveriges-stod-till-ukraina/
Government Offices of Sweden. (2023b). *Rysslands invasion av Ukraina*. www.regeringen.se/regeringens-politik/rysslands-invasion-av-ukraina/?page=1
Government Offices of Sweden. (2023c, December 12). *Humanitarian and Civilian Support to Ukraine*. www.government.se/government-policy/swedens-support-to-ukraine/humanitarian-and-civilian-support-to-ukraine/
Højskolerne [Website]. (n.d.). www.hojskolerne.dk/
Human Rights Careers. (2023). *13 Types of Activism*. www.humanrightscareers.com/issues/types-of-activism/

Lithuanian Development Cooperation. (2023). *2022 Report on the Implementation of the Development Cooperation and Democracy Promotion Programme.* https://ltaid.urm.lt/data/public/uploads/2023/09/vbpdp-ataskaita-2022-m.-en-atnaujinti-opv-duomenys_rugsejis.pdf

Mjøset, L. (2018). Old and new social movements in the Nordic Countries: History and future in an international perspective. In F. Engelstad, C. Holst & G. C. Aakvaag (Eds.), *Democratic State and Democratic Society. Institutional Change in the Nordic Model* (pp. 118–150). De Gruyter Open.

Moyer, B. (1987). The movement action plan: A strategic framework describing the eight stages of successful social movements. *History Is a Weapon.* www.historyisaweapon.com/defcon1/moyermap.html

Nordic Council of Ministers. (2021a). *The Nordic Council of Ministry, the Nordic Region – Towards Being the Most Sustainable and Integrated Region in the World Action Plan for 2021 to 2024.* www.norden.org/en/publication/towards-sustainable-and-integrated-nordic-region

Nordic Council of Ministers. (2021b). *Support Programme for NGO Cooperation between the Nordic and Baltic Countries.* www.norden.lt/en/programmes/support-programme-for-non-governmental-organisations-cooperation-between-the-nordic-and-baltic-countries/

Nordic Council of Ministers. (2021c). *For-In (Fostering Refugee and Immigrant Integration/For Integration).* www.norden.lt/en/projects/for-in-fostering-refugee-and-immigrant-integration-for-integration/

Nordic Council of Ministers. (2023). *Public Administration's Mobility Program Opens Up for Participants from Ukraine.* www.norden.lt/en/public-administrations-mobility-program-opens-up-for-participants-from-ukraine/

Politiets Efterretningstjeneste. (2023a, May). *Spionagetruslen mod Danmark, Færøerne og Grønland.* https://pet.dk/-/media/mediefiler/pet/dokumenter/analyser-og-vurderinger/vurdering-af-spionagetruslen-mod-danmark/vsd_2023_dk_web.pdf

Politiets Efterretningstjeneste. (2023b). *Vurdering af Spionagetruslen mod Danmark, Færøerne og Grønland.* https://pet.dk/aktuelt/publikationer/vurdering-af-spionagetruslen-mod-danmark

Radziszewski, D. (2023, August 24). Leczenie stomatologiczne dla 121 dzieci z Ukrainy. *Rotary Dystrykt 2231.* https://rotary.org.pl/leczenie-stomatologiczne-dla-121-dzieci-z-ukrainy/

Riabchuk, M. (2023). War in Ukraine: Peace-talking versus peace-making. In *CIDOB. Notes Internacionals CIDOB* (288/03/2023). www.cidob.org/publicaciones/serie_de_publicacion/notes_internacionals_cidob/288/war_in_ukraine_peace_talking_versus_peace_making

Rotary [Website]. (n.d.). www.rotary.org/en

Schaffer, J. (2020). The self-exempting activist: Sweden and the international human rights regime. *Nordic Journal of Human Rights*, 38(1), 40–60. DOI: 10.1080/18918131.2020.1773065

Stockholm International Peace Research Institute. (2022, May 24). *Environment of Peace: Security in a New Era of Risk.* www.sipri.org/research/peace-and-development/environment-peace/

Stockholm International Peace Research Institute. (2023). *Stockholm Forum on Peace and Development.* www.sipri.org/events/2023/2023-stockholm-forum-peace-and-development

Stockholm International Peace Research Institute. (2023a). *More Investment in Nuclear Deterrence Will Not Make Europe Safer.* www.sipri.org/commentary/essay/2023/more-investment-nuclear-deterrence-will-not-make-europe-safer

Sustainable Peace Manifesto Never Again 2.0. (2022). https://sustainablepeacemanifesto.org/

136 *Magdalena Lachowicz*

Tænketanken EUROPA. (2023, March 16). *Ny meningsmåling: Danmark er blandt Europas 'hardliners' i synet på krigen.* https://thinkeuropa.dk/meningsmaaling/2023-03-ny-meningsmaaling-danmark-er-blandt-europas-hardliners-i-synet-paa-krigen

Tænketanken EUROPA. (2023a, June 7). *Ny måling: Krigen skubber danskerne tættere på USA, men øger støtten til et stærkere europæisk forsvar.* https://thinkeuropa.dk/meningsmaaling/2023-06-ny-maaling-krigen-skubber-danskerne-taettere-paa-usa-men-oeger-stoetten-til

Teperik, D. (2023, October 12). The Beacon model for resilience building in the Baltics: Key lessons to learn from Ukraine. *Latvian Transatlantic Organization.* www.lato.lv/the-beacon-model-for-resilience-building-in-the-baltics-key-lessons-to-learn-from-ukraine/

Tilly, C., & Tarrow, S. (2015). *Contentious Politics.* Oxford University Press.

United Nations High Commissioner for Refugees. (2023a). *Ukraine Situation: Regional Refugee Response Plan: January-December 2023.* https://data.unhcr.org/en/documents/details/97958

United Nations High Commissioner for Refugees. (2023b). *UNHCR in the Baltic Countries.* www.unhcr.org/neu/about/unhcr-in-the-baltic-countries

Wcisła, D. (2022). Skoordynowana pomoc dla Ukrainy. *Rotary Dystrykt 2231.* https://rotary.org.pl/skoordynowana-pomoc-dla-ukrainy/

9 'When peace comes'

Activities undertaken in the Baltic region states to preserve Ukraine's cultural capital

Małgorzata Madej, Małgorzata Myśliwiec and Karolina Tybuchowska-Hartlińska

Introduction

What characterises Central and Eastern Europe is its turbulent history with numerous armed conflicts, frequent shifting of borders, and states appearing and disappearing. These dynamic changes have been a challenge to individual communities that have demonstrated the will to preserve and protect their identities while often harbouring an ambition to establish and defend a sovereign state of their own.

One of the factors that enabled the creation of an independent Ukrainian state in 1991 were almost two centuries of work by local elites developing a separate cultural identity. The 19th century was the era of Ukrainian national renaissance and the shaping of the modern Ukrainian language. The works of Taras Shevchenko and the later activity of such figures as Mykhailo Drahomanov and Mykhailo Hrushevsky were essential for shaping Ukrainian national identity and the emerging ambition to establish an independent state. It should be remembered that such activities are a distinctive feature of communities defined as *nations* (Myśliwiec, 2014, pp. 57–61).

It is worth analysing the events currently taking place in Europe in this context. Supposing that sharing a common culture is one of the most important factors shaping national identities in the reality of Central and Eastern Europe, the authors have resolved that the main objective of this chapter will be the identification of activities undertaken by state institutions, social organisations, private entities and volunteers in order to sustain, develop and promote Ukrainian culture in the states of the Baltic region.

Cultural capital during the war in Ukraine

The concept of cultural capital sets the theoretical framework for this text. War and its consequences have led to the weakening of Ukrainian social capital, which also includes cultural capital, particularly important in the context of the research subject. Questions regarding social capital became the focus of theoretical and empirical interest towards the end of the 20th century. Among the pioneers of this research were Pierre Bourdieu (1986), James

DOI: 10.4324/9781003558040-12

138 *Madej et al.*

Samuel Coleman (1988) and Robert Putnam (Putnam et al., 1993), although the concept itself had appeared in theoretical discussions slightly earlier. The main purpose of its introduction was to facilitate understanding of the rules of the social world, particularly concerning the levelling of social inequalities.

According to Pierre Bourdieu, cultural capital is the knowledge and skills that a person, that is a specific subject of social life, has at their disposal; the main feature of cultural capital is its accumulation, which then drives development through the gathering and allocation of resources. Potential obstacles to this process are primarily changes of ideological contexts as well as suddenly occurring situations that change society's point of view (such as war, system change). Bourdieu differentiated three types of cultural capital: embodied, objectified and institutionalised (Bourdieu, 1986, pp. 241–258). Embodied cultural capital is a resource that can be carried only by an individual who has knowledge, competences and professional qualifications; objectified capital encompasses the material elements of the human environment that are closely connected with culture and are its carriers (e.g. works of visual art, literature and music); while the last category refers to all the elements of culture the possession of which is defined by formal institutions, such as appropriate diplomas and certificates, which usually give specific powers or licences.

The war in Ukraine has caused immense material and social losses. In addition to the death toll from the conflict, which is difficult to estimate, according to data published by the United Nations High Commissioner for Refugees (UNHCR), 6,268,000 citizens have left the territory of Ukraine since February 2022 in search of aid and shelter in other states all over the world (UNHCR, 2023), 64% of them, that is 4,065,615, reside in the EU (Eurostat, 2023), with 60% of these staying in the states of the Baltic region (Table 9.1).

Table 9.1 Non-EU citizens who had fled Ukraine and received temporary protection in the states of the Baltic region (end of June 2023)

State	Number of refugees	Percentage of refugees
Germany	1,133,420	27.88%
Poland	977,740	24.04%
Lithuania	70,650	1.74%
Finland	56,145	1.39%
Norway	47,200	1.16%
Latvia	44,260	1.09%
Sweden	39,190	0.97%
Denmark	35,640	0.87%
Estonia	35,215	0.86%
Total Baltic region states	**2,439,460**	**60%**
Total EU	**4,065,615**	**100%**

Source: Authors based on Eurostat (2023, August 9), *30 June 2023: 4.07 million with temporary protection* (https://ec.europa.eu/eurostat/web/products-eurostat-news/w/ddn-20230809–1)

The unique cultural heritage of Ukraine has been seriously threatened by Russian aggression. As demonstrated by the experience of Central and Eastern European states, particularly affected by the events of World War II, it is not possible to fully regain lost heritage, such as architectural monuments and art collections, that have been destroyed; nor is it easy for eminent artists, so important for the functioning of the society, to resume their activity. As emphasised by Magdalena Pasikowska-Schnass (2022), an expert working for the European Parliament, the goals of Russian aggression include such destruction of heritage. Academic researchers also point out that one of the objects of this war is 'Ukrainian-ness' and Ukrainian identity: 'Ukraine's own national imaginary and the right to its own national imaginary' (Knott, 2022). It should be therefore concluded that a threat to Ukrainian culture is something to which the Ukrainian state and its allies must react, as losing Ukrainian cultural capital may cause serious difficulties during the post-war reconstruction.

A testimony to the importance of preserving cultural capital during the war is the joint declaration of the ministers of culture of Poland, Latvia, Lithuania, Estonia and Ukraine, signed on 9 July 2023 in Riga. The parties declared a 'common interest in enhancing coordinated international efforts in the safeguarding, promotion and transmission of Ukraine's intangible cultural heritage as an integral part of the cultural heritage of Europe, as well as of Humanity, in the face of Russia's unforgivable attacks upon it', and proposed establishing an International Culture Heritage Protection Fund for Ukraine under UNESCO's auspices as well as an increased commitment of the European Commission and member states in aiding Ukraine through a dedicated fund for the protection of Ukrainian heritage ('Joint Declaration', 2023).

There is another important argument for undertaking research in this area: the current research gap. So far, issues regarding cultural capital have been presented in the literature in different aspects highlighting its role in the process of migration and social integration (Nagopoulos et al., 2023) as well as the role of women refugees in sustaining it (Carlbaum, 2022). Important aspects are access to education for children and teenagers (Miller et al., 2021) and the taking up of gainful employment (Eggenhofer-Rehart et al., 2018). Attention has been drawn to the role of social capital in the professional and social mobility of migrants (Gericke et al., 2018). In the context of this research, conducted in the time of peace, the topic of actions aimed at sustaining, developing and promoting the cultural capital of Ukraine during the war are a problem deserving academic analysis. Considering that the previous full-scale armed conflict in Europe had taken place in the Balkans in the early 1990s, in 2022, no one was conceptually prepared to launch and implement well-thought-out patterns of operating in such a situation. During the 30-year gap between conflicts, there have been significant changes in the reality in which artists representing different arts work. During the Yugoslav Wars, most of today's means of communication were not available, and the

140   Madej et al.

neighbouring states were not members of the European Community/European Union.

The main objective of the research was to identify the activities undertaken in support of Ukrainian culture in the states of the Baltic region. Its detailed goals have provided for the identification of both the actors involved in these undertakings and the recipients of these actions.

Starting from the discussed definition of Pierre Bourdieu, the following research questions were formulated:

1. What types of activity were undertaken during the investigated period in the states of the Baltic region in order to sustain the embodied, objectified and institutionalised cultural capital of Ukraine?
2. What types of activity were undertaken during the investigated period in the states of the Baltic region in order to develop the embodied, objectified and institutionalised cultural capital of Ukraine?
3. What types of activity were undertaken during the investigated period in the states of the Baltic region in order to promote the embodied, objectified and institutionalised cultural capital of Ukraine?

A preliminary analysis has allowed the authors to assume that help for Ukraine at war cannot be limited to supplying weapons and other forms of material assistance. It is equally important to support culture as a factor contributing to the preservation of the unity and national identity of Ukrainians, which consequently has become a foundation for actions aimed at rebuilding the country after peace is restored. The following analysis will focus on three fundamental activities: sustaining, developing and promoting cultural capital. 'Sustaining' is defined here as activities focused on preserving existing culture and access to it, as well as creating conditions that ensure the survival of artists and leaders of cultural life. 'Developing' cultural capital involves cultivating conditions in which Ukrainian artists, either on their own or in collaboration with local artists, are able to create new work. Finally, 'promotion' refers to making use of existing or new forums and tools in order to popularise Ukrainian artists and their works. Applying this frame to the three types of cultural capital, the authors have formulated a hypothesis that in the states of the Baltic region there exist recurring forms of activity related to every aim and every type of cultural capital (Table 9.2).

The territorial scope of the research covers the states of the Baltic region. Thus, the analysis will focus on Denmark, Estonia, Finland, Germany, Latvia, Lithuania, Poland and Sweden as countries that have provided temporary protection for as many as 60% of Ukrainian refugees currently residing in EU member states.

The research was carried out during the period February–July 2023. The initial date is the symbolic beginning of the second year of the war and this has allowed the authors to analyse the source materials created during the first 12 months of the conflict; while the end date is the day of signing the

'When peace comes' 141

Table 9.2 Types of activities undertaken in the states of the Baltic region by state institutions, social organisations, private entities and volunteers in support of Ukrainian cultural capital in the period 2022–2023

Aim of activity	Type of cultural capital	Forms of activity
Sustaining	embodied	Supporting relocation
		Residencies
		Grants
	objectified	Ensuring access to existing works of art
	institutionalised	Cooperation with local institutions
		Employment in local institutions
Developing	embodied	Grants for activity and promotion of Ukrainian culture
	objectified	Screenings and broadcasts of films
	institutionalised	Cooperation with cultural and art institutions
Promoting	embodied	Providing an environment for Ukrainian artists to present their work
	objectified	Providing an environment for the presentation of Ukrainian works of art
	institutionalised	Providing an environment for existing or newly established institutions to operate

Source: Authors

joint declaration on international support for the protection of Ukrainian cultural heritage mentioned earlier.

Answering the research questions required analysing the relevant source materials. In the first phase, based on information made public by cultural institutions and organisations, as well as on press releases, sample initiatives undertaken in the investigated area were identified. The second phase involved an analysis of publicly available information and documents from selected institutions. If some information was missing (particularly details regarding practical implementation), the data was completed by direct contact (by e-mail or a phone call) with those responsible for implementing the particular initiative. Selecting the source material was not an easy task, as the range of measures introduced varied from state to state. Due to the urgency of the situation and the scale of Ukrainian migration, actions were taken rapidly, often spontaneously. Hence, the only task possible to be completed within the adopted timeframe was to check what activities had been undertaken and to attempt to evaluate their potential benefits and risks. The source materials also encompassed statistical data published by Eurostat and the UNHCR office, with the study primarily employing the comparative method. Subsequent to a careful analysis of these sources, conclusions were drawn to enable responses to the research inquiries. Furthermore, the study used desk research to analyse relevant documents and data accessible on the websites of institutions supporting Ukrainian artists.

142 *Madej et al.*

Activities aimed at sustaining Ukrainian cultural capital

The primary area of activity to support Ukrainians in the first period after the outbreak of war was direct organisational and material help for artists who became refugees or were otherwise affected by war. This should be linked to the concept of embodied cultural capital. The purpose of such activities was to rescue and support individual artists and cultural leaders, and in many cases the activities were grassroot initiatives, implemented spontaneously. If they were launched by cultural institutions, it was often at the initiative of employees of those institutions. These fall within the area of sustaining cultural capital, as they focused on survival in the new refugee conditions.

In some cases, this meant practical assistance in relocating. Immediately after the outbreak of war, the Latvian Ministry of Culture provided aid to musicians fleeing Ukraine in terms of transportation, housing, humanitarian aid, food, clothing, schools and kindergartens, along with psychological, legal and medical assistance. Helping the refugees included opening the labour market and establishing contacts with Latvian musical institutions, orchestras, choirs, schools and government organisations (Ministry of Culture: Republic of Latvia, 2023). Support for Ukrainian refugees was also provided by groups that organised spontaneously. An example of this was an international group of classical musicians who used their personal and professional contacts to build a network of musical friends who raised funds, paid for visas, COVID-19 tests, clothing and essentials, while arranging safe travel to further destinations and emergency funds. Assistance was also provided with submitting visa applications, hosting musicians or arranging safe lodging in local musicians' homes. Other areas of support included continuing education or getting a job, as well as application procedures (Help musicians Ukraine, 2023). The Polish Filmmakers' Association in the early days of the war offered practical assistance in the form of permanent or temporary accommodation, provision of supplies, equipment and transportation, as well as support in translating documents (Stowarzyszenie Filmowców Polskich, 2022).

Another way of assisting refugee artists, allowing for the sustaining of embodied cultural capital, were residencies. Such activities were undertaken in all the investigated countries and fields. In cooperation with other organisations, the Swedish Institute prepared ten-month scholarships for female filmmakers to help them relocate to safety. The humanitarian nature of this measure is evidenced by the inclusion of those with children in their care. An important distinction was the absence of any requirement related to the outcomes of the residency programme as the goal of the activity was to 'allow the women filmmakers to work at their own pace' (B2B Doc, 2022). Another residency offer, a three-month stay for Ukrainian filmmakers with housing, a stipend and workspace provided, was organised by the Göteborg Film Fund with support from the Västra Götaland Region. In 2022, four directors and cinematographers were selected from 35 applicants (Göteborg Film

Festival, 2022), and the following year another three directors and screen-writers received the residency (Göteborg Film Festival, 2023b). The Polish Institute of Literature ran an artistic and translation residency programme and in 2022 more than 200 applications were received, of which 37 were selected. Residents participated in a Polish language course, and attended literary meetings, concerts, art therapy workshops and integration meetings organised for them (Instytut Literatury, 2023).

Residency opportunities have sometimes been combined with scholar-ships to enable survival, which is related to another type of activity focused on embodied capital, the provision of resources. The Writers' Union Foun-dation in Lithuania prepared a scholarship programme for Ukrainian writ-ers and translators of literature in Lithuania, Ukraine and abroad. The programme comprised providing support for four people in the form of residence in Vilnius for one month and a stipend of 650 euros (Lithuanian Writers' Union, 2023).

In many cases, the support provided was purely financial and took the form of scholarships awarded without the requirement to account for a spe-cific result. An example concerning literature is the 'Stand with Ukrainian Writers' project initiated by Wrocław UNESCO City of Literature (Poland) in cooperation with Sharjah UNESCO World Book Capital, where support consisted of financial assistance to Ukrainian writers, translators and oth-ers remaining in Ukraine who have lost their livelihoods (Wrocławski Dom Literatury, 2022). In some cases, grants were allocated to representatives of multiple fields rather than of a single specific discipline. A grant offer from the Estonian Creative Residency Network (LOORE) included a residency for Ukrainian artists in 2023–2024 (LOORE, 2023), while the Lithuanian Ministry of Culture prepared three-month stipends of 600 euros per month. Artists and other cultural workers such as translators, renovators and guides, were eligible to apply for the stipends. The support was intended to fund the creative activities of Ukraine's professional arts and culture creators, but it also involved encouraging their cooperation with the Lithuanian cultural community (Ministry of Culture of the Republic of Lithuania, 2023).

There were fewer projects related to sustaining objectified capital, focus-ing on the cultural capital of Ukrainian audiences. The main objective of such activities was the preservation of continued access to existing Ukrainian culture. Examples include projects implemented in Poland, Lithuania and Germany to support Ukrainian readers in exile. As part of the Goethe Insti-tute's project 'Ein Koffer voll mit Büchern', books in Ukrainian, representing both Ukrainian literature and translations from world literature, were deliv-ered to places in Germany where Ukrainians, especially Ukrainian youth, were staying, and to Goethe Institutes in other host countries. Of the 800 applications, it was possible to secure the delivery of books to more than 600 (Goethe Institut, 2023). Polish and Lithuanian publishers initiated coopera-tion with publishing houses from Ukraine (Ranok, Urbino and VSL) and the cooperation consisted of printing and distributing books to more than three million Ukrainian refugees. Fairy tales for children was the first book published (Nawotka, 2022).

Support for the evacuation of artworks from Ukrainian museums has also served to sustain objectified cultural capital. Among the many European institutions that have undertaken such activities was the Royal Castle Museum in Warsaw, which took in 38 works from the National Art Museum in Kiev and has undertaken their conservation. The museum's director also announced that these works will be exhibited in Poland (Royal Castle in Warsaw, 2023).

Support for institutionalised cultural capital has been facilitated in host countries by establishing permanent units to work for the benefit of the Ukrainian diaspora such as Ukraine House, established in Copenhagen in 2023, which acts as a cultural centre for Ukrainian refugees in Denmark, responding to the needs of both creators and audiences (Ukraine House, 2023).

A particular form of activity aiming to sustain the institutionalised cultural capital of Ukrainian filmmakers has been assistance in the form of networking and leveraging the professional capabilities of local filmmakers' organisations. One example is the Polish Filmmakers' Association, which hired four refugee women directly, and also acted as an intermediary between Ukrainian filmmakers and potential employers in Poland.

Another element connected to sustaining institutionalised capital was the provision of chances for young artists to continue their education. The Estonian Academy of Music and Theatre offered study opportunities to Ukrainian refugees, with guaranteed social assistance, in cooperation with the Ministry of Education and Research and other Estonian universities (Estonian Academy of Music and Theatre, 2023).

Activities aimed at developing Ukrainian cultural capital

Significantly more projects have emphasised the importance of the production of Ukrainian cultural capital by allowing artists from the invaded country to continue creating. Such projects have usually taken the form of grant competitions, where artists were given funds to carry out a specific project to be delivered as part of the grant settlement. Other forms have included short-term stipends, which would give the grantee time to complete the chosen creative task, as well as access to equipment and materials.

In the context of the development of Ukrainian culture, support for the embodied cultural capital has manifested itself primarily in initiatives related to financial support for filmmakers. An example is the Lithuanian Film Centre programme, launched in 2022 and funded by the Lithuanian Ministry of Culture. Filmmakers who obtained temporary protection status in Lithuania could apply for three months of support (1,800 euros) (Lithuanian Film Centre, 2023). A similar solution was implemented in Latvia. Since the outbreak of the war, the State Cultural Capital Fund (Valsts Kultūrkapitāla fonds) has held two competitions under a Creative Scholarship Programme for Ukrainian citizens. Its objective was to support the creative work of those residing in Latvia as refugees and promote cooperation between Ukrainian and Latvian artists. Three-month scholarships of 1,800 euros were awarded on the basis of an application indicating the Latvian cultural institution with which the candidate would collaborate (State Culture Capital Foundation, 2022). The 17 grantees that received support in 2023 included three music events and six filmmakers. The cinematography projects involved co-production of films, script writing and production of a short film. Music-related projects involved participation in 'Jazz Jam' sessions and original programmes for concerts (State Culture Capital Foundation, 2023). As of April 2022, the Lithuanian Council for Culture had allocated nearly 240,000 euros to fund 133 Ukrainian artists who had found refuge in Lithuania. The purpose of the grants was to support artists' creative activities and promote cooperation with the Lithuanian cultural community (Lithuanian Council for Culture, 2023). An example of developing objectified cultural capital is the Göteborg Film Fund initiative which supports the implementation of advanced film projects by Ukrainian artists with grants of up to SEK 75,000 (6,800 euros) for film-making projects. In exchange for providing financial assistance, the Göteborg Film Festival was to hold the rights to organise the world premieres of those films (Göteborg Film Festival, 2023a).

Support for development of creativity has been intended primarily for creators, but not exclusively. Frankfurter Buchmesse GmbH, with funding from the German Foreign Ministry, organised a special programme for publishers from Ukraine and neighbouring countries, which comprised workshops and networking meetings intended to facilitate publishing activities (Frankfurter Buchmesse, 2023).

Institutionalised forms of assistance to Ukrainian artists include initiating and coordinating activities by state cultural institutions. In the case of Lithuania and Latvia, lists of organisations have been created that offer refugees opportunities to take up work in line with their interests in various branches of culture ('Cooperation offers', 2023; Ministry of Culture of the Republic of Lithuania, 2023). The Ministry of Culture together with the Lithuanian Council for Culture has compiled a list of contacts for Lithuanian cultural and art institutions, encouraging partnerships between the local NGO sector and Ukrainian art/culture individuals and institutions that had to find temporary refuge there due to the Russian invasion of Ukraine. The Lithuanian list includes 125 institutions willing to enter cooperation. An LKNVOA mentoring programme has also been developed for cultural workers seeking refuge in Latvia. NGO members of the Latvian Association of Contemporary Culture offered artists and cultural workers arriving in Latvia support in integrating into the local cultural environment, contacts and networking with local colleagues, assistance in practical matters, and other support as needed (*Laikmetīgās kultūras nevalstisko organizāciju asociācija*, 2023).

Recognition of diplomas plays an important part in developing institutionalised cultural capital by creating opportunities for work and self-realisation

146 *Madej et al.*

in the host country. This procedure applies to academic artistic qualifications just as it does to authorisations and licences in other fields. No special facilities have been implemented in this area, but the Polish National Agency for Academic Exchange has published a relevant guide in Ukrainian (*Narodowa Agencja Wymiany Akademickiej*, 2022).

Activities aimed at promoting Ukrainian cultural capital

For the survival of Ukraine's cultural capital, it is important not only to sustain and develop, but also to promote Ukrainian art. An important aspect of the threat to Ukrainian cultural capital, potentially damaging to creators and to audiences, is the situation of individual refugees. This applies both to artists and to leaders of cultural life, for whom it can be difficult to find work in their own profession in a foreign country, and to Ukrainians-recipients of culture. For them, the loss of contact with national art can be an additional source of stress in a difficult situation. Some researchers point to the lack of contact with the culture of origin as a factor in psychological difficulties among migrants, even using the term 'cultural bereavement' (Burgha & Becker, 2005). Therefore, helping promote Ukrainian culture contributes to strengthening the integration of migrants with the host community, as well as to their well-being as refugees.

Promotion of embodied and objectified capital is particularly important. During the ongoing war, the recipients of such activities are both the Ukrainian refugees residing in the states of the Baltic region and the citizens of these countries. Only some of the activities promoting Ukrainian culture were launched as a direct response to the outbreak of war. In other, numerous cases, successive editions of recurring events were devoted to this topic, which in the context of the war gained a much broader social resonance.

The popularisation of Ukraine's embodied cultural capital during the period under review was primarily associated with enabling Ukrainian artists to present themselves in the countries where they arrived. The first group of activities in this regard entailed the special inclusion of the work of Ukrainian artists into events organised periodically. An example is the 'Ukraine! Film Festival' organised in Poland, which in 2022 had its seventh run, with 'Between War and Hope' as its theme. The event was also noticeably larger than previous ones, presenting 50 works, compared to 30-plus in the previous two years (*Ukraina! Festiwal Filmowy*, 2022). The number of participants, which had previously grown slowly and gradually, increased rapidly in 2022 (by 40% compared to the previous year), reaching 10,000 attendees at the event in Warsaw and screenings in other Polish cities as well as through online access. One of the main goals of the initiative was to present the profiles of Ukrainian filmmakers.

Other areas of cyclical activity that offered opportunities to spread information about Ukrainian authors were nominations and awards in well-established literary contests. The prestige of the prizes awarded was connected

'When peace comes' 147

to their monetary value and recognition in cultural circles, which usually translated into recognition for the authors in the awarding country. In Poland, for example, the 'European Poet of Freedom', a biennial Literary Award of the City of Gdansk since 2010, was presented in 2022 to Marianna Kiyanovska, a Ukrainian poet, (Kijanowska & Pomorski, 2022). A year earlier, in 2021, Ukrainian writer Kateryna Babkina, the author of *My Grandfather Danced the Best*, received the prestigious ANGELUS Central European Literature Award (mjz//now, 2021), founded in 2006 by the city of Wroclaw and awarded for prose works written in or translated into Polish. In 2022, the recipients of the awards for the Poland-Lithuania Cooperation and Dialogue Forum included Serhiy Zhadan, a poet, writer, musician and translator whose books have been published in Poland and Lithuania for many years; since the Russian invasion he has remained in Kharkiv, describing the daily life of the shelled city on social media (W, 2022). Also in 2022, the Ukrainian writer Andrey Kurkov received the German *Geschwister-Scholl-Preis*, established in the 1980s by the city of Munich and the German Booksellers Association (*Börsenverein des Deutschen Buchhandels*), for his *Diary of an Invasion* (Gopalakrishnan, 2022).

There have also been new initiatives undertaken to promote Ukraine's embodied cultural capital, such as the concert 'Baltic Music in the Service of Ukraine', in which orchestras and choirs of the Baltic countries live and in a video recording played works of Ukrainian and Baltic composers. The event involved the State Academic Choir LATVIJA, Latvian National Symphony Orchestra, Estonian National Symphony Orchestra, Kaunas State Choir and Lithuanian State Symphony Orchestra, Latvian Radio Choir and State Chamber Orchestra Sinfonietta Riga; Liepaja Symphony Orchestra (Sinaisky, 2022). On the basis of this event, and on the initiative of people associated with the Metropolitan Opera in New York and the Grand Theatre-National Opera in Warsaw, the Ukrainian Freedom Orchestra was formed in 2022; it included leading Ukrainian instrumentalists who were refugees from Kyiv, Lviv, Kharkiv, Odessa and other parts of the country as well as Ukrainian musicians who had been members of major European orchestras before the war (Teatr Wielki–Opera Narodowa, 2023; Wilson, 2022). Thus the new initiative, launched as a response to Russia's aggressive actions, not only became an activity aimed at promoting Ukraine's embodied cultural capital but also helped introduce the newly institutionalised form to a wide audience.

Other examples of promoting Ukraine's embodied cultural capital have included increases in the number of copies of published translations of works by Ukrainian authors in Latvia (Kuške, 2023), funding grants for translations of Ukrainian literature into Finnish (Finnish Literature Exchange, 2022), and the organisation of a series of meetings which involved reading of Ukrainian literary works (Svenska Pen, 2022). One of the purposes behind those events was to familiarise local audiences with the literary profiles of the authors of the translated works.

148 *Madej et al.*

The situation was similar in the case of the promotion of objectified cultural capital. After the war broke out in Ukraine, the easiest measure to implement in this regard was to expand existing cultural formats, such as competitions or festivals, by adding a Ukrainian component. An example of such an expansion was the solution implemented by Industry@Tallinn & Baltic Event, a cyclical forum for film and audio-visual industry professionals, which was implemented as part of the Tallinn Black Nights Film Festival. During the 21st edition in 2022, a series of events dedicated to Ukrainian cinema was organised in cooperation with the Ukrainian Film Academy, the Goethe Institute and the Odesa International Film Festival (Industry@Tallinn & Baltic Event, 2022). This offered an opportunity to promote the works of Ukrainian film art.

The second group of activities promoting the objectified cultural capital of Ukraine in the Baltic States involved new initiatives of varying forms launched after the beginning of the war. For instance, in 2022 and 2023, numerous Ukrainian cinema reviews were organised in Poland in such cities as Gliwice, Koszalin, Krakow, Lublin, Olsztyn, Wroclaw and Zielona Gora. An example of a similar type of activity is the promotion of works by Ukrainian composers during concerts of the Ukrainian Freedom Orchestra.

Conclusion and potential for future research

Ukrainian artists have been present in the Baltic region countries for many years, yet Russian aggression and the beginning of the war in 2022 became an impulse for new actions in support of Ukrainian culture with three groups of beneficiaries, the first being artists from Ukraine, the carriers of embodied cultural capital. They are opinion leaders with regard to initiatives undertaken and works produced; their ability to act and remain active is to a large extent a condition for sustaining the unity of the Ukrainian national community. Their activity produces new works that enrich objectified cultural capital and this translates into obtaining specific licences and authorisations, confirmed with diplomas and certificates, which in turn allows the creation of institutionalised cultural capital.

The second group of beneficiaries were Ukrainian recipients of such activities, many of whom became refugees after the start of the war; due to territorial and cultural proximity, they resided in the states of the Baltic region. Thus, activities aimed at supporting Ukrainian culture became a form of material and moral support for Ukraine and its citizens, which in Central and Eastern Europe has a significant symbolic meaning.

Finally, the third group of recipients for whom such activities turned out to be very important are the inhabitants of the states in the Baltic region. They were faced with the necessity to familiarise themselves with the presence of a large group of new residents with a different national identity. Support for activities that facilitated spreading knowledge about Ukrainian culture was of fundamental importance for the processes of integration of refugees within new societies.

'*When peace comes*'   149

The assistance described was provided by public administration entities and cultural institutions under the supervision of the former (such as museums, art galleries, philharmonics) as well as by NGOs and volunteers. Non-institutionalised activities were of great significance; they were often spontaneous and focused on practical assistance in surviving the first days and weeks of refuge. On the other hand, organisations of a creative or artistic provenance tried to undertake activities related to their area of specialisation. Undoubtedly, this contributed to significant support for the cultural and social capital of Ukraine.

The study has revealed that the help given to artists from Ukraine had three main objectives. The first was sustaining, development and promotion of embodied cultural capital, which primarily meant offering Ukrainian artists the opportunity to settle down and find a source of income in a new place, as well as promotion of their artistic profiles in new environments. The second goal was the sustaining, developing and promotion of objectified cultural capital, which mainly translated into an opportunity for artists from Ukraine to create new work. To this aim, calls were prepared in the form of grants for the making, presentation or publication of specific works, as well as for collaboration with organisations of local artists. The third goal was the promotion of Ukrainian culture among war refugees and within communities that hosted numerous refugee groups. The primary form of such activity was the organisation of new events promoting Ukrainian culture as well as of sections dedicated to this issue during regular festivals, fairs and exhibitions. During the period under review, art competitions often gave awards to Ukrainian artists and writers.

The activities undertaken in support of Ukrainian artists and their work have brought the benefits assumed, and by strengthening Ukrainian identity they have contributed to the strengthening of cultural capital which will be needed in peacetime during restoration of the country. However, there are also related risks. Enterprises focused on sustaining cultural capital have the largest humanitarian impact as they involve direct aid for refugee artists and audiences, yet due to their passive character they will not increase Ukrainian society's capacity for post-war restoration. Projects that concentrate on developing cultural capital, encouraging artists and enabling them to create in a new environment and location, seem to be more promising in this context. Fears related to such activities are connected with the problem of sustaining immigrants' relations with their homeland and the risk of acculturation in the case of collaborative activities undertaken together with artists from host countries. However, strong emphasis on maintaining the relation of Ukrainian audiences with the culture of their country of origin can bring the threat of ghettoisation, isolation from the host environment, and difficulties in integration. All these risks should be included both in the planning of long-term activities and in the evaluation of undertakings implemented ad hoc, directly after the outbreak of the war.

It is thus justified to point out that the cultural capital brought by refugees from Ukraine can bring benefits and pose risks to the host societies as well.

150 *Madej et al.*

The undoubted benefits include its integrative function, creating opportunities for development and building group identity. On the other hand, threats include the risk of social conflicts, exclusion and labour market problems. In this context, it is important that countries hosting refugees introduce appropriate measures, such as integration programmes, cultural education and social support, to maximise the benefits and minimise the risks associated with preserving the cultural capital of refugees.

As has been demonstrated, the preservation of cultural heritage is of utmost significance for sustaining a nation's identity, unity and, consequently, its social capital. This task is particularly important in the reality that involves resisting armed aggression and progressive depopulation, as well as in the context of rebuilding not only infrastructure but also social resources when peace is re-established after the end of the war. Actions taken by public administration institutions and non-governmental organisations in the states of the Baltic region hosting the largest number of refugees from Ukraine have the potential to contribute to strengthening the state's post-war capacity to rebuild not only physical resources but also Ukrainian society.

The forms of activities presented in the study, aimed at helping embattled Ukraine, were undertaken almost immediately after the start of Russia's armed aggression. The scale of needs related to the mass exodus of civilians from the areas attacked, resulted in the speedy introduction of specific solutions rather than implementation of pre-planned procedures.

It should also be emphasised that the described forms of assistance were characteristic not only of Baltic region states. Similar measures were taken in other countries reached by Ukrainian refugees. However, the examination of this specific area, where a particularly large group of Ukrainians fleeing the war has gathered, makes it possible to identify the most characteristic patterns of action.

The research task set by the authors was to check the forms of measures taken in the Baltic region states in order to help sustain the potential of the cultural capital of Ukraine. The short time range of the work, as well as the fact that the Russian-Ukrainian war is still ongoing, does not allow drawing conclusion as to which forms of assistance have proved most effective and could be considered as model solutions. Without a doubt, it would be worthwhile to conduct such a study after the end of the armed conflict.

References

B2B Doc. (2022). *Emergency Residency for Female Ukrainian Filmmakers.* https://b2bdoc.se/news/emergency-residency-for-female-ukrainian-filmmakers

Bourdieu, P. (1986). The forms of capital. In J. E. Richardson (Ed.), *Handbook of Theory of Research for the Sociology of Education* (pp. 241–258). Greenwood Press.

Burgha, D., & Becker, M. A. (2005). Migration, cultural bereavement and cultural identity. *World Psychiatry, 4*(1), 8–24.

Carlbaum, S. (2022). Refugee women's establishment in the rural north of Sweden: Cultural capital in meeting local labour market needs. *Journal of Ethnic and Migration Studies, 48*(5), 1210–1227. DOI: 10.1080/1369183X.2021.1933402

Coleman, J. S. (1988). Social capital in the creation of human capital. *The American Journal of Sociology, 94*, 95–120.

Cooperation Offers for Ukrainian Cultural Professionals. (2023). https://docs.google.com/spreadsheets/d/1zNzE_YswDk5MCrtcd71NXA5FNz3j4OQrzfFLvKjTctw/edit#gid=0 [access: 21.12.2023].

Eggenhofer-Rehart, P. M., Latzke, M., Pernkopf, K., Zellhofer, D., Mayrhofer, W., & Steyrer, J. (2018). Refugees' career capital Welcome? Afghan and Syrian refugee job seekers in Austria. *Journal of Vocational Behavior, 105*, 31–45. DOI: 10.1016/j.jvb.2018.01.004

Estonian Academy of Music and Theatre. (2022, March 1). *Estonian Academy of Music and Theatre is Ready to Offer Study Opportunities to Ukrainian Refugees.* https://eamt.ee/en/the-estonian-academy-of-music-and-theater-is-ready-to-offer-study-opportunities-to-ukrainian-refugees/

Eurostat. (2023, August 9). *30 June 2023: 4.07 Million with Temporary Protection.* https://ec.europa.eu/eurostat/web/products-eurostat-news/w/ddn-20230809-1 [access: 17.8.2023].

Finnish Literature Exchange. (2022, March 14). *Additional Funding for the Translation of Ukrainian Literature into Finnish.* https://fili.fi/en/additional-funding-for-the-translation-of-ukrainian-literature-into-finnish/

Frankfurter Buchmesse. (2023). *Special Programme for Publishers from Ukraine and Neighbouring Countries.* www.buchmesse.de/en/fellowship-and-grant-programmes/special-programme-publishers-ukraine

Gericke, D., Burmeister, A., Löwe J., Deller, J., & Pundt, L. (2018). How do refugees use their social capital for successful labor market integration? An exploratory analysis in Germany. *Journal of Vocational Behavior, 105*, 46–61.

Goethe Institut. (2023). *Ein Koffer voll mit Büchern.* www.goethe.de/ins/ua/de/kul/uap/kof.html

Gopalakrishnan, M. (2022, November 28). *Ukrainian Author Andrey Kurkov Honored with German Award.* www.dw.com/en/ukrainian-author-andrey-kurkov-honored-with-german-literary-award/a-63882632

Göteborg Film Festival. (2022, November 3). *Göteborg Film Fund 2022 Presents Development Grants for Ukrainian Filmmakers.* https://goteborgfilmfestival.se/en/goteborg-film-fund-2022-presents-development-grants-for-ukrainian-filmmakers/

Göteborg Film Festival. (2023a, May 19). *Recipients of Development Grants Selected & New Residency Programme Opens for Ukrainian Filmmakers.* https://goteborgfilmfestival.se/en/recipients-of-development-grants-selected-new-residency-programme-opens-for-ukrainian-filmmakers/

Göteborg Film Festival. (2023b, July 4). *Three Ukrainian Directors and Screen Writers Have been Selected for Residencies at Göteborg Film Festival.* https://goteborgfilmfestival.se/en/tre-ukrainska-filmskapare-utvalda-for-residensvistelse-hos-goteborg-film-festival/

Help Musicians Ukraine [Website]. (2023). www.helpmusiciansukraine.com/

Industry@Tallinn & Baltic Event. (2022, November 21). *Ukraine Today.* https://industry.poff.ee/about/ukraine-today/

Instytut Literatury. (2023). *Rezydencje Artystyczne i Translatorskie dla osób z Ukrainy 2023 – wyniki 1. tury.* https://instytutliteratury.eu/2023/02/06/rezydencje-artystyczne-i-translatorskie-dla-osob-z-ukrainy-2023-wyniki-1-tury/

Joint Declaration of the Ministers of Culture on the 9th of July 2023 in Rīga, Latvia. (2023, July 9). www.km.gov.lv/lv/media/33603/download?attachment

152 *Madej et al.*

Kijanowska, M., & Pomorski, A. (2022). *2022: Marianna Kijanowska.* https://europejskipoetawolnosci.pl/winners/2022-marianna-kijanowska/
Knott, E. (2022). Existential nationalism: Russia's war against Ukraine. *Nations and Nationalism*, 1–8.
Kuške, B. (2023, February 21). Ukrainas gads – arī literatūrā. Kā Krievijas īstenotais karš atspoguļojies Latvijas grāmatniecībā. *Latvijas Sabiedriskie Mediji.* www.lsm.lv/raksts/kultura/literatura/ukrainas-gads-ari-literatura-ka-krievijas-istenotais-kars-atspogulojies-latvijas-gramatnieciba.a497439/
Laikmetīgās kultūras nevalstisko organizāciju asociācija. (2023). *Par Mums.* www.lknvoa.lv/
Lithuanian Council for Culture. (2023, January 16). *EUR 240,000 Allocated for the Creative Activities of Ukrainian artists in Lithuania.* www.ltkt.lt/en/news/719-eur-240-000-allocated-for-the-creative-activities-of-ukrainian-artists-in-lithuania-.html
Lithuanian Film Centre. (2023). *Call for Applications for Grants from Ukrainian Citizens, Film Culture or Art Creators.* www.lkc.lt/en/financing/call-for-applications-for-grants-from-ukrainian-citizens-film-culture-or-art-creators
Lithuanian Writers' Union [Website]. (2023). https://rasytojai.lt/en/
LOORE. (2023). *Open Call Results Announced.* www.loore.ee/ukraine-residency
Miller, E., Ziaian, T., Melanie, B. M., & de Anstiss, H. (2021). Recognition of refugee students' cultural wealth and social capital in resettlement. *International Journal of Inclusive Education.* DOI: 10.1080/13603116.2021.1946723
Ministry of Culture of the Republic of Lithuania. (2023). *Lithuanian Organizations Are Open to Project based and Long-Term Cooperation with Ukrainian Artists and Institutions.* https://lrkm.lrv.lt/uploads/lrkm/documents/files/LIST-EN(1).pdf
Ministry of Culture: Republic of Latvia. (2023, March 3). *Help Available to Displaced Musicians from Ukraine.* www.km.gov.lv/en/article/help-available-displaced-musicians-ukraine
mjz//now. (2021, October 17). Nagrody Angelus i Silesius wręczone. *TVN24.* https://tvn24.pl/kultura-i-styl/wroclaw-nagrody-angelus-i-silesius-wreczone-jacek-sutryk-wreczyl-nagrody-5454812
Myśliwiec, M. (2014). *Pozycja partii regionalnych w systemie politycznym współczesnej Hiszpanii.* Wydawnictwo Uniwersytetu Śląskiego.
Nagopoulos, N., Sarsour, O., & Paraskevopoulois, D. (2023). Intercultural capital and social integration of refugees. *Open Journal of Social Sciences, 11*, 353–365.
Narodowa Agencja Wymiany Akademickiej. (2022). *Nostryfikacja dyplomów ukończenia studiów.* https://nawa.gov.pl/uznawalnosc/informacje-dla-uczelni/nostryfikacja-dyplomow
Nawotka, E. (2022, March 16). Ukraine update: Ukrainians publish in Poland, Lithuania; StreetLib Offers Help. *Publishers Weekly.* www.publishersweekly.com/pw/by-topic/international/international-book-news/article/88777-ukraine-update-ukrainians-publish-in-poland-lithuania-streetlib-offers-help.html
Pasikowska-Schnass, M. (2022, April). Russia's war on Ukraine's cultural heritage. *European Parliamentary Research Service.* www.europarl.europa.eu/thinktank/en/document/EPRS_ATA(2022)729377
Putnam, R. D., Leonardi, R., & Nanetti, R. Y. (1993). *Making Democracy Work: Civic Traditions in Modern Italy.* Princeton University Press.
Royal Castle in Warsaw. (2023). *Dzieła sztuki z Kijowa w Zamku Królewskim w Warszawie.* https://zamek-krolewski.pl/strona/aktualnosci-i-komunikaty/1779-dziela-sztuki-z-kijowa-w-zamku-krolewskim-w-warszawie
Sinaisky, V. (2022). Statement by honorary conductor of the LNSO, Vasily Sinaisky. *Latvian National Symphony Orchestra.* www.lnso.lv/ukrainas-atbalstam
State Culture Capital Foundation. (2022). *Finansētie mērķprogrammu projektu konkursi.* https://vkkf.lv/index/finansētie-projekti/mērķprogrammas-fp.html?nozare=444&gads=2022

'When peace comes'   153

State Culture Capital Foundation. (2023). *Finansētie mērķprogrammu projektu konkursi*. https://vkkf.lv/index/finans%C4%93tie-projekti/m%C4%93r%C4%B7 programmas-fp.html?nozare=444&gads=2023

Stowarzyszenie Filmowców Polskich. (2022, February 26). *SFP oferuje pomoc uchodźcom z Ukrainy*. www.sfp.org.pl/SFPpomaga

Svenska Pen. (2022). *Läsningar för Ukraina*. www.svenskapen.se/senaste-nytt/2022/2/27/lsningar-fr-ukraina

Teatr Wielki–Opera Narodowa. (2023). *Koncert Ukrainian Freedom Orchestra 28 lipca w Teatrze Wielkim – Operze Narodowej w Warszawie*. https://teatrwielki.pl/ukrainian-freedom-orchestra/

Ukraina! Festiwal Filmowy [Website]. (2022). https://ukrainaff.com/

Ukraine House in Denmark [Website]. (2023). www.ukrainehouse.dk/

United Nations High Commissioner for Refugees. (2023). *Refugees from Ukraine Recorded Globally*. https://data2.unhcr.org/en/situations/ukraine

W. (2022, August 17). Serhij Żadan laureatem Nagrody Forum Współpracy i Dialogu Polska-Litwa. *Rynek książki*. https://rynek-ksiazki.pl/aktualnosci/serhij-zadan-laureatem-nagrody-forum-wspolpracy-i-dialogu-polska-litwa/

Wilson, K.-L. (2022). *Ukrainian Freedom Orchestra*. www.keri-lynnwilson.com/ukrainian-freedom-orchestra-1

Wrocławski Dom Literatury. (2022). *Stand with Ukrainian Writers*. https://literatura.wroclaw.pl/projekty/stand-with-ukrainian-writers/

10 'It's not our war'

Social movements against state involvement in aid to Ukraine

Marzena Cichosz, Elżbieta Szyszlak and Renata Podgórzańska

Introduction

After Russia's aggression against Ukraine, the prevailing sentiment across European societies strongly aligned with Ukraine while condemning the actions of the Russian Federation (cf. Flash Eurobarometer, 2022). This situation was mirrored in the states of the Baltic region. Support for Ukraine and the need to provide military assistance to the beleaguered state also received backing from numerous pacifist organisations, marking a departure from their erstwhile stance of 'no to any war' to 'yes to a just war'. This chapter examines social movements comprising groups and individuals whose views contrasted and continue to contrast sharply with the mainstream, particularly in their opposition to state-sponsored aid to Ukraine, mainly in military terms. These social movements are commonly referred to as anti-involvement movements (AIMs), and their activism has become the focal point of the inquiry into 'pathways to peace', given that the rhetoric espoused by their members often includes anti-war slogans and calls for the immediate establishment of peace and security. However, their conceptions of peace, and the rationale underlying their position, differ from those articulated elsewhere in this discourse. In analysing AIMs, the authors shed light on the factors that fostered their emergence in the states of the Baltic Sea region, their characteristics, available resources, relations with other actors (particularly political parties) and the framework underpinning their narrative. Furthermore, the authors analyse the degree of institutionalisation within AIMs, seeking to ascertain whether they possess the potential, through their alternative paradigms, to permeate the mainstream discourse on peace and security in Europe. Such a scenario would necessitate a geopolitical reconfiguration in at least some countries within the region.

The authors verify the hypothesis that AIMs represent incipient movements that can evolve and influence the strategies of other actors in the political arena, that is political parties, through policies and tactics of resource acquisition, imitation, audience capture and the use of the organisational capacity of other social movements.

DOI: 10.4324/9781003558040-13

The analysis is based on theories of social movements, particularly on the work of researchers investigating mobilisation theory, which is a middle-range theory rooted in the rational choice paradigm. The authors conceptualise social movements as conscious actors making rational choices (della Porta & Diani, 2006) whose development is linked to the accumulation of various resources, be they economic, cultural or symbolic, through social movements (McAdam & Scott, 2012; McCarthy & Zald, 1973; Olson, 2012; Tilly, 1999).

The issues discussed in this chapter have not yet been the subject of academic inquiry; thus, the analysis will principally rely upon desk research and qualitative discourse analysis. Data collected from various sources, including social media platforms, websites of social movements and newspaper articles, have been utilised.

Political, social and cultural determinants of AIM activity in the states of the Baltic region

The main stimulus for the emergence of AIMs was Russia's aggression against Ukraine in February 2022. This event, alongside its consequences, such as the redefinition of security strategies by the vast majority of European states, coupled with the solidarity extended to Ukraine's quest for sovereignty by democratic states within the Baltic region, provided the opportunity to create new political divisions around geopolitical concerns ('allied' states, 'enemy' states), the nature and scale of support extended to Ukraine, and the provision of aid to refugees fleeing the war. AIMs have actively participated in shaping these new political divisions. However, it is noteworthy that while a distinct characteristic narrative is noted within each country included in this analysis, the development of these movements varies in its extent across these countries.

In the view of the authors, one of the factors potentially most conducive to the growth of AIMs in the Baltic region is the size of the Russian or Russian-speaking diaspora.[1] However, the region encompasses countries as diverse in this regard as the Nordic states and Poland which host relatively small Russian communities, whereas Germany[2] and the Baltic states are characterised by substantial Russian-speaking minorities. This minority demographic also includes Ukrainians, Belarusians and Tatars, yet for this study's subject matter, Russians are the most relevant group due to their susceptibility to Kremlin influence. Compared to the 1989 census (Bobryk, 2023, p. 177; Bonusiak, 2022, p. 66), the number of Russians living in the Baltic states has decreased, yet their presence remains noticeable. In Lithuania, they constitute merely 4.5% of the population, while in Estonia and Latvia, the figure stands at 25% (Coolican, 2021, p. 6). The Russian minority is characterised by a high degree of territorial concentration, higher levels of unemployment, poverty, social marginalisation and emigration, surpassing those of the majority population. Important challenges, particularly in Estonia and Latvia, include citizenship issues, with part of this demographic remaining stateless or holding Russian citizenship. Moreover, the persistence of ethnic divisions within society poses yet another problem for these states.

Russia's actions in Ukraine have led to a growing polarisation within the Russian-speaking population residing in the Baltic states. Consequently, there is an observable increase in unequivocal stances ranging from total approval for the Kremlin to embracing political orientations characteristic of residents of their host countries (Chmielewski, 2022).

Russian propaganda serves as an important tool for influencing the societies in the region of the Baltic Sea. Employing a variety of mechanisms which include both traditional and online media platforms, Russia's propaganda efforts vary across countries. Notably, its influence appears most pronounced within the Baltic states, owing partially to the presence of a substantial Russian-speaking demographic, among whom pro-Kremlin Russian-language media enjoy greater popularity than their counterparts in the national languages. For instance, in 2019, the Russian-language and pro-Kremlin First Baltic Channel (*Perviy Baltiyskiy Kanal*) ranked as the second most popular television channel in Latvia (Brauß & Rácz, 2021, p. 16). Nevertheless, following the escalation of the full-scale conflict in Ukraine, a visible decline in trust towards Russian media sources has been observed (Kuczyńska-Zonik, 2022; Vänttinen, 2022).

These media outlets repeat arguments used by the Kremlin's propaganda, presenting scenarios such as the potential expansion of the conflict to the Baltic states. They also claim that the governments of the Baltic states are contributing to the escalation, aid provision to Ukraine only prolongs the war, and the Ukrainian leadership is mired in corruption and driven solely by its vested interest. Additionally, they highlight rampant Russophobia in the Baltic states, alongside 'the widespread violation of rights of their Russian-speaking residents' (Pawela, 2023). These arguments, as discussed next, can be found in the narratives created by AIMs.

In turn, an aspect that could potentially impede the development of the movements in question is the historical and contemporary experience of the region's states with the Russian Federation. Historically, the countries of the Baltic Sea region (Finland, the Baltic states and Poland) faced Soviet occupation and an existential threat from Moscow, and their relations with Russia have been fraught with conflicts and wars. Presently, their attitudes towards Russia are full of distrust and a dearth of illusions, compounded by concerns regarding the ongoing conflict in Ukraine, and Russia's efforts to escalate it. In the authors' view, this apprehension is one of the principal determinants shaping their societies' support for Ukraine in its conflict with Russia, while constraining the activities of AIMs in the region (Andrejsons, 2022; Auers, 2023, pp. 206–207; Ulinskaitė & Garškaitė-Antonowicz, 2023, p. 218).

On the other hand, historical legacies can also foster the development of AIMs. For instance, such a dynamic is visible in Poland where it concerns relations with Ukraine. Over the years, Poles and Ukrainians have presented different interpretations of historical events, accusing each other of nationalism as the root of conflict which peaked in 1943. The national-patriotic message perpetuated in both countries reinforces mutual animosities, thereby constituting a factor that mobilises certain factions in Poland and Ukraine (see Szeptycki, 2020, 2010, pp. 298–299).

Processes of resource acquisition by AIMs

According to research on resource mobilisation theory, resources are the key factor determining the emergence and development of a social movement. Traditionally, these encompassed a spectrum of tangible and intangible assets, typically including people (members and leaders) and economic resources (connections and financial support) (Peoples, 2019, p. 24). However, this perspective has been revised, partly due to advancements in internet technology, new media platforms and the new field of studies researching cyber/digital activism. Social media has been recognised as an important space for advancing the objectives of social movements. Nevertheless, as noted by Castañeda and others, offline social ties and interpersonal relationships remain crucial (Castañeda, 2019, p. 167).

The degree of development of AIMs varies across different countries. In the Nordic states, such organisations are virtually non-existent. Instead, the landscape includes investigative journalists, watchdog organisations and activists, such as Vatnik Soup, who focus on individuals (so-called 'Vatniks')[3] or a network comprising 152 people (as of May 2023) spreading pro-Kremlin content online. These individuals are members of the extreme right/left with links to Russian state media or intelligence services (Olsen, 2023). It is noteworthy that activists from the Nordic countries predominantly engage in digital activism, not only on a national scale but also, significantly influenced by the size of their movement's membership, in a 'Nordic' format. Joint initiatives are broadcast by all parties involved, with organisers rotating roles as hosts and invited 'experts'. Similar attempts at joint transnational projects by individual activists are also observed in the Baltic states. The Lithuanian-Belarusian International Good Neighbourhood Forum (*Международный форум добрососедства*), founded in 2022 and overseen by Algidras Paleckis, and the Baltic anti-fascists group active on Telegram (*Антифашисты Прибалтики*; 'Baltic anti-fascists') are noteworthy examples ('*Obschestvennoe objedinenie*', 2023; '*Sud v Vilniuse*', 2023). It is also worth mentioning in this context the activities of pro-Kremlin influencers who react online to actions taken by the authorities in the Baltic states to remove post-Soviet cultural heritage – perceived as symbols of USSR imperialism – from public spaces. In their commentary, these influencers refer to such actions as 'renazification' and 'normalisation of fascism in Europe', echoing the Kremlin's narrative. These influencers boast a large group of followers, often numbering tens of thousands or even exceeding 100,000 ('Recurring Pro-Kremlin', 2022).

158   *Marzena Cichosz, Elżbieta Szyszlak and Renata Podgórzańska*

Organisations established by AIM activists are relatively few and lack extensive structures and membership bases. Nevertheless, AIMs often leverage the industry of other social movements, such as the organisational framework and human resources of anti-vaccination and anti-COVID-19 movements. Movements that integrate opposition to their states supporting Ukraine into their agendas include the *Querdenker* in Germany (cf. also Kamińska-Korolczuk & Piotrowska, in this volume) and the Kamrat movement in Poland, for example, *Bydgoskie Bractwo Kamratów* [the Bydgoszcz Kamrat Brotherhood] (Mąka, 2021). Moreover, broadly networked movements and organisations that emerged during the 2020–2021 pandemic, articulating demands either denying the existence of the pandemic or contesting the state's vaccination policy, have expanded their objectives to challenge engagement in aid efforts for Ukraine and Ukrainians.

Another segment of the AIMs industry comprises factions within the pacifist movement, or more precisely, organisations that claim to espouse pacifist principles. A case in point is the Polish Anti-war Movement, established in 2023.

AIMs are also supported by an extensive network of media connections. As noted by German columnists, platforms such as *Anti-Spiegel*, *NachDenk-Seiten*, and the extremist magazine *Compact* have assumed the role previously played by the Russian foreign broadcaster, *RT* (formerly: *Russia Today*),[4] in disseminating content that portrays Russia's aggression against Ukraine as a form of 'Russian self-defence' (Meisner, 2022). In Poland, support for AIMs comes from far-right media, such as the weekly *Myśl Polska*.

Political parties towards AIMs

The existing literature offers many propositions for analysing the relationship between political parties and social movements (cf. Heinze & Weisskircher, 2022). One particularly clear concept is Downs' framework, which distinguishes between engaged and disengaged strategies adopted by political parties towards social movements. The engaged strategy, as conceptualised by Downs, involves substantive cooperation and the adoption of movement demands by political parties. This can extend to cooperative efforts at legislative, executive and electoral levels. Non-engagement, on the other hand, involves disregard for the movement, isolating it as well as the imposition of restrictions and coalition-building efforts aimed at impeding it (Downs, 2001). Applying Downs' framework, it can be argued that in most countries in the region, mainstream parties adopt disengagement strategies towards AIMs, with responses ranging from indifference and isolation to restrictions (Sweden, Denmark, Finland, Latvia and Lithuania). Only a few politicians from the extreme left or right, known for their pro-Russian sympathies, engage with AIM activists.

Particularly visible instances of cooperation and support for AIM by certain political actors can be found in three countries in the region, Estonia,

'It's not our war' 159

Germany and Poland and they include cooperation in the electoral arena as well as the presentation of the movement's demands in parliamentary settings (Germany, Poland). In Estonia, the social movement, *Koos/Vmiestie* (Together), formed in 2022 by pro-Russian activists from AIM, declared its establishment as a political party. It subsequently formed an electoral coalition with the Estonian United Left Party (*Objedinionnaja lewaja partija Estonii, EÜVP*) in the 2023 parliamentary elections. However, this alliance was not successful in terms of parliamentary seats.

In Germany, AIMs receive support from the right-wing populist Alternative for Germany (Al*ternative für Deutschland, AfD*), which has its representation in both federal and state parliaments. As noted by researchers, AfD gains electoral backing from a substantial number of Russians (Sablina, 2023, p. 4; Spies et al., 2023), however, it remains an isolated entity within the legislative and executive branches. In Poland, support for AIMs is extended by the Confederation of the Polish Crown (*Konfederacja Korony Polskiej, KKP*) party, a member of the radical-right (nationalist, anti-EU and traditionalist) Confederation coalition, which has held parliamentary representation since 2019. Through the Confederation of the Polish Crown, the initiative 'Stop the Ukrainisation of Poland' was tabled in the national parliament on 14 July 2022. It is worth noting, however, that other parties within the Confederation coalition refrained from unequivocal support for the activities of their partner. During the campaign preceding the 2023 parliamentary elections, the ruling Law and Justice (*Prawo i Sprawiedliwość, PiS*) coalition also adopted a narrative aligning closely with AIMs' demands. In the pre-election period, the PiS coalition voiced support both for refugees from Ukraine and the Ukrainian state. This shift in the PiS narrative placed the issue of state support for Ukrainian refugees at the centre of the electoral discourse of all relevant right-wing and far-right parties.

Political messages and forms of AIM activity

The emergence and development of social movements involve communicative processes, formulating concrete claims and arguments, giving meaning to unfolding events as well as constructing narratives that not only explain the causes of the movement but also identify its goals and mobilise members and supporters to action (cf. Benford & Snow, 2000, p. 613). This process is ongoing and involves multiple actors, with movement leaders and social movement organisations playing a central role, and the resulting messages are the outcome of negotiations between these actors (Caiani, 2023; Castells, 2015; Earl, 2019; Lindekilde, 2014). In resource mobilisation theory, a strand of research has emerged linking the mobilisation and success of social movements to their capacity to develop interpretive/narrative frames that can effectively connect the movement and its cause with the interests, perceptions and ideologies of specific social groups (cf. Benford & Snow, 2000; Koopmans & Statham, 1999, p. 288; Snow et al., 1986, p. 466). This perspective emphasises the importance of cultural factors influencing the framing process (van Dijk, 2023) and the nature of the audience to which appeals are directed (Benford & Snow, 2000, pp. 629–630). The premise that a social movement's message hinges on these factors appears particularly salient, especially in comparative studies, as it effectively explains the observed disparities in the narratives of AIMs across different countries of the region.

The communicative processes initiated by a social movement and its leaders entail the construction of interpretive schemas (frames), which Snow and Benford categorise into diagnostic, prognostic and motivational (Snow & Benford, 1988). In indicating the narrative frames proposed by AIMs, we include both those that identify the problem and the genesis of the 'harm' (grievance) that gives rise to the movement (i.e. diagnostic frame), as well as those about strategies, tactics and modes of action (prognostic frames), along with the 'call to arms' (motivational frames). Simultaneously, we employ the concept of 'master' frames, that is general labels that encompass discourse and cognitive processes, and point to key values, ideologies, themes and norms (cf. also the critique: van Dijk, 2023, pp. 166–168).

Diagnostic framing

Between March 2022 and September 2023, AIMs' messages encompassed three primary diagnostic frames. The first was axiological, centred on human rights values, including the right to life, liberty, personal security and the right to live in a healthy environment. Within this narrative, discourses argued that military aid provided to Ukraine in its war with Russia was against life, as Ukrainians and Russians were being killed with weapons from Western/NATO countries. Ukraine was depicted as a victim of a war between superpowers, a country facing threat of depopulation. Moreover, the narrative warned of the broader risk to humanity posed by the potential use of nuclear weapons in the conflict. In the Baltic states, it was asserted that authorities opportunistically exploited the war in Ukraine to curtail the rights of the Russian-speaking and Russian minority communities and to erase their cultural heritage from public spaces. This claim was supported by instances such as the removal of Soviet monuments from public areas (Chmielewski, 2022), restrictions on Russian-language education, and the rapid transition to state language instruction. Allegations were made that Russians living in these states were being expelled under the guise of security threats, but in reality as part of a deliberate effort to reduce the Russian population (Askew, 2022; 'Recurring Pro-Kremlin', 2022).

The second frame centred on ethnocentrism and was based on the othering dichotomy of 'us vs. them'. In the AIM narrative, there was a strong emphasis on distancing from Ukraine and the propagation of negative stereotypes and clichés about the Ukrainian people. The narrative placed blame for the outbreak of war on 'the other', Ukrainian elites who endangered 'our' soldiers, while accentuating the perceived threat posed by refugees or Ukrainian immigrants. A significant portion of the AIM discourse sought to demonstrate that Ukrainians were not refugees but mere economic migrants. For instance, the leader, Koos Aivo Peterson, said in one of his speeches addressed to Ukrainians: 'This is your war, your tragedy, the decision of your rulers' (*Koos Vmeste*, 2022). The narrative also underscored negative attitudes towards refugees from Ukraine and in countries hosting refugees, they were depicted as promoting views against the interests of the host country's citizens. The narrative also included references to well-known conspiracy theories, such as the 'Great Replacement' theory, popular among the far right (cf. Camus, 2011). For instance, in Poland, the threat of the 'Ukrainisation of Poland', that is 'takeover of Polish lands' by the Ukrainian population 'in a relatively short period', was pointed out.

The third diagnostic frame, termed 'economic calculation', bears some resemblance to 'ethnocentrism'. However, the authors decided to discuss it separately due to the distinct emphasis within the narrative and its rational argumentation grounded in the calculation of gains and losses. Losses encompassed economic concerns as well as military security issues. For instance, economic sanctions imposed on Russia were construed as a de facto declaration of economic warfare, with the primary impact felt by citizens of Western states. The ensuing economic crisis, escalated the cost of living, and soaring energy prices were attributed to the breakdown in relations with Russia. The costs of the crisis fell upon 'ordinary citizens', while corrupt elites, both in Ukraine and EU member states, were alleged to be profiting from the conflict (JiiPee, 2023). This narrative also raised concerns about the perceived 'preferential treatment' of Ukrainian refugees. Leaders of the Estonian KOOS, for instance, argued that aid to war refugees should be reassessed, as there remained pressing unresolved domestic issues such as housing, inflation and the citizenship status of stateless people (Mishina, 2023).

Prognostic framing

Among the articulated goals that AIMs set for themselves were the end of the war, the lifting of sanctions against Russia and the withdrawal of support for Ukraine. Since the main objective was to foster 'peace and security in the region' to ensure stable development, the priority was seen as ending the 'economic war' with Russia and establishing friendly relations with this state, which was emphasised, for example, by the *Vatniks* from the Nordic countries as well as leaders of the Confederation of the Polish Crown in Poland. Citizens were also urged to exert pressure on their respective governments to advocate the expeditious signing of peace treaties, signifying the restoration of security, even if it entailed Ukraine ceding certain territories. A key element of the narrative was to underscore Russia's economic significance while highlighting both the real and perceived failures of the Ukrainian state. Another objective was to diminish public support and thereby compel regional governments to curtail assistance to refugees. Efforts to discredit Ukrainians were designed to advance this aim.

The activities of AIMs varied, including both conventional and unconventional methods. Conventional actions involved the organisation of peaceful demonstrations and rallies, submitting petitions in support of peace as well as publishing brochures such as 'Stop the Ukrainisation of Poland', issued by the Confederation of the Polish Crown in 2022 ('*Oświadczenie*', 2022). On the other hand, unconventional actions were also evident, for example, football fans from Poznan, organised what they called 'educational sessions' for Ukrainian refugees. During these sessions, they gave advice to the refugees, including reminders to 'be good' and suggestions to 'go to the front' (Żytnicki, 2023).

While members of the movements were active both offline and on social media platforms, the predominant arena of activity was the virtual sphere. Platforms such as Facebook, Instagram, MINDS, Gap, MeWe, YouTube, Telegram and Vkontakte, websites and blogs served as the main channels for engagement. Online activities ranged from sharing and disseminating information sourced from Russian state media, including conspiracy theories propagated by the Kremlin, to generating original content in line with arguments advanced by Russian propaganda. Additionally, arguments from circles not strictly associated with AIMs but closely linked, such as pacifist and feminist statements against the war, were also promoted.

An example of offline activity is the anti-Ukrainian campaign initiated in February 2023 by the aforementioned Polish Anti-war Movement. This campaign included billboards bearing slogans such as 'This is not our war' in various Polish cities.

Motivational framing

The call for 'urgent' action and citizens' involvement was justified primarily by the gravity of the conflict, including the threat it posed to the security and lives of individuals in the region, as well as its substantial economic costs. Additionally, there were warnings about the potential rapid escalation of the conflict. Another key argument mobilising support for action was the adoption of populist rhetoric, contrasting the interests of ordinary people with those of perceived corrupt and war-rich elites. Furthermore, encouragement for action was fostered through the promotion of the slogan 'better a poor peace than the best war' (*Koos Vmeste*, 2022).

It is essential to acknowledge the diversity within the narratives of AIMs, which is likely to have stemmed from an effort to attract support from various organisations and social movements. This inclusivity has extended across a spectrum that includes feminists, pacifists, environmentalists, nationalists and chauvinists, indicating an attempt to construct a comprehensive AIM industry.

In summary, as of September 2023, there was a notable lack of consistency in the narratives proposed by AIMs. The message was continuously developed by AIM members, but with different aspects of the narratives

'It's not our war' 163

gaining prominence based on evolving circumstances and the available facts for interpretation. Nevertheless, the overarching framework of the message and the roles ascribed to various actors and states involved in the conflict remained relatively consistent. According to this narrative, EU/NATO states were depicted as latent aggressors responsible for triggering the conflict. Ukraine was portrayed as a 'fascist state' partly responsible for the outbreak of war. While this version, propagated by the Kremlin, was not uniformly adopted by AIMs in every country, a recurring theme in their message was the depiction of the Ukrainian regime as 'fascist'. Conversely, Russia was portrayed as a victim of the conflict, forced into a just war against fascism.

Conclusion

The long-term achievement of social movement goals is facilitated by its institutionalisation, which involves the establishment of formal structures with professional leadership (cf. Staggenborg, 1988, pp. 597–599; Staggenborg, 2022). Herbert Blumer (1951, p. 203) outlined four stages in the typical life cycle of a social movement. The first stage, termed 'social ferment', is characterised by unorganised and undirected agitation, with considerable emphasis on the activities of 'agitators'. This is followed by the phase of 'popular agitation', in which the fundamental causes of discontent and the objectives of action become more clearly defined. In the third phase, known as 'formalisation', disciplined participation and coordinated strategies to achieve the social movement goals are realised through the establishment of initial organisational structures. Finally, in the 'institutionalisation' stage, the social movement is assimilated into society and consolidated into a professional structure (della Porta & Diani, 2006, p. 150).

In the context of AIMs, there is an observable variability in their level of institutionalisation across the Baltic Sea states. In the Nordic countries, Lithuania and Latvia, AIMs are in their early stages, with individuals (also operating through established organisations and co-founded networks) seeking to agitate members and create ferment. Meanwhile, in Estonia, Poland and Germany, AIMs have moved on to the next stage of development, gaining support from other social movements and political entities. As noted by Scholzman (2015), it is often a fruitful strategy for political movements to seek alliances with existing political parties. Indeed, some AIMs have forged such alliances, thereby increasing their prospects of advancing the movement's goals, including in the electoral (in Estonia) and parliamentary (in Germany and Poland) arenas. However, such alliances do not necessarily guarantee the full institutionalisation of the AIM as a whole. Instead, the resources can be used to strengthen the potential of already established political structures or to contribute to the work of another social movement.

Regardless of their level of institutionalisation, AIMs in the Baltic Sea region primarily exploit the opportunities offered by modern technology and the political landscape of the countries in which they operate. The internet

164 Marzena Cichosz, Elżbieta Szyszlak and Renata Podgórzańska

has emerged as a key platform for the dissemination of disinformation and anti-Ukrainian narratives, with Twitter, Facebook, YouTube and various online portals playing a central role (Mierzyńska, 2023). Importantly, the use of these digital tools not only facilitates the spread of anti-Ukrainian messages but also accelerates the mobilisation of groups and individuals. On the other hand, the conflict in Ukraine has posed challenges for movements linked to or associated with Russia, particularly in their online operations. Both security services and societies have become more vigilant and sensitive to such online activities, making it more difficult for these movements to operate effectively (Karčiauskas, 2023, p. 5).

The master frame of the narrative spread by various AIM movements, despite their nuanced emphases and national differences, shows a significant degree of convergence, particularly at the diagnostic level, the most extensively elaborated. Discourse analysis suggests ongoing discussion, supplementation and testing of the narrative frames among members and supporters. While not necessarily carbon copies, these narratives often allude to strands formulated by the Russian Federation. AIMs use a wide range of arguments, reflecting their efforts to seek allies across diverse organisations and social movements, including feminists, pacifists, environmentalists, liberals, nationalists and chauvinists. This, in the author's assessment, represents an attempt to build a comprehensive AIM industry.

The solutions to the issue of the war, advocated by AIMs through the slogans of non-alignment, appear to be in line with Russia's interests, since, as a member of the Security Council, it legitimises the failed United Nations system. The ultimate value of this system is to ensure global peace, so narratives that distance themselves from the conflict in Ukraine fit perfectly with this concern. As a result, audiences who fail to see the broader context may easily accept the viewpoint presented by AIMs. However, the issue is more complex than that.

Notes

1 Russia boasts one of the largest diasporas in the world, ranking fourth in terms of size as of 2020 (Coolican, 2021, p. 5).
2 In the Nordic countries and Poland, the number of Russians fluctuates between several and tens of thousands, while in Germany it is 1.5 million people. Cf.: Statistikbanken (statbank.dk); https://pxdata.stat.fi:443/PxWeb/api/v1/en/StatFin/vaerak/statfin_ vaerak_pxt_11rp.px; Statistic Finland; Population statistics (scb.se); Statistisches Bundesamt (2023): Statistischer Bericht – Mikrozensus – Bevölkerung nach Migrationshintergrund – Ersterbebnisse 2022, LINK, Tabelle 12211–03, eigene Berechnung; https://stat.gov.pl/spisy-powszechne/nsp-2021/nsp-2021-wyniki-ostateczne/ tablice-z-ostatecznymi-danymi-w-zakresie-przynaleznosci-narodowo-etnicznej-jezyka-uzywanego-w-domu-oraz-przynaleznosci-do-wyznania-religijnego,10,1.html.
3 The term, referring to a poor-man's cotton-padded jacket, came from a popular 2011 meme depicting a blindly patriotic supporter of the Russian government, but soon was embraced by pro-Putin bloggers as well.
4 RT was banned from operating in Germany in February 2022.

References

Andrejsons, K. (2022, January 11). Baltic citizens worry they're next on Russia's menu. *Foreign Policy Magazine*. https://foreignpolicy.com/2022/01/11/baltics-russia-aggression-collective-security-ukraine/

Askew, J. (2022, June 14). Why Lithuania is polarised over Russia's war in Ukraine. *EuroNews.com*. www.euronews.com/my-europe/2022/06/14/why-lithuania-is-polarised-over-russia-s-war-in-ukraine

Auers, D. (2023). The Russia-Ukraine war and right-wing populism in Latvia. In G. Ivaldi & E. Zankina (Eds.), *The Impacts of the Russian Invasion of Ukraine on Right-Wing Populism in Europe* (pp. 201–209). European Center for Populism Studies. DOI: 10.55271/rp0023

Benford, R. D., & Snow, D. A. (2000). Framing processes and social movements: An overview and assessment. *Annual Review of Sociology, 26*, 611–639. www.jstor.org/stable/223459

Blumer, H. (1951). Social movements. In A. McClung Lee (Ed.), *Principles of Sociology* (pp. 199–220). Barnes & Noble.

Bobryk, A. (2023). The cultural security of Lithuania. In R. Wiśniewski, E. Szyszlak & R. Zenderowski (Eds.), *Cultural Security: Theory – Selected Aspects – Case Studies* (pp. 175–187). Peter Lang.

Bonusiak, G. (2022). Ochrona praw mniejszości narodowych w państwach powstałych w zachodniej części byłego Związku Radzieckiego. *Rocznik Instytutu Europy Środkowo-Wschodniej, 20*(4), 59–83. DOI: 10.36874/RIESW.2022.4.4

Brauß, H., & Rácz, A. (2021, January 7). Russia's strategic interests and actions in the baltic region: DGAP report no. 1. *German Council on Foreign Relations*. https://dgap.org/en/research/publications/russias-strategic-interests-and-actions-baltic-region

Caiani, M. (2023). Framing and social movements. *Discourse Studies, 25*(2), 195–209. DOI: 10.1177/14614456231154734

Camus, R. (2011). *Le Grand Remplacement*. David Reinharc.

Castañeda, E. (2019). Analyzing contemporary social movements. In C. Tilly, E. Castañeda & L. J. Wood (Eds.), *Social Movements 1768–2018* (pp. 167–176). Routledge.

Castells, M. (2015). *Networks of Outrage and Hope: Social Movements in the Internet Age*. Polity Press.

Chmielewski, B. (2022, June 24). Łotewskie batalie o pomniki. *Ośrodek Studiów Wschodnich*. www.osw.waw.pl/pl/publikacje/komentarze-osw/2022-06-24/lotewskie-batalie-o-pomniki

Coolican, S. (2021, October 10). *The Russian Diaspora in the Baltic States: The Trojan Horse That Never Was*. www.lse.ac.uk/ideas/publications/updates/russian-diaspora-baltic-states

della Porta, D., & Diani, M. (2006). *Social Movements: An Introduction*. Blackwell Publishing.

Downs, W. (2001). Pariahs in their Midst: Belgian and Norwegian parties react to extremist threats. *West European Politics, 24*(3), 23–42.

Earl, J. (2019). Symposium on political communication and social movements: Audience, persuasion, and influence. *Information, Communication & Society, 22*(5), 754–766. DOI: 10.1080/1369118X.2019.1568519

Eurobarometer. (2022, May). *Flash Eurobarometer 506: EU's Response to the War in Ukraine*. https://europa.eu/eurobarometer/surveys/detail/2772

Heinze, A.-S., & Weisskircher, M. (2022). How political parties respond to pariah street protest: The case of anti-corona mobilisation in Germany. *German Politics, 32*(3), 1–22. DOI: 10.1080/09644008.2022.2042518

JiiPee. (2023, September 4). Ukraina on pohjaton kaivo. *MVLehti.net*. https://mvlehti.net/2023/09/04/ukraina-on-pohjaton-kaivo-kolumni/

166 *Marzena Cichosz, Elżbieta Szyszlak and Renata Podgórzańska*

Karčiauskas, J. (2023). Lithuania social briefing: Fifth Columnists in Lithuania. *Weekly Briefing, 58*(3). https://china-cee.eu/wp-content/uploads/2023/02/2023s01_Lithuania.pdf

Koopmans, R., & Statham, P. (1999). Ethnic and civic conceptions of nationhood and the differential success of the extreme right in Germany and Italy. In M. Giuni, D. McAdam & C. Tilly (Eds.), *How Social Movements Matter* (pp. 225–251). University of Minnesota Press.

Koos Vmeste. (2022, December 5). Aivo Peterson s publichnym obrashcheniyem ko vsem prozhivayushchim v Estonii ukraintsam [Video]. *YouTube.* www.youtube.com/watch?v=OdROHTmh6Lc

Kuczyńska-Zonik, A. (2022, March 08). Mniejszości rosyjskojęzyczne w państwach bałtyckich a agresja Rosji na Ukrainę. *Instytut Europy Środkowej.* https://ies.lublin.pl/wp-content/uploads/2022/03/ies-komentarze-551-63-2022.pdf

Lindekilde, L. (2014). Discourse and frame analysis: In-depth analysis of qualitative data in social movement research. In D. della Porta (Ed.), *Methodological Practices in Social Movement Research* (pp. 195–227). Oxford University Press. DOI: 10.1093/acprof:oso/9780198719571.003.0009

Mąka, W. (2021, November 17). Wojciech O. został zatrzymany w Kaliszu za antysemityzm. Zaistniał także w Bydgoszczy. *To on m.in. zaatakował gazem białoruskiego studenta. BydgoszczNaszeMiasto.pl.* https://bydgoszcz.naszemiasto.pl/wojciech-o-zostal-zatrzymany-w-kaliszu-za-antysemityzm/ar/c1-8549779

McAdam, D., & Scott, W. R. (2012). Organizations and movements. In G. F. Davis, D. McAdam, S. Mayer & N. Zald (Eds.), *Social Movements and Organization Theory* (pp. 4–40). Cambridge University Press. DOI: 10.1017/CBO9780511791000

McCarthy, J. D., & Zald, M. N. (1973). *The Trends of Social Movements in America: Professionalization and Resource Mobilization.* General Learning Press. https://deepblue.lib.umich.edu/bitstream/handle/2027.42/50939/164.pdf?sequence=1&isAllowed=y

Meisner, M. (2022, July 29). Immer mehr Parallelmedien: Angriffe aufs System. der *Tagesspiegel.* www.tagesspiegel.de/gesellschaft/medien/angriffe-aufs-system-8542357.html

Mierzyńska, A. (2023, January 12). Wzrosła liczba wpisów z antyukraińską narracją. Znamy niechlubnych "liderów". *OkoPress.* https://oko.press/wzrosla-liczba-wpisow-z-antyukrainska-narracja-znamy-niechlubnych-liderow

Mishina, A. (2023, June 29). Lider Koos Oleg Ivanov: Estoniya gotovit voennuyu provokatsiyu protiv Rossii. *BaltNews.com.* https://baltnews.com/v-ehstonii/20230629/1026014638/Lider-Koos-Oleg-Ivanov-Estoniya-gotovit-voennuyu-provokatsiyu-protiv-Rossii.html

Obschestvennoe objedinenie „Mezhdunarodnyj forum dobrososedstva" zaregistrirovano v Minjuste. (2023, March 6). *Belta.by.* www.belta.by/society/view/obschestvennoe-objedinenie-mezhdunarodnyj-forum-dobrososedstva-zaregistrirovano-v-minjuste-554058-2023/

Olsen, M. (2023, May 16). Nordic media coalition uncovers Russian disinformation campaign. *Courthouse News Service.* www.courthousenews.com/nordic-media-coalition-uncovers-russian-disinformation-campaign/

Olson, M. (2012). *Logika działania zbiorowego: dobra publiczne i teoria grup.* Scholar.

Oświadczenie na temat pokoju na Ukrainie. (2022, June 26). *Gloria.tv.* https://gloria.tv/post/AUrVDnd6Dpcq3yWfyXg8m7oQa

Pawela, M. (2023, April 25). Rosyjska propaganda w Europie Środkowo-Wschodniej, część 2 (20–26.03.2023). *FakeNews.pl.* https://fakenews.pl/badania/rosyjska-propaganda-w-europie-srodkowo-wschodniej-czesc-2-20-26-03-2023/

Peoples, C. D. (2019). Classical and contemporary conventional theories of social movements. In B. Berberoglu (Ed.), *The Palgrave Handbook of Social Movements, Revolution, and Social Transformation* (pp. 17–34). Palgrave Macmillan.

Recurring Pro-Kremlin Rhetoric Linking Baltic States with Nazism. (2022, September 2). *Institute for Strategic Dialogue.* www.isdglobal.org/digital_dispatches/recurring-pro-kremlin-rhetoric-linking-baltic-states-with-nazism/

Sablina, L. (2023). The role of social media in facilitating minority mobilisation: The Russian-language pro-war movement in Germany amid the invasion of Ukraine. *Nations and Nationalism, 29*(4), 1–17. DOI: 10.1111/nana.12982

Scholzman, D. (2015). *When Movements Anchor Parties: Electoral Alignments in American History.* Princeton University Press.

Snow, D. A., & Benford, R. D. (1988). Ideology, frame resonance, and participant mobilization. *International Social Movement Research, 1,* 197–217.

Snow, D. A., Rochford, E. B., Worden, S. K., & Benford, R. D. (1986). Frame alignment processes, micromobilization, and movement participation. *American Sociological Review, 51*(4), 464–481.DOI: 10.2307/2095581

Spies, D. C., Mayer, S. J., Elis, J., & Goerres, A. (2023). Why do immigrants support an anti-immigrant party? Russian Germans and the alternative for Germany. *West European Politics, 46*(2), 275–299. DOI: 10.1080/01402382.2022.2047544

Staggenborg, S. (1988). The consequences of professionalization and formalization in the prochoice movement. *American Sociological Review, 53*(4), 585–605. DOI: 10.2307/2095851

Staggenborg, S. (2022). Institutionalization of social movements. In D. A. Snow, D. della Porta, B. Klandermans & D. McAdam (Eds.), *The Wiley-Blackwell Encyclopedia of Social and Political Movements.* DOI: 10.1002/9780470674871.wbespm113.pub2

Sud v Vilniuse podtverdil likvidatsiiu "Foruma dobrososedstva". (2023, May 17). *lrt.lt.* www.lrt.lt/ru/novosti/17/1991230/sud-v-vil-niuse-podtverdil-likvidatsiiu-foruma-dobrososedstva

Szeptycki, A. (2010). Nowa odsłona polskiego mesjanizmu na Wschodzie? In S. Bieleń (Ed.), *Polityka zagraniczna Polski po wstąpieniu do NATO i do Unii Europejskiej. Problemy tożsamości i adaptacji* (pp. 288–313). Difin.

Szeptycki, A. (2020). Stosunki polsko-ukraińskie: ku nowemu "strategicznemu partnerstwu"? *Batory.org.pl.* www.batory.org.pl/wp-content/uploads/2020/11/Stosunki-polsko-ukrainskie_Komentarz.pdf

Tilly, C. (1999). From interactions to outcomes in social movements. In M. Giugni, D. McAdam & C. Tilly (Eds.), *How Social Movements Matter* (pp. 253–270). University of Minnesota Press. https://voidnetwork.gr/wp-content/uploads/2016/09/How-Social-Movements-Matter-edited-by-Marco-Giugni-Doug-McAdam-and-Charles-Tilly.pdf

Ulinskaitė, J., & Garškaitė-Antonowicz, R. (2023). The populist far right in Lithuania during Russia's war against Ukraine. In G. Ivaldi & E. Zankina (Eds.), *The Impacts of the Russian Invasion of Ukraine on Right-wing Populism in Europe* (pp. 211–221). European Center for Populism Studies. DOI: 10.55271/rp0024

van Dijk, T. A. (2023). Analyzing frame analysis: A critical review of framing studies in social movement research. *Discourse Studies, 25*(2), 153–178. DOI: 10.1177/14614456231155080

Vänttinen, P. (2022, March 23). Rosyjska mniejszość w Estonii coraz bardziej przeciwna Putinowi. *Euractiv.pl.* www.euractiv.pl/section/bezpieczenstwo-i-obrona/news/rosyjska-mniejszosc-w-estonii-coraz-bardziej-przeciwna-putinowi/

Żytnicki, P. (2023, July 24). Kibole Lecha Poznań polują na młodych Ukraińców. "Nasz kraj, nasze zasady". *Gazeta Wyborcza.* https://poznan.wyborcza.pl/poznan/7,36001,30002953,nasz-kraj-nasze-zasady-kibole-lecha-poznan-poluja-na-mlodych.html

11 Between just and unjust war

Social movements in Germany and their attitude to the Russian-Ukrainian war

Katarzyna Kamińska-Korolczuk and Marlena Piotrowska

Introduction

The subject of the research presented in this chapter is socio-political movements in the Federal Republic of Germany (FRG, Germany), focusing on their attitude towards the Russian-Ukrainian conflict as it has evolved into a full-scale war. The authors analyse the changes in the German political landscape in the context of *Zeitenwende*, a policy referring to a statement made by the German Chancellor Olaf Scholz during a speech to the Bundestag on 27 February 2022 (Scholz, 2022). Given Germany's location in the Baltic Sea region, its inclusion in this study is essential due to the significant shift in policy towards Russia, previously a key economic and political partner, and the longstanding tradition of the German pacifist movement which plays a crucial role in articulating interests within the country.

This chapter aims to examine the significance of social movements in the German public sphere. The authors identify these movements and present their activities within the changing geopolitical landscape. The starting point for the analysis is the state of the German political system before the outbreak of war in Ukraine (Bräuninger et al., 2019; Kamińska-Korolczuk, 2021; Schmidt et al., 2019). Initial findings suggest that the Russian-Ukrainian armed conflict has not profoundly affected the overall functioning of the German state or the attitudes of segments of society organised into various social movements. However, there is evidence that certain interest groups have taken a different stance in response to Russia's aggression against Ukraine, adopting a narrative with explicit populist overtones (De Vreese et al., 2018). The actions of the main social groups addressing the Russian-Ukrainian war appear to be consistently against aggression, closely aligned with Germany's strategy implemented since the reconstruction of German statehood after the end of World War II. Among the many questions that arise, a central one is whether Germany's response to the war, as coming from one of the most influential European states, is sufficient to maintain the authority of the government in the eyes of its citizens.

To assess the validity of the above assumptions, the following research questions were formulated: What are the characteristics of pacifist movements

DOI: 10.4324/9781003558040-14

in Germany in the context of the Ukrainian conflict? Is it possible to observe a bottom-up development in the discourse on war and peace in Germany following the escalation of the Ukrainian-Russian conflict? Can it be inferred that social movements trigger changes in the rhetoric of the state and other movements; or do they only represent the perspectives of a minority within the society, with negligible influence on the ideological assumptions of the policy pursued by Germany?

The chapter draws on the research tradition of neo-institutionalism, examining both institutionalised norms and values and the behaviour of political actors, the key figures who shape the rules that govern how other actors within social movements perceive domestic and global circumstances. The study was approached from two perspectives. Firstly, a comprehensive contextual understanding was established through an ongoing literature review and analysis in the fields of political systems, social movements and social sciences. This perspective allows the system to be viewed holistically and through David Easton's (1953) systems theory. Systemic analysis was complemented by qualitative research methods (Wodak & Meyer, 2001, p. 65) whose findings include direct and indirect observations, as well as insights from content interpretation analyses of the official communication channels of selected movements.

The text structure comprises an analysis of key events in German politics, including a discussion on the German concept of civilian power (*Zivilmacht*). It examines the origins of peace movements with a long tradition within the German political landscape, their contemporary engagements and the main actors involved in intra-parliamentary politics in the context of the Russian-Ukrainian conflict. Attention is given to social movements and churches embedded in the tradition of pacifist and non-pacifist ideologies. In addition, political parties are considered as social movements representing different perspectives within German society (Katz & Mair, 1994).

The literature on the peace movement in West Germany is rich, although dominated by German-language debate. The most important works are by Andreas Buro (1977, 2005, 2011), Dieter Riesenberger (1985), Ulrike C. Wasmuht (1987) and Rüdiger Schmitt (1990). More recent contributions include Alexander Leistner's article (2022) in which he analyses the peace movement in Germany in the context of the Russian-Ukrainian war and identifies three main areas of activity. In addition, a relevant work for the following discussion is an article by Larissa Meier and Priska Daphi (2022), who examined the limited mobilisation potential of the Easter marches.

Pacifist movement in Germany

The German socio-political identity has its origins in the conception of foreign policy formulated after World War II within the newly established state emerging from the three occupation zones of the FRG. This conception aimed to reconcile the expectations of the powers involved in the reconstruction of

Germany and German society which was integrating itself into the newly formed state. Given German society's responsibility for the outbreak of the World War, the determination of an appropriate role on the international stage required particular caution.

German society operates according to governance principles (Jann, 2003; Mayntz, 2017). As a result, West German foreign policy and its correlated domestic policies have been shaped by both external expectations and internal social demands. Their key features include actions based on the concept of *Zivilmacht* and the collective trauma stemming from Germany's experience in World War II (Colvin, 2014; Fuchs et al., 2006). Coined by political scientist Hanns W. Maull in 1990, the term '*Zivilmacht*' (a civil power) posits that a state's foreign policy is determined not only by objective factors such as geography, size and wealth but also by the ideas it seeks to represent (Maull, 2019). Since reunification in 1991, Germany has sought to maintain such an attitude (Kirste & Maull, 1996; Maull, 2007, 2019). However, shifts in approaches to ongoing global conflicts are discernible. According to the author of the *Zivilmacht* concept (Maull, 2019) and other scholars (Bunde, 2020; Kamińska-Korolczuk, 2021), Germany remains a civil power that advocates alliances and seeks peaceful global solutions. However, a change in attitude towards this concept is underway, partly due to Russia's aggression against Ukraine. While there was initially a hesitant acknowledgement that alliance policy and dealings with Russia were misguided (Atai, 2019; Lough, 2022), the need for a shift in German perceptions of Russia was articulated in the *Zeitenwende* statement (Scholz, 2022). Studies have highlighted a shift away from *Zivilmacht* principles, manifested in increased military spending, with a focus not only on security provision but also on military procurement (Bernarding et al., 2021, p. 5). However, scepticism about military force is deeply rooted in Germany, both in the policies of the FRG and the GDR and in the post-war German social consciousness.

Perceptions of German foreign policy have been closely linked to the involvement of social movements, particularly peace movements opposed to militarisation and related actions. The tradition of German pacifist movements dates back to the turn of the 20th century, initially marginal and represented by a small group of middle-class individuals. However, its importance increased after World War I and it developed into a divisive ideology within German society between those who advocated demilitarisation and those who maintained military aspirations (Riesenberger, 1985, p. 99f). The notion of peace movements gained prominence in the 1950s during Germany's efforts to rebuild its military capacity and its accession to NATO in 1955 (Bundesministerium, 2020). This period saw the emergence of the '*Ohne-mich*' ('Without Me') movement whose ideas were short-lived (Wasmuht, 1987) but influenced the development of new concepts. In 1957, Eirene was founded by the peace churches of Mennonites and the Brethren (*Brüderkirche*) (*Eirene*, n.d.) to focus on ecumenical efforts for international peace and development. Two years later, a conference of the Evangelical Academy in Berlin established the

Weltfriedensdienst (World Peace Service, *WFD*), an organisation of politically active Christians committed to peace and reconciliation (*Weltfriedensdienst*, n.d.). Further impulses for peace activism came from international events. The first Easter marches in the UK in 1958, protesting against nuclear proliferation and war (Nehring, 2005), resonated in West Germany and led to similar marches. In 1960, Konrad Tempel organised an Easter march in northern Germany, supported by the Association of Conscientious Objectors (*Verband der Kriegsdienstverweigerer, VK*), (*War Resisters' International (Internationale Kriegsdienstverweigerer, IdK)*) and the German Peace Society (*Deutsche Friedensgesellschaft, DFG*) ('60 *Jahre Ostermaersche*', 2020). By the late 1960s, nationwide demonstrations were commonplace, attracting around 200,000 participants (Buro, 1977) and establishing the marches as the largest peace movement in Germany (Buro, 2011).

Naturally, there were other important peace organisations that shaped German social structures. In the late 1960s, the Working Group Service for Peace (*Arbeitsgemeinschaft Dienst für den Frieden, AGDF*) was founded to support peace organisations in various areas of social life. Next, in the late 1980s, the West German public engaged in the anti-nuclear movement (*Anti-Atomraketen-Bewegung*) (Buro, 2005). In addition, citizens actively participated in the Workshop for Non-violent Action (*Werkstatt für Gewaltfreie Aktion*), which offered training in peaceful civil disobedience from 1984 (*Werkstatt für Gewaltfreie* Aktion, n.d.). The protest movements employed various forms of activism to express their dissent and commitment to Germany's international arms policy, including marches, demonstrations, human chains and acts of civil disobedience. It has been argued that the actions of these movements contributed to the positive outcome of disarmament negotiations and the signing of the Intermediate-Range Nuclear Forces Treaty between the United States and the USSR in the late 1980s, thereby playing an important role in shaping European security policy (Schweitzer & Johansen, 2014).

Peace movements were also active in Germany's communist neighbour, the German Democratic Republic (GDR), founded in October 1949 in the Soviet occupation zone. Coordination of the movements in this part of Germany was facilitated by the involvement of the Protestant and, to a lesser extent, Catholic churches, which were the only entities capable of organising outside the state-monopolised social structures. Ehrhart Neubert explicitly states that East German peace movements, and later also environmental movements, were dependent on church structures (Neubert, 2011, p. 17). The East German peace movement operated in parallel to the West German movement, focusing primarily on promoting peace ideas without addressing global events. The history of the Easter marches in the GDR is short, spanning from 1966 to 1968. In August 1968, however, Warsaw Pact troops crushed the Prague Spring in Czechoslovakia (Bischof et al., 2010), leading to the cessation of the marches. As a result, the peace movements in the GDR became intertwined with the student movement and gradually lost relevance

172   *Katarzyna Kamińska-Korolczuk and Marlena Piotrowska*

('*Muff unter den Talaren*', 2022). The idea of Easter marches briefly resurfaced in the GDR in the late 1970s and early 1980s. At the beginning of 1982, the dissident Robert Havemann and the Protestant pastor Rainer Eppelmann published an eight-point Berlin Appeal (*Berliner Appell*) entitled 'Make Peace without Weapons' ('*Frieden schaffen ohne Waffen*'), proposing concepts for achieving long-term peace through demilitarisation (Robert Havemann Gesellschaft, n.d.). However, with the fall of the Berlin Wall and the collapse of the bipolar world, interest in this form of activism in the GDR waned.

The systemic transformations in Central and Eastern European countries, the end of the Warsaw Pact on 1 July 1991, German reunification and the dissolution of the USSR have reduced the importance of peace movements. Their focus has shifted to helping those affected by conflicts and disasters as well as advocating the principles of peaceful and constructive conflict resolution. For example, the League for Social Defence (*Bund für Soziale Verteidigung, BSV*) was active during the conflicts in the former Yugoslavia, and peace movements organised large-scale demonstrations and formed coalitions against the Iraq war in 2001, 2003 and 2004, but ultimately lost momentum due to their limited influence on government decisions (Deutsche Geschichte in Dokumenten und Bildern, 1991; '*Anti-Kriegs-Kundgebungen*', 2003; wp.pl, 2004). While actions also addressed conflicts and interventions in the Balkans and Afghanistan, they lacked the visibility of earlier efforts, partly because the world had shifted towards peacekeeping, resulting in less intense engagement by peace movements (Meier & Daphi, 2022). It is noteworthy that since the 1950s, anti-war demonstrations have taken place every year on 1 September, with slogans promoting peace, freedom, solidarity and democracy (Deutscher Gewerkschaftsbund, 2023). In turn, the long period of peace has fostered a link between peace movements and climate activism. This intersection is evident in citizen-led initiatives advocating 'No Peace with Climate Change' ('*Kein Frieden mit dem Klimawandel*') (Bund für Soziale Verteidigung, 2021). Climate change is now recognised as one of the most pressing threats and challenges facing nations. German social movements have been effective in highlighting this issue, leading to an increased awareness of its importance in security policy.

Pacifist movement organisations in Germany in the face of the Russian-Ukrainian war – a redefinition of positions?

There were limited Easter marches in 2019 as well as during the COVID-19 pandemic, when disarmament demands were put forward mainly in virtual protests. However, demonstrations returned to the streets and regained importance in the context of Russia's declaration of war against Ukraine (Scheffran, 2020). L. Meier and P. Daphi studied the motivations and attitudes of participants in a march in Bielefeld. The analysis showed that the majority on the 2022 march were people with experience in demonstrating in previous years. The most common reasons were support for disarmament/ anti-armament sentiments (42% of respondents), a pacifist stance (34%) and opposition to war (16%). Only 13% of respondents indicated solidarity with Ukraine/opposition to Russian aggression (Meier & Daphi, 2022, p. 591).

The mobilising capacity of the Easter marches prompts consideration of the pacifist movement in Germany. There is not complete unanimity among various circles on how to end the war and what role Germany should play in the peace process. Some circles advocate opposition to the war and call for a ceasefire, while others stress the need to stop the transfer of weapons and heavy military equipment to Ukraine, and to intensify diplomatic efforts. Alexander Leistner outlines three main areas of action for the peace movement in Germany during the ongoing war in Ukraine: (1) opposing armament and violence; (2) expressing solidarity with Ukraine; and (3) seeking peace with Russia (2022).

The activities of the peace movement focus on campaigns, actions and demonstrations. One prominent organisation is the *Netzwerk Friedenskooperative* (Network of the German Peace Movement), which emerged from the *Koordinierungsausschuss der Friedensbewegung* in the late 1980s (Friedenskooperative, 2023a). The organisation stands in solidarity with all people threatened by war and recognises Ukraine's right to self-defence, but advocates diplomatic efforts to end the conflict, particularly by the German government. On its website, it stresses the importance of keeping channels of dialogue open between Ukraine and Russia:

> Ukraine and Russia regularly negotiate prisoner exchanges and grain deals, so there are channels for talks that must be kept open. It is particularly important to show Russia a possible way out of the conflict. The goal must be the end of the war and the withdrawal of Russian troops.
>
> (Friedenskooperative, 2023b)

The actions taken by peace activists since 24 February go beyond the conflict in Ukraine. They include opposing the war, demonstrating for peace, questioning the allocation of additional funds to the Bundeswehr, and opposing the export of arms and heavy equipment to Ukraine. In addition, these efforts address broader concerns such as combating climate change, phasing out fossil fuels and moving away from nuclear technology. Initially, there were discussions about imposing or lifting sanctions on Russia and the possible establishment by NATO of a no-fly zone over Ukraine which could escalate into a global conflict. Some of the positions taken by peace movements relate to the banning of specific weapons, such as nuclear weapons, and opposition to the supply of cluster munitions from the United States, with calls for the German government to intervene to stop this, particularly important as Germany is a signatory to the Convention on Cluster Munitions (Pax Christi, 2023).

When discussing pacifism, the positions of the churches in Germany should not be overlooked. As early as 24 February, representatives of the country's two largest churches – the Evangelical Church in Germany (*Evangelische Kirche in Deutschland, EKD*) and the German Bishops Conference (*Deutsche Bischofskonferenz*) – issued a joint appeal calling on Russia to stop its aggression:

> We are appalled by the current developments and call on the Russian Federation to refrain from further aggression. Russia must immediately stop its military attacks and fully respect the territorial integrity of Ukraine. Russia's attack on Ukraine jeopardises the European peace project.
>
> (quoted in *Pressestelle der EKD*, 2022)

At the same time, Annette Kurschus, chairwoman of the EKD Council, remarked that she could not accuse politicians responsible for decisions on arms supplies to Ukraine of acting unchristianly (EKD, 2022a). On the anniversary of the attack on Ukraine, she reiterated the need for a strategy leading to peace alongside arms supplies to protect the Ukrainian people (EKD, 2023). The EKD also organised large demonstrations on 13 March 2022 in Berlin, Frankfurt, Leipzig, Stuttgart and Hamburg under the slogan 'Stop the war! Peace and solidarity for the people of Ukraine' (EKD, 2022b). It is noteworthy that the demonstration was jointly organised by over 40 organisations, including trade unions, churches, environmental, peace and human rights organisations such as the EKD, Netzwerk Friedenskooperative, Pax Christi, Greenpeace and ver.di. The announcement of the demonstrations emphasised solidarity with individuals protesting against the war in Russian cities: 'Our goal is peace negotiations leading to a nuclear-free Europe, common security, peace and disarmament, including Ukraine and Russia' (Stoppt den Krieg, 2022). The demonstration provided a platform to advocate for energy and climate policies to reduce Germany's dependence on coal, oil and gas from autocratic states, and to promote greater energy efficiency and climate protection. Opposition to armament was also emphasised. Around 125,000 people took part in the demonstrations in the five cities ('*Polizei soll*', 2022).

At least 30 pro-Russian demonstrations have taken place in Germany since Russia attacked Ukraine, but they have attracted fewer supporters than those in favour of Ukraine's actions ('*Polizei soll*', 2022; ktz/dpa, 2023). For example, in early April 2022, a vehicle demonstration took place in Berlin under the slogan 'No propaganda in schools – protection for Russian speakers, no discrimination' ('*Keine Propaganda in der Schule – Schutz für russischsprechende Leute, keine Diskriminierung*'), attracting around 900 participants ('*Autokorso mit russischen*', 2022). It is relevant to consider movements that do not explicitly identify as peace activists, but whose demands oppose aid to Ukraine. The Querdenker movement emerged during the COVID-19 pandemic, with members resisting government-imposed restrictions, including mandatory vaccination. In August 2020, the movement showed high mobilisation potential, with tens of thousands participating in organised demonstrations; by the end of the month, around 38,000 people were protesting, according to the authorities ('*Fast 40.000 Menschen*', 2020). However, as public health regulations changed, the mobilisation potential waned. In August 2022, about 6,500 people participated in a Berlin demonstration (Sundermeyer, 2022), and a year later, three years after the first major anti-pandemic demonstration, the movement organised another protest in Berlin against vaccination and aid to Ukraine (Huesmann, 2023). Around 4,600 people took part under the slogan 'Peace, Freedom, Truth, Joy' (Frieden, Freiheit, Wahrheit, Freude) ('*Rund 4.600*', 2023), indicating a decline in the number of Querdenker protestors.

Social movements in Germany and their place in state policy

Against the background of the conflict in Ukraine, the motto of the peace movement of the 1980s '*Frieden schaffen ohne Waffen*', as expressed in the appeal by Havemann and Eppelmann (Robert Havemann Gesellschaft), is resounding once again. While the dozens of organisations agree on the need for peace, they have not reached a consensus as to the strategies for achieving it. Initially, after Russia's invasion, demonstrations called for peace and an end to the war. However, as subsequent government decisions unfolded, there were growing calls to resist the delivery of heavy military equipment. This is in line with earlier stances against nuclear armament and calls for increased diplomatic efforts to end the conflict. Despite the declaration of the '*Zeitenwende*', for several months public opinion, social movements and the international community criticised the German government for its perceived sluggishness in providing heavy military support to Ukraine (Hasselbach, 2022). Nevertheless, from 24 February 2022 to the beginning of July 2023, the German government provided Ukraine with €22 billion in assistance (excluding contributions from federal states, local authorities, companies and individuals) (Presse und Informationsamt der Bundesregierung, 2023).

Public debates also address the extent to which pacifism is present in the German peace movement and how a pacifist approach is currently expressed (Meyer-Blankenburg & Pitzer, 2022). These discussions are rooted in the historical experiences outlined earlier in this chapter. Objections to Germany's involvement in military aid to Ukraine are raised not only during demonstrations. Since the escalation of the war in Ukraine, the Petitions Committee of the German Bundestag has received numerous petitions from citizens related to the ongoing conflict. These petitions are published on the Bundestag's dedicated website and cover various aspects of public life, including Germany's support for Ukraine through the supply of heavy weapons (Petition 132019, 2022), the non-delivery of heavy weapons to Ukraine (Petition 133021, 2022) and the approval of the delivery of Leopard 1 tanks to Ukraine (Petition 135218, 2022). The content of the petition regarding the non-delivery of heavy weapons to Ukraine, as well as its justification, was succinct. However, the authors mentioned that supplying heavy equipment would involve Germany in the war, with possibly unpredictable consequences. The petition was supported by 161 internet users (Petition 133021, 2022). It is worth noting that, in general, most petitions do not attract significant attention, and the support of 50,000 citizens within four weeks is required to initiate a public committee hearing (Deutscher Bundestag, 2021). The aforementioned petitions are not the only public demands addressed to German politicians regarding the war in Ukraine. Open letters to the Chancellor are also widespread. For example, in April 2022, 28 intellectuals and artists sent a letter to Olaf Scholz in which they stressed that the escalation of the conflict between Russia and Ukraine could lead to World War III. They expressed their hope that Scholz would return to his original stance against arms deliveries and called for an immediate ceasefire. The appeal was signed by more than 511,000 people on the petition platform change.org (Offener Brief, 2022). Another significant letter calling for an end to arms supplies and the initiation of peace negotiations was the 'Manifesto for Peace' ('*Manifest für Frieden*'), initiated by feminist activist Alice Schwarzer and Sahra Wagenknecht, a politician from Die Linke, the party in opposition to the Scholz government. The letter was signed by 69 individuals and was supported by over 850,000 people on a petition portal (Schwarzer & Wagenknecht, 2023). The manifesto also inspired Schwarzer and Wagenknecht to organise the 'Rising for Peace' ('*Aufstand für Frieden*') demonstration on 25 February 2023. According to the organisers, 50,000 people participated, although the Berlin police reported a turnout of 13,000 (Aufstand für Frieden, 2023).

As in other countries, the slogan 'This is not our war' ('*Das ist nicht unser Krieg*') began to appear on walls in Germany. This sentiment was also echoed during a plenary session of the Bundestag. Tino Chrupalla of the New Right party Alternative for Germany (*Alternative für Deutschland*, *AfD*) uttered this slogan during a discussion summarising the '*Zeitenwende*' year. Notably, during the same meeting, Olaf Scholz stated that Germany would support Ukraine for as long as necessary (Deutscher Bundestag, 2023a). On that day, a motion from Die Linke MEPs titled 'Diplomacy instead of tanks – a negotiating initiative to end the war of the Russian Federation against Ukraine' ('*Diplomatie statt Panzer – Für eine Verhandlungsinitiative zur Beendigung des Krieges der Russischen Föderation gegen die Ukraine*') was also considered (Deutscher Bundestag, 2023b). The motion proposed that the Bundestag call on the federal government to 'advocate an immediate ceasefire and a diplomatic initiative for further peace negotiations ... through which the withdrawal of Russian troops should take place, the sovereignty, territorial integrity and security of Ukraine should be guaranteed, and a common European security system with Russia should be made possible in the long term' (Deutscher Bundestag 2023c). Die Linke supported the motion, but the Social Democratic Party of Germany (SPD), Bündnis 90/Die Grünen (Alliance 90/Green), Free

Between just and unjust war 177

Democratic Party (FDP), and the largest opposition party Christian Democratic Union/Christian Social Union (CDU/CSU) were against it. The AfD abstained from the vote. Consequently, the motion was rejected (Deutscher Bundestag, 2023a).

Conclusion

The chapter has aimed to address three key questions. Firstly, it has examined the defining characteristics of the pacifist movements that developed in Germany against the backdrop of the war in Ukraine. Notable among these characteristics were expressions of opposition to the war and calls for an immediate ceasefire, alongside the observation of a limited mobilisation potential. The present activities of these movements concentrate on conducting campaigns, organising actions and staging demonstrations.

Secondly, the research into whether a bottom-up shift in the narrative of war and peace is evident in Germany following the outbreak of the full-scale Ukrainian-Russian war indicates that the demands made by pacifist social movements in response to it echo the slogans prevalent in the early days of the movement in Germany. These demands include opposition to war, exploration of alternative methods of conflict resolution and a consistent adherence to familiar slogans from the 1980s. However, as the Russian-Ukrainian war has developed, the range of demands articulated by the peace movement has expanded, for example, to question the allocation of additional funds to the Bundeswehr, to oppose the export of arms and heavy equipment to Ukraine, and to demand the government take diplomatic initiatives to end the war. Furthermore, during the energy crisis caused by the war and its aftermath, these movements also expressed an interest in energy and climate policy. This aspect of their activism underscores ongoing concerns about nuclear disarmament and European security, alongside calls to address climate change and transition away from fossil fuels. These demands are not only a response to the unfolding climate crisis but also a response to Germany's previous reliance on Russian energy sources.

The third research question examined whether social movements bring about a shift in the rhetoric of the state and other groups, or whether they remain representative of a minority opinion without influencing the ideological underpinnings of German policy. The analysis suggests that despite visible public mobilisation and concerted protest efforts, peace-oriented social movements do not have a decisive influence on the German government's decisions regarding the provision of military equipment and weapons to Ukraine, and thus do not change the ideological foundations of government policy. Despite discussions and numerous demonstrations, opponents of the supply of arms have not succeeded in obstructing the military aid sanctioned by the German government (Bundesregierung, 2023). Moreover, pacifist movements do not enjoy majority support among the population and their mobilisation efforts remain relatively modest. Opinion polls underline

178 *Katarzyna Kamińska-Korolczuk and Marlena Piotrowska*

the prevailing sentiment in favour of government-supported arms provision, with 35% of respondents seeing this as adequate, 29% as insufficient and 27% as excessive in April 2022. By comparison, in March 2023 the figures had shifted: 47% thought the support was appropriate, 16% thought it was insufficient and 31% thought it was excessive. However, peace movements still serve to amplify ethical concerns and advocate for a shift in government orientation from pro-war to pro-peace. By bringing issues such as aid to Ukraine, including arms supplies, sanctions against Russia and diplomatic efforts to end the conflict to the fore and into public discourse, they play a role in shaping the debate. It is worth noting that peace movements also work to strengthen the authority of the state, as a strong government allows citizen participation in decision-making.

References

60 Jahre Ostermaersche, "Zur Not gehe ich allein". (2020, April 12). *Der Spiegel.* www.spiegel.de/geschichte/corona-und-60-jahre-ostermaersche-zur-not-gehe-ich-allein-a-831c9aad-44c4-4425-9c97-f72c559c612e
Anti-Kriegs-Kundgebungen. Größte Friedens- Demonstration in der Geschichte der Bundesrepublik. (2003, February 15). *Der Spiegel.* www.spiegel.de/panorama/a-235314.html
Atai, G. (2019). *Die Wahrheit ist der Feind: Warum Russland so anders ist\ nominiert für den Grimme-Preis.* Rowohlt Verlag GmbH.
Aufstand für Frieden [Website]. (2023). https://aufstand-fuer-frieden.de/
Autokorso mit russischen Fahnen rollt durch Berlin. (2022, April 3). *rbb24.* www.rbb24.de/politik/thema/Ukraine/beitraege/autokorso-russland-ukrainei-demonstration.html
Bernarding, N., Menninger, J., Provan, A., Scheyer, V., & Standke-Erdmann, M. (2021). Wie militarisiert ist die deutsche Außenpolitik. *The Centre for Feminist Foreign Policy.* www.boell.de/sites/default/files/2021-09/CFFP-HeinrichBoll-DE-Final2.pdf
Bischof, G., Karner, S., & Ruggenthaler, P. (2010). *The Prague Spring and the Warsaw Pact Invasion of Czechoslovakia in 1968.* Lexington Books.
Bräuninger, T., Debus, M., Müller, J., & Stecker, C. (2019). Party competition and government formation in Germany: Business as usual or new patterns? *German Politics, 28*(1), 80–100. DOI: 10.1080/09644008.2018.1538362
Bunde, T. (2020, June). Einleitung. Der Münchner Konsens. In T. Bunde, L. Hartmann, F. Stärk, R. Carr, C. Erber, J. Hammelehle & J. Kabus (Eds.), *Zeitenwende | Wendezeiten: Sonderausgabe des Munich Security Report* (pp. 17–25). Münchner Sicherheitskonferenz. DOI: 10.47342/YSUC7634
Bundesministerium der Verteidigung. (2020, May 4). *Vor 65 Jahren: Beitritt der Bundesrepublik Deutschland zur NATO.* www.bmvg.de/de/vor-65-jahren-beitritt-bundesrepublik-deutschland-nato
Bundesregierung. (2023). *Liste der militärischen Unterstützungsleistungen.* www.bundesregierung.de/breg-de/schwerpunkte/krieg-in-der-ukraine/lieferungen-ukraine-2054514 [access: 24.6.2023].
Bund für Soziale Verteidigung. (2021, June). *Es wird heiß – kein Frieden mit dem Klimawandel: Dokumentation einer Tagung vom 19.-20. März 2021.* www.soziale-verteidigung.de/heiss-kein-frieden-klimawandel
Bund für Soziale Verteidigung. (n.d.). *Über uns.* www.soziale-verteidigung.de/bund-soziale-verteidigung-bsv

Buro, A. (1977). Die Entstehung der Ostermarsch-Bewegung als Beispiel für die Entfaltung von Massenlernprozessen. In R. Steinweg (Ed.), *Friedensanalysen 4. Schwerpunkt Friedensbewegung* (pp. 50–70). Suhrkamp.

Buro, A. (2005). Die Friedensbewegung in der Bundesrepublik in ihren historischen Etappen. *Netzwerk Friedenskooperative.* http://archiv.friedenskooperative.de/netzwerk/histo114.htm

Buro, A. (2011). Friedensbewegung. In H. Gießmann & B. Rinke (Eds.), *Handbuch Frieden* (pp. 113–124). VS Verlag für Sozialwissenschaften.

Colvin, S. (Ed.). (2014). *The Routledge Handbook of German Politics & Culture.* Routledge

De Vreese, C. H., Esser, F., Aalberg, T., Reinemann, C., & Stanyer, J. (2018). Populism as an expression of political communication content and style: A new perspective. *The International Journal of Press/Politics, 23*(4), 423–438.

Deutscher Bundestag. (2021). *Grundsätze des Petitionsausschusses über die Behandlung von Bitten und Beschwerden (Verfahrensgrundsätze).* www.bundestag.de/ausschuesse/a02_Petitionsausschuss/verfahrensgrundsaetze-867806

Deutscher Bundestag. (2023a). *Plenarprotokoll 20/88.* https://dserver.bundestag.de/btp/20/20088.pdf

Deutscher Bundestag. (2023b). *Diplomatie statt Panzer – Für eine Verhandlungsinitiative zur Beendigung des Krieges der Russischen Föderation gegen die Ukraine.* https://dip.bundestag.de/vorgang/diplomatie-statt-panzer-f%C3%BCr-eine-verhandlungsinitiative-zur-beendigung-des/296950?f.deskriptor=Waffenruhe&rows=25&pos=15&ctx=e

Deutscher Bundestag. (2023c, February 28). *Krieges der Russischen Föderation gegen die Ukraine, Drucksache 20/5819.* https://dserver.bundestag.de/btd/20/058/2005819.pdf

Deutsche Geschichte in Dokumenten und Bildern. (1991, January 26). *Protest gegen Irakkrieg.* https://ghdi.ghi-dc.org/sub_image.cfm?image_id=3387&language=german

Deutscher Gewerkschaftsbund. (2023, September 1). *Aufruf des DGB zum Antikriegstag 2023. Antikriegstag 2023: Die Welt braucht Frieden!* www.dgb.de/termine/++co++8acfd9f4-01e1-11ed-8b48-001a4a160123

Easton, D. (1953). *The Political System: An Inquiry into the State of Political Science.* Alfred A. Knopf.

Eirene. (n.d.). *Über uns.* https://eirene.org/ueber-uns

Evangelische Kirche in Deutschland. (2022a). *Kurschus: Entscheidung zu Waffenlieferung nicht unchristlich.* www.ekd.de/kurschus-entscheidung-zu-waffenlieferung-nicht-unchristlich-74047.htm

Evangelische Kirche in Deutschland. (2022b). *Mehr als 100.000 Menschen bei Demos gegen Ukraine-Krieg.* www.ekd.de/mehr-als-100-000-menschen-bei-demos-gegen-ukraine-krieg-72062.htm

Evangelische Kirche in Deutschland. (2023). *Kurschus: "Keine Waffe allein wird den Frieden schaffen".* www.ekd.de/kurschus-zum-jahrestag-des-russischen-angriffskriegs-77513.htm

Fast 40.000 Menschen bei Corona-Demos – Sperren am Reichstag durchbrochen. (2020, August 29). *rbb24.* www.rbb24.de/politik/thema/2020/coronavirus/beitraege_neu/2020/08/demonstrationen-samstag-corona-querdenken-gegendemos.html

Friedenskooperative. (2023a). *Wofür steht das Netzwerk Friedenskooperative?* www.friedenskooperative.de/ueber-uns

Friedenskooperative. (2023b). *Überblick über Friedensinitiativen zum Ukraine-Krieg.* www.friedenskooperative.de/ueberblick-ueber-friedensinitiativen-zum-ukraine-krieg

Fuchs, A., Cosgrove, M., & Grote, G. (2006). *German Memory Contests: The Quest for Identity in Literature Film and Discourse Since 1990.* Camden House.

180   Katarzyna Kamińska-Korolczuk and Marlena Piotrowska

Hasselbach, C. (2022, October 19). Na jaką broń z Niemiec może liczyć Ukraina – a na jaką nie. *Rzeczpospolita*. www.rp.pl/konflikty-zbrojne/art37264741-na-jaka-bron-z-niemiec-moze-liczyc-ukraina-a-na-jaka-nie

Huesmann, F. (2023). Gegen Corona-Impfungen und Ukraine-Hilfen: "Querdenker" demonstrieren wieder. *Redaktionsnetzwerk Deutschland*. www.rnd.de/politik/ querdenker-demo-in-berlin-wogegen-die-szene-heute-demonstriert-LWOD 667R5VFXRHEHZCE7GHVZMM.html

Jann, W. (2003). State, administration and governance in Germany: Competing traditions and dominant narratives. *Public Administration, 81*, 95–118. DOI: 10.1111/1467-9299.00338

Kamińska-Korolczuk, K. (2021). *Polityka i media a kryzys zaufania: polityka informacyjna mocarstw w czasie zagrożenia*. Wydawnictwo Uniwersytetu Gdańskiego.

Katz, R. S., & Mair, P. (Eds.). (1994). *How Parties Organize: Change and Adaptation in Party Organizations in Western Democracies*. Sage.

Kirste, K., & Maull, H. W. (1996). Zivilmacht und Rollentheorie. *Zeitschrift für internationale Beziehungen*, H. 2, 283–312.

ktz/dpa. (2023, August 20). Prorussischer Autokorso in Köln fällt deutlich kleiner aus als geplant. *Der Spiegel*. www.spiegel.de/panorama/gesellschaft/koeln-prorussischer-autokorso-faellt-deutlich-kleiner-aus-als-geplant-a-49b455c1-0d4b-4473-bee6-24659512bdad

Leistner, A. (2022). Wo steht die Friedensbewerbung und was steht an? *Forschungsjournal Soziales Bewegungen, 35*(4), 596–612. DOI: 10.1515/fjsb-2022-0051

Lough, J. (2022). Deutschlands Russlandproblem. *SIRIUS – Zeitschrift für Strategische Analysen, 6*(2), 150–164. DOI: 10.1515/sirius-2022-2003

Maull, H. W. (2019). Deutschland und Japan: Noch immer Zivilmächte? In K. Brummer, F. Kießling (Eds.), *Zivilmacht Bundesrepublik? Bundesdeutsche außenpolitische Rollen vor und nach 1989 aus politik- und geschichtswissenschaftlichen Perspektiven* (pp. 51–83). Nomos.

Maull, H. W. (2007). Deutschland als Zivilmacht. In S. Schmidt, G. Hellmann & R. Wolf (Eds.), *Handbuch zur deutschen Außenpolitik* (pp. 73–84). VS Verlag für Sozialwissenschaften.

Mayntz, R. (2017). From government to governance: Political steering in modern societies. In D. Scheer & F. Rubik (Eds.), *Governance of Integrated Product Policy* (pp. 18–25). Routledge.

Meier, L., & Daphi, P. (2022). Friedensbewegung und Krieg: Warum konnte die Ostermarschbewegung kaum von der öffentlichen Empörung über den russischen Angriffskrieg auf die Ukraine profitieren? *Forschungsjournal Soziale Bewegungen, 35*(4), 580–595. DOI: 10.1515/fjsb-2022-0050

Meyer-Blankenburg, L., & Pitzer, S. (2022, June 5). *Die deutsche Friedensbewegung – Was bleibt vom Pazifismus?* www.swr.de/swr2/wissen/deutsche-friedensbewegung-was-bleibt-vom-pazifismus-swr2-wissen-archivradio-2022-06-06-100.html

"Muff unter den Talaren": Vom Protestbanner zur Studentenbewegung. (2022, November 9). *Norddeutscher Rundfunk*. www.ndr.de/geschichte/chronologie/Muff-unter-den-Talaren-Vom-Protestbanner-zur-Studentenbewegung,studentenbeweg ung2.html

Nehring, H. (2005). The British and West German protests against nuclear weapons and the cultures of the Cold War, 1957–64. *Contemporary British History, 19*(2), 223–241.

Neubert, E. (2011). *Kościół i opozycja w NRD: Raporty Fundacji Konrada Adenauera 18*. Konrad Adenauer Stiftung.

Offener Brief an Bundeskanzler Scholz. (2022, April 29). *Change.org*. www.change. org/p/offener-brief-an-bundeskanzler-scholz

Pax Christi (2023, July 11). *"Keine Streumunition für Ukraine!"*. www.paxchristi.de/
meldungen/view/5222961917198336/Keine%20Streumunition%20f%C3%BCr%
20Ukraine!

Petition 132019, Unterstützung der Ukraine von Deutschland mit der Lieferung schwerer Waffen vom 16.03.2022. (2022, March 16). *Deutscher Bundestag.* https://
epetitionen.bundestag.de/petitionen/_2022/_03/_16/Petition_132019.nc.html

Petition 133021, Keine Lieferung schwerer Waffen an die Ukraine vom 13.04.2022.
(2022, April 13). *Deutscher Bundestag.* https://epetitionen.bundestag.de/petitionen/_
2022/_04/_13/Petition_133021.nc.html

Petition 135218, Genehmigung etc. bzgl. der Lieferung von Leopard 1-Panzern an die
Ukraine vom 21.06.2022. (2022, June 21). *Deutscher Bundestag.* https://epetitionen.
bundestag.de/petitionen/_2022/_06/_21/Petition_135218.nc.html

Polizei soll bei Verstößen eingreifen. (2022, April 9). *Tagesschau.* www.tagesschau.de/
inland/innenpolitiker-prorussische-demos-101.html

Pressestelle der EKD. (2022, February 24). "Sind in Gedanken bei den Menschen
in der Ukraine": Präses Kurschus und Bischof Bätzing rufen zum Frieden in der
Ukraine auf. *Evangelische Kirche in Deutschland.* www.ekd.de/ekd_de/ds_doc/
220224_PM_Praeses_Kurschus_und_Bischof_Baetzing_rufen_zum_Frieden_in_
der_Ukraine_auf.pdf

Presse und Informationsamt der Bundesregierung. (2023, July 11). *Bilaterale Unterstützungsleistungen der Bundesregierung für die Ukraine und Menschen aus der
Ukraine.* www.bundesregierung.de/resource/blob/2008726/2201464/a94d8b3bf3e
77798c926c1649612ddf6/2023-07-11-liste-ukr-bilaterale-hilfe-data.pdf?
download=1

Riesenberger, D. (1985). *Geschichte der Friedensbewegung in Deutschland. Von den
Anfängen bis 1933.* Vandenhoeck & Ruprecht.

Robert Havemann Gesellschaft. (n.d.). *"Frieden schaffen ohne Waffen" – 40 Jahre
Berliner Appell.* Archiv der DDR-Opposition. www.havemann-gesellschaft.de/
aktuelles/aus-dem-archiv/frieden-schaffen-ohne-waffen-40-jahre-berliner-appell

Rund 4.600 "Querdenker" demonstrieren in Berlin-Mitte. (2023, August 5). *rbb24.*
www.rbb24.de/politik/beitrag/2023/08/berlin-demonstration-querdenker-protest-
bundesregierung-ballweg.html

Scheffran, J. (2020, May 27). Kollaps und Transformation: Die Corona-Krise und
die Grenzen des Anthropozäns. *Universität Hamburg.* www.cen.uni-hamburg.de/
about-cen/news/11-news-2020/2020-05-27-kollaps-und-transformation.html

Schmidt, T. S., Schmid, N., & Sewerin, S. (2019). Policy goals, partisanship and paradigmatic change in energy policy – Analyzing parliamentary discourse in Germany over
30 years. *Climate Policy, 19*(6), 771–786. DOI: 10.1080/14693062.2019.1594667

Schmitt, R. (1990). *Die Friedensbewegung in der Bundesrepublik Deutschland.
Ursachen und Bedingungen der Mobilisierung einer neuen sozialen Bewegung.*
Springer Fachmedien. DOI: 10.1007/978-3-663-09707-5

Scholz, O. (2022). Reden zur Zeitenwende. *Die Bundesregierung.* www.bun
desregierung.de/resource/blob/992814/2131062/78d39dda6647d7f835bbe76
713d30c31/bundeskanzler-olaf-scholz-reden-zur-zeitenwende-download-bpa-
data.pdf

Schwarzer, A., & Wagenknecht, S. (2023). *Manifest für Frieden.* www.change.org/p/
manifest-f%C3%BCr-frieden

Schweitzer, C., & Johansen, J. (2014, July 26). Kriege verhindern oder stoppen.
Der Beitrag von Friedensbewegungen. IFGK Arbeitspapier. *Institut für Friedensarbeit und Gewaltfreie Konfliktaustragung e.V.* https://nbn-resolving.org/
urn:nbn:de:0168-ssoar-393106

Stoppt den Krieg. (2022). https://stoppt-den-krieg.de/

Sundermeyer, O. (2022). Querdenker und Montagsspaziergänger proben den Aufstand. *rbb24*. www.rbb24.de/politik/thema/corona/beitraege/2022/08/berlin-demonstration-querdenker-corona-regeln.html

Wasmuht, U. C. (1987). *Friedensbewegungen der 80er Jahre: Zur Analyse ihrer strukturellen und aktuellen Entstehungsbedingungen in der Bundesrepublik Deutschland und den Vereinigten Staaten von Amerika nach 1945: Ein Vergleich*. Focus Verlag.

Weltfriedensdienst. (n.d.). *Über uns*. https://wfd.de/ueber-uns

Werkstatt für Gewaltfreie Aktion. (n.d.). *Für eine Kultur der Gewaltfreiheit*. https://wfga.de.

Wodak, R., & Meyer, M. (Eds.). (2001). *Methods of Critical Discourse Analysis*. Sage Publications.

wp.pl. (2004, April 10). *Wielkanocne marsze w Niemczech*. https://wiadomosci.wp.pl/wielkanocne-marsze-w-niemczech-6031673351804033a

12 Between fear and courage

Russians vis-à-vis the oppressive state

Anna Jach and Magdalena Lachowicz

The oppressive state and non-violent behaviour

An oppressive state is one that on a large scale uses violence against its own citizens, residing both within and without its borders. 'Non-violent behaviour' means 'fighting without resorting to violence' or 'non-violence socio-technique' (Grzegorczyk, 1984, p. 6), also known as 'civil disobedience', 'political disobedience' and 'passive resistance' (Karwat, 2014, pp. 263–279). This issue has drawn attention from numerous researchers specialising in civil activity in countries with well-established democracies (Rawls, 2009; Thoreau, 2017) as well as in states failing to meet this criterion (Arendt, 1998; Sharp, 2013).

While the use of passive resistance is nothing extraordinary in democratic states, in authoritarian ones it becomes an act of courage that few dare to risk. The essence of civil disobedience, thus understood, is a public expression of a dissenting opinion or a rejection of specific regulations in the belief that they blatantly violate values that are of great importance to those who practise civil disobedience. Such citizens, on the one hand, are fully aware of the possible legal repercussions, yet on the other, they also consider submitting to these consequences as another demonstration of their objection (Jach, 2016, p. 126).

An analysis of civil disobedience must not forget the circumstances in which it is used. This kind of social activity is undertaken by various social movements as a way in which citizens can call authorities to order; it is used when the authorities go beyond their mandate, abuse their powers, or violate basic values, principles and social norms. There are also situations when this form of civil resistance becomes an instrument for removing a government whose power is illegitimate or loses the mandate of society for these reasons. If non-violent struggle is carried out within the framework of an oppressive state, it not only becomes a form of resistance, dissent and social protest but above all serves as a measure of self-defence for underprivileged communities threatened by violence. It helps resist the temptation to meet oppression with violence and offers an alternative to ineffective forms of purely passive resistance. For this community, it becomes an active form of the 'art of survival'.

DOI: 10.4324/9781003558040-15

184 Anna Jach and Magdalena Lachowicz

In such cases, we are dealing with social resistance that takes the form of a protest or counter-action in the extreme conditions of a repressive system of government (Karwat, 2014, pp. 264–265).

In practice, as has been observed many times, the pressure a state exerts on its citizens through the resistance of the latter can be reversed. In specific conditions, under the pressure of growing civil resistance, a repressive state can be forced to abandon such policies or even to submit to the will of its citizens (Karwat 2014, p. 269).

Approving attitudes in Russian society towards the 'special military operation'

In the Russian Federation, the cult of war is being strengthened both in real-life projects and in virtual space. There are visible grassroots civic, local-government, municipal and institutional initiatives that aim to strengthen the polarisation of society against the West in order to increase support for the idea of 'Russkiy mir' (*Русский Мир*) and defend the conservative trend of 'Orthodox civilisation'. The development dynamics of these projects clearly point to a deliberate linking of the so-called 'special military operation' with the strong myth of the Great Patriotic War promoted by the state and its subordinate research institutions. The objective of this process is social polarisation, and figures of external and internal enemies are used. Its visual symbol has become the letter 'Z', the use of which signifies support for Putin's regime and thus for the Russian-Ukrainian war.

According to surveys from the Russian Public Opinion Research Center (VCIOM), support for the Russian-Ukrainian war is high. The level of support for the decision to conduct the 'special military operation' in January 2023 was 68% (in February 2022, it was 65%), while the percentage of non-supporters in January 2023 was only 20% (in February 2022–25%). The degree of readiness among the respondents to provide assistance to residents of the new territories, Russian soldiers, conscripts and refugees, in January 2023 was 72–79%. Compared to 2021, in 2022, there was a marked increase in the approval of the activities of the president (+15 pp.) and the main political institutions, that is the government of the Russian Federation, the Federation Council and the State Duma (+10–14 pp.) (VCIOM, 2023). High level of support for the war is confirmed by independent sociological studies which demonstrate that the supporters of the conflict outnumber its convinced opponents by approximately four to one ('*Pogruzheniye v voynu*', 2023, p. 3). According to data from the Levada Center, social polarisation and the radicalisation of opinions is progressing, with the ratio of supporters and opponents remaining stable over time (Levada Center, 2022, 2023). Nevertheless, next to groups approving Russian aggression and state policy, there is an emerging one opting for peace, end of conscription and demobilisation, with a number of other groups demonstrating attitudes that fall in between these two stances. The picture is therefore not clear-cut. It should be remembered, however, that respondents in these surveys are citizens of an authoritarian state, so they cannot be said to faithfully represent the actual distribution of pro- and anti-war sentiments (Human Rights Watch, 2022; Spetsial'naya voyennaya operatsiya na Ukraine, 2023).

A two-level analysis allows a distinction between the so-called declarative majority who support the war (60%) of which a 'non-objecting majority' (40%) are respondents who avoid answering or declaring support, but in their other answers do not support pro-war decisions or convictions. According to sociologists, the attitude of the 'non-opposing majority' lets the pro-war minority (35–40%) confidently dominate the public sphere ('*Pogruzheniye v voynu*', 2023, pp. 3–4).

The majority of Russians at the same time both support and do not support the war; they are a 'categorically de-politicised' society (Yudin & Medvedev, 2023). Qualitative studies also demonstrate that Russian attitudes to the war resemble an internally contradictory patchwork, compiled from the arguments and narratives of both sides, while the tendency to focus on arguments for support/non-support can itself change depending on circumstances. Furthermore, declarative and imposed attitudes should be separated from social practice. Hence Krastev seems to be correct in his assumption that we are dealing here with a 'post-sacrifice' society, in which citizens support the regime but are not ready to sacrifice themselves for its sake. What supports this argument is the difficulty in winning over citizens to accept conscription, and even in convincing the army to sign the contract and participate in the war (Krastev, 2022).

It is also important to understand the objective of Russian aggression in Ukraine. According to the Athena Project, in 2022, as many as 38% of respondents watching the TV news identified the main purpose of the intervention as protecting the population of the Russian-backed quasi-republics in Donetsk and Luhansk (The Athena Project, 2022). Additional reasons included responding to a threat from the West; defending the people of Donbas; getting ahead of an enemy that was preparing to attack; fighting fascism; the necessity to support one's country in any situation; and delegating competences to the political elite (Yerpyleva, 2023).

Attitudes approving of the war are systematically strengthened and sustained by the propaganda machine, instruments of external intervention, and the main social actors. For example, support for Russian aggression against Ukraine has been expressed by the Orthodox Church (Moscow Patriarchate) since 2014. The forms of expressing an attitude of approval are based on a shared idea of celebrating the war that refers to the Soviet and imperial tradition of affirming the system, which is part of Russian propaganda. Concerts, performances, official letters of support, organised groups (e.g. children and students) writing supportive letters to individual soldiers in the front zone, documentaries and visualisations aimed at raising the fighting spirit, solidarity projects and actions to provide material help to soldiers at the front, veterans and their families, are all duplications of formats already known. Other

186 *Anna Jach and Magdalena Lachowicz*

instruments of support are activities aimed at providing for the families of war victims as well as the soldiers fighting, and the so-called compatriots or new arrivals from the Donbas and Ukraine; carried out within the framework of the 2022 special competition for presidential grants dedicated to NGOs (493 projects in progress) ('*Spetsial'nyy konkurs*', 2023).

Forms and instruments of civil disobedience used by Russian civil society in relation to the Russian-Ukrainian war

Since 24 February 2022, a number of grassroots-inspired anti-war initiatives have emerged in the Russian Federation. The crucial question is whether their intensification can and will result in setting a path to peacefully end the ongoing war. Essentially, these initiatives are of a mixed nature: traditional (offline) forms co-occur with or otherwise complement contemporary (online) forms. Social media like Facebook, Twitter, Telegram, Instagram, YouTube, VKontakte (*ВКонтакте*) have become very helpful means of communication, especially under a police state that uses a series of repressive measures against objectors. Internet platforms and services have also emerged that allow banned civil society structures as well as cultural, civic and political activists to publish their own materials, to present an alternative reality to that propagated by the Kremlin, and to inform global public opinion and Russian citizens about the events taking place. Examples include the application Samizdat (*Самиздат*)[1] as well as the portals Levada-Center, Meduza, Colta.ru., OVD-Info, Lenta.ru, Novaya Gazeta (*Новая газета*),[2] Navalny LIVE (*Навальный LIVE*), Mediazona, TV Rain (*ДО///ДЬ*), Radio Svoboda (*Радио Свобода*), Radio Sakharov (*Радио Сахаров*) and The Insider. They are a complementary or even the sole space for promoting Russian citizens' traditional means and methods of protest in virtual reality and in hybrid form, with the latter using such alternative sources of information as independent newspapers published by anti-war circles, for example, *Zhenskaya Pravda* (*Женская правда*) and *Obshchestvenno-politicheskaya organizatsiya* (*Molodëzhnoye Demokraticheskoye Dvizheniye* 'Vesna', n.d.; Radio Sakharov, n.d). A number of online consultation and training sites have been launched as well, covering all spheres of political, social, economic and cultural life. Instructional campaigns on the internet and in social media have focused on training citizens in how to bypass blockades and use coded communication channels, instructing on how to speak about the war to be heard and how to behave during arrest or detention (*Młodzi Rosjanie*, 2022). The institutions mentioned operate in Russia whenever possible, but predominantly outside RF borders in the territories of the Baltic region states, other EU members or third countries.

The repertoire of forms and instruments of non-violent struggle waged by Russians in their country against the RF's aggression onto Ukraine can be assessed from the perspective of the methods of nonviolent protest and persuasion, social non-cooperation and non-violent intervention applied (Sharp,

2013, pp. 98–107). The analysis of these methods with regard to forms of civil resistance and actions carried out has revealed several rudimentary features. Firstly, they exemplify both individual and collective resistance to the decisions of the president and his administration. Secondly, for security reasons, they have been transferred to the internet; actions of passive resistance previously undertaken in person by specific protesters give credence to the current protest. According to the models popularised by former Soviet and Russian dissidents, any type of protest must be a publicly expressed form of disobedience for two reasons: (1) it is to set an example of solidarity and shared responsibility with the group with which a citizen identifies, and (2) not just the immediate environment but the maximum number of people, both inside and outside the country, should be informed about the nonviolent action. Consequently, such a strategy of civil dissent gives, if not a guarantee, at least the hope that someone will speak in favour of the protesters, that they will not be silently eliminated by the machinery of state repression.

Other forms of protest include petitions, open letters, rallies and protest marches. In response to the bending, bypassing and violating of civil rights, social groups come up with legislative initiatives and projects, such as 'Impeachment 2.0' (of Vladimir Putin), attempts to restore democratic legal solutions in different regions of the RF and to repeal anti-democratic federal laws, tightening the provisions of the Criminal Code and the Code of Administrative Procedure of the Russian Federation (*Molodëzhnoye Demokraticheskoye Dvizheniye* 'Vesna', n.d.) or referendum initiatives on whether regions inhabited by the indigenous peoples of the Russian Federation should remain within the Russian state ('*Zayavleniya predstavitel'_nits*', 2022).

Among visual anti-war propaganda actions, those of a symbolic nature deserve attention. Due to involvement in this type of protest, an informal grassroots movement emerges, uniting participants. The array of opposition symbols to the war includes first and foremost the white-blue-white flag, which is a symbol of Russians opposing Russia's invasion of Ukraine and the rule of Vladimir Putin (Katonina, 2022; 'Flag of the Wonderful Russia of the Future', n.d.).

Other recognisable signs of the opponents of the war with Ukraine and of Putin's rule, authoritarianism and territorial expansion include green ribbons; anti-war slogans ('For war – No!', 'For genocide – No!', 'Mothers against war', 'It's Putin's war, not mine!', 'Ukraine, forgive us!', 'Putin is war!', 'It's war!', 'Nation, arise!'); photo actions (with faces covered/out of frame); satirical cartoons, leaflets and stickers, graffiti, posters and placards; writing anti-war slogans on banknotes; using toys and children's clothes to strengthen the message of banners and slogans; replacing shop price tags with ones bearing anti-war messages; sticking information on the war on one's own clothing (so-called silent protest); hand-made toys ridiculing war and Putin; spraying/painting over propaganda banners, posters and the 'Z' symbol; leaving in public places books containing anti-war slogans; writing anti-war slogans on trees; leaving flowers with placards against Russian aggression in Ukraine at the monuments of the Great Patriotic War; distributing leaflets about independent Russian media; agitation through comments under internet posts, podcasts and discussions; putting on Yandex Maps service information about heavy traffic with tags pointing to Putin as the culprit of high fuel prices; using anti-war bots such as Brave Partizan (*Храбрый партизан*) ('*Vidimyy protest*', 2022).

An important form of resistance is non-cooperation, such as boycotting official state ceremonies, moving the activities of banned cultural institutions to the internet, posting applications from outlawed cultural institutions on international platforms for downloading to the computer and/or phone, and organising underground (or bypassing mainstream state cultural policy) concerts and theatrical performances by artists who oppose the war (Nazarov, 2022).

The RF citizens involved in protests come from all social groups, regardless of their education, occupation, place of residence or national and ethnic affiliation. They use their own resources to improve publicity and recognition. Crucial in this process are media personalities (Alexei Navalny, Marianna Ovsyannikova) and celebrities (Ksenia Sobchak), politicians (Andrei Kozyrev), social activists, entrepreneurs, artists (Alla Pugacheva, Andrei Makarevich), groups of financial oligarchs (Yeltsin's backers: Tatiana and Maria Yumasheva, Sofia Abramovich), and groups of political oligarchs (Putin's backers: Oleg Deripaska, Yelizaveta Peskova) ('*Sem'ya protiv voyny*', 2022).

A civil resistance phenomenon that decision-makers consider dangerous is the attitudes of those who enjoy widespread respect and authority in society, such as war veterans (European Bureau for Conscientious Objection [EBCO], n.d.) and Orthodox hierarchs and scholars who, contrary to the official position of the Russian Orthodox Church, issued an appeal condemning the concept of 'Russkiy mir' and its use to justify the war in Ukraine ('A Declaration on the "Russian World"', 2022). In protest, 'well-informed' citizens (Guriev & Treisman, 2023, pp. 63, 363) publicly tender resignations from their jobs and membership of prestigious cultural, social and charity organisations (EBCO, n.d.).

The protests have also taken an institutionalised form. A number of civil society institutions (NGOs of various profiles, media, social organisations, religious associations) openly expressed their condemnation of the war against Ukraine and/or spoke out against Putin's rule; however, they were quickly dissolved, banned and/or forced to move their activities into exile. Among them were *Движение 'Мир, Прогресс и Права человека' им. Сахарова* (Andrey Sakharov's Movement 'Peace, Progress and Human Rights'), *Феминистское антивоенное сопротивление* (Feminist Anti-war Resistance), and *Фонд борьбы с коррупцией* (Anti-corruption Foundation) (Vagner, 2023) as well as some of Russia's oldest human rights movements of Soviet origin such as *Международное историко-просветительское, правозащитное и благотворительное общество Мемориал* (Memorial

Society) (Russia's Supreme Court, 2022), the Russian branch of Amnesty International (*Международная амнистия*) (RKN ob'yasnil blokirovku saytov "Golosa", 2022), and the Moscow Helsinki Group (*Московская Хельсинкская Группа*) (The Decision of Moscow City Court, April 27, 2023).

A separate form of institutionalised, group civil objection that is worth mentioning is the anti-war movement in the regions of the RF. They are a major source of policy-maker worries. Since the beginning of the Russian-Ukrainian war, frustration has been growing among such nations as the Buryats, Yakuts, Dagestanians, Tuvans, Bashkirs, Chechens, the residents of Tatarstan and other groups of indigenous peoples living within the borders of the RF. They are organising themselves to prevent a 'holocaust of Russia's indigenous peoples' ('*Voyna protiv Ukrainy ili genotsid*', 2023), which is being carried out 'by Putin and his supporters', as it is not ethnic Russians that are sent to the Ukrainian front, but rather other peoples and nations of the Russian Federation. Hence such groups establish, either on their own or with the support of ethnic structures operating in exile, anti-war committees aimed not only at protecting a specific native population. There are postulates of withdrawing from the federated state (Free Buryatia Foundation, n.d.; '*Zayavleniya predstavitel'_nits*', 2022; Teluk, 2022). They see also their activity as a fight against the stigmatisation that accompanies the war campaign in Ukraine: any wrongs, misdemeanours and war crimes committed there are blamed on the representatives of those nations: 'a Buryat has raped . . ., a Tuvan has murdered' and so forth (Beda Collective, 2022; Free Yakutia Foundation, n.d.).

Another symptom of the social discontent resulting from the ongoing war is civil disobedience actions among prisoners not only those incarcerated for political reasons but also those serving time for criminal offences. Riots in detention centers and penal colonies are becoming a very dangerous phenomenon for those in power, for the threat of losing control of the penitentiary system could end in events of a revolutionary nature (Volkov, 2023).

The 'special military operation' (as Putin's propaganda announced it) and de facto war against Ukraine has encountered two more fundamental problems: the conscription of recruits into the army and the refusal of soldiers of the Russian Federation to fight on the Ukrainian front. Individual citizens, informal and formal social groups as well as the representatives of indigenous peoples have spoken out against the conscription[3] (Makarowa, 2022). Detailed instructions were prepared for young men on how to avoid it. Military registration and conscription offices were set on fire, and people pulled draft cards out of neighbours' mailboxes and destroyed them (Kochkina, 2022; 'W Rosji ogłoszono protest', 2022; Pavlova, 2022). Meanwhile the refusal to fight was manifested by the soldiers of units transferred to the Belarusian area after operations who refused to return to the front (Salenkov, 2022).

The degree of publicly expressed civic opposition to the war with Ukraine neither was a phenomenon of stable long-term intensity nor took a

190   Anna Jach and Magdalena Lachowicz

homogeneous form. While for the first two months of the invasion (February and March 2022), protests were numerous (Dudek, 2022; Roman-Rawska, 2022), later the majority of them moved to the internet due to the risks the participants faced. According to OVD-Info, the human rights organisation, 15,441 people were detained in Russia in connection with anti-war activities between 24 February and 9 May 2022 ('*Rafaelki, sinyaya kofta*', 2022). The use of oppressive methods has led to long-term negative consequences for Russia in the forced migration of skilled, educated people with financial resources.

Attitudes and activities of the new Russian dissidents in the Baltic region

The Russian invasion of Ukraine in 2022 led to migration on a hitherto unprecedented scale that is difficult to estimate (according to experts, between 500,000–600,000 and 1.2 million people have left Russia) (Domańska, 2023, p. 5; Gulina, 2023, p. 2). Two waves were clearly visible: right after the outbreak of war and after the announcement of mass conscription in September 2022. There is no trustworthy data on returns. Until 2022, RF citizens migrated mostly for economic reasons (sanctions against Russia and lack of prospects for highly qualified employees after the withdrawal of Western companies and innovative projects; lack of prospects for small- and medium scale businesses) as well as for political ones (human rights activists who were persecuted or threatened with persecution; independent journalists; activists, particularly those with the status of 'foreign influence agents').

The emigrants of the 2022/2023 waves who moved to the Baltic region states, particularly to Germany, encountered well-established emigration groups that offered social potential for development and opposition to the war (cf. the activities of Mikhail Khodorkovsky, Zhanna Nemtsova, the Russian-speaking minorities in Riga and Tallinn, as well as activists in Vilnius). Another important factor was the traditional ties of German public institutions (Heinrich Boll and Adenauer foundations, the DAAD programme, universities and German-Russian exchanges including *Austausch e.V.* and *Deutsche-Russischer Austausch*, etc.) as well as the attitude of the German authorities and society, without signs of Russophobia. In Latvia and Estonia, the procedural ease of border crossing together with traditional Russian-speaking diasporic centres played an important role in the first stage of migration. Other attractive destinations were Turkey, the South Caucasus and Central Asia (ICMPD Migration Outlook Eastern Europe and Central Asia, 2023, pp. 1–31; Statista, 2022; Turkish Statistical Institute, 2022).

Russian migrants focus on several main areas of activities directed at creating and strengthening the potential for civic resistance to the war and Putin's regime: (1) expressing public opposition to the war; (2) respecting the lives and dignity of war victims and expressing solidarity of Russian migrants with Ukrainians (e.g. Congress of Civic Anti-war and Humanitarian Initiatives,

Between fear and courage 191

Berlin 2022); and (3) linking and consolidating the image of the Russian migrant with democratic values.

Russian emigrants in Baltic-region countries are engaged in assisting refugees from Ukraine (through their own initiatives or within structures already existing in the host state) and migrants from Russia. The model of assistance varies from ad hoc aid to a multifaceted, transnational network of cooperation between professionals from different areas (psychologists, lawyers, human rights defenders, IT specialists and doctors). The last category includes such entities as *Kovtcheg*, *Diaspora molodëzhnogo demokraticheskogo dvizheniya 'Vesna'*, Free Russia, Russia against War, Russian Antiwar Committee as well as *Antikrigskommittén* and Sverige Russians Against War. Activists make use of their achievements and work experience from their time in Russia, while often maintaining horizontal networks of connections with the regions of the RF and anti-war circles (e.g. *Feministskoye antivoyennoye soprotivleniye – Litva*).

Protest actions and long-term anti-war campaigns, both stationary and virtual, making use of free Russia symbols (the white-blue-white flag) are considered by migrants as tools of intervention, aiming to demonstrate an active anti-war stance in the public space. In the long term, Russian migrants are joining the third sector as dynamic social actors in the target countries, successfully establishing local foundations and associations, building international networks, consolidating the structure of anti-war initiatives in individual countries and creating effective communication networks between such entities. At both local and trans-border levels, working groups are formed and informal education projects are launched, teams are established to monitor the situation in the Russian Federation, especially in the area of human rights, repressions, the situation of so-called foreign influence agents and political prisoners (such groups include OVD-Info, Reform Space Tallinn, Danish Friends of a Democratic Russia, *Demokraticheskoye soobshchestvo Yugo-vostochnoy Finlyandii*, and PANDA platform Berlin). The process is mutually beneficial: for the community of the host country it is a source of knowledge, an integration factor and a way to combat disinformation, while for activists, it is an effective way to increase competences in the area of European solutions, instruments of democracy and professionalisation of volunteerism.

The multiplicity of forms and tools of e-participation concerning innovative projects escapes basic classifications and takes hybrid forms (ranging from individual security standards, instruction on fact checking, 'hack-a-thons' and use of VPNs/defence against DDoS attacks, to the creation of effective independent media in virtual space). The involvement of the IT sector is evident in all the locations analysed. The migrant community is offered the opportunity to raise awareness and skills through courses, training and instructional actions. The parallel process of increasing migrants' awareness of the effective implementation of human rights, personal security and instruments of civic participation seems to be of the greatest importance for the future, providing potential for forging stable pro-democratic Russian structures in the Baltic region countries (and, more broadly speaking, in the West) as well as (distant) prospects for the democratisation and transformation of Russia (e.g. Roundtable with Russian Opposition, June 2023) (European Parliament Brussels, 2023). This also offers an opportunity for constructive dialogue, provided that these entities are actively included in the existing structure of the third sector in host countries and become integrated with European actors. Significantly, representatives of the scientific and analytical communities (including Yekateryna Shulman, Sergey Utkin, Vasilyj Zarhkov, Olga Gulina and others) have joined in research on the state and potential of Russian migration as well as in the exchange of knowledge in the field of Russian studies (Foxt, 2023; 'Sciences Po Welcomed Political Scientist', 2023).

As a migration of resistance, Russians have created/continued a movement for free media and channels of communication with Russian society to combat disinformation and propaganda. The countries of the Baltic region have become a field of activism for Russian journalists and human rights defenders with the status of 'foreign influence agents'. Latvia has become a hub for independent Russian-language media (including Medusa Project SIA, TVRain (until December 2022), *Novaya Gazeta*, and even the local *Gubernia* from Pskov), while the Baltic region states have become an important centre for individual legal assistance in the protection of human rights and the rights of political prisoners, as well as financing such activity (PTS Memorial, 2023).

Financing does remain a problem, and so does the dispersion of emigration democratic circles among the Baltic countries, disputes over forms of resistance against the regime and instruments of support for Ukraine during the war, as well as matters related to political awakening and activism in opposition forces (e.g. the Anti-war Committee and the 'Free Russia' Congress). An important issue is how to maintain stable and systematic contacts inside Russia in the face of the restrictions imposed by the regime: the status of an undesirable organisation was assigned for instance to 'Organization for a Free Russia' operating in Poland; the Russian authorities revoked the registration of 15 foreign NGOs and foundations (including Human Rights Watch and Amnesty International) that actively supported the Russian opposition, forcing them to close their offices in Russia. A pressing problem is also the censorship of selected content on social media such as *VKontakte*, which impedes communication among anti-war and migrant communities (Knockel et al., 2023). There have been actions to break the information blockade, for example the Lithuanian #CallRussia initiative aimed at making ordinary Russians aware of the RF's illegal invasion of Ukraine. However by July 2023, divisions among anti-regime circles in exile had become apparent (there is an ongoing debate among oppositionists in exile, and attempts are made at consolidation in the form of congresses, closed meetings, conferences with representatives of the EU and host countries (e.g. the Congress of People's

Between fear and courage 193

Deputies, seminars at NUPI/The Norwegian Institute of International Affairs, debates about the future of Russia by the organisation *Demokraticheskoye soobshchestvo Yugo-vostochnoy Finlyandii* and conventions of activists working for freedom for the indigenous peoples of the Russian Federation). The positive effect is a significant increase in knowledge and awareness of the Russian regime among European political, intellectual and social circles.

Conclusion

The analysis in this chapter has concentrated on the process of the engagement of Russians, both those residing in the RF and those living in the diaspora in the countries of the Baltic region, in civil disobedience activities aimed not only at ending the Russian-Ukrainian war but also at gathering grassroots civic support for peace.

Is such conversion possible in the case of the relations of the Russian state with its citizens in the country and abroad? In search for an answer, the concept of social networking (Sierocki, 2020) should be recalled; it involves creating a number of connections between groups and/or individuals that share a way of thinking, values or even fate. In the case of a society in an oppressive state, which the Russian Federation undoubtedly is, there emerge strings of social connections due to which citizens, both supporters and opponents of the war, can share the communality of goals from their own group. This translates into a level of effectiveness of operations undertaken by a given group as well as a sense of empowerment and agency. What are the chances that the developed network of social connections between civil society institutions that practice passive resistance (non-governmental, non-commercial sector, media, religious communities and informal social structures) (Jach, 2019) will be sustained and will become a cornerstone of a new reality, as happened several times in the 20th century? It is difficult to find satisfactory answers to these questions. In an authoritarian state, the entities organising social protests care first and foremost about the safety of their own members, with demands to correct the course of the government coming second.

The contemporary world has provided civic resistance activists with new possibilities to safely express their opinions in the new environment of the internet with all the opportunities it offers. Thus, we are witnessing a blending of traditional and non-traditional forms of civil disobedience. The mixed non-violent system is based both on in-person physical appearances and on virtual ones, which have a much greater reach and scope of influence. This, too, is a very important step in constructing a system of social networking, which can become a viable resource for developing, within the community thus generated, effective paths to peace and mechanisms to safeguard against another war of attrition.

In this situation, it is worth noting the effects and significance of the attitudes adopted by Russians towards the ongoing war in the context of developing mechanisms to lead to an end of the conflict, restoring peace

194 Anna Jach and Magdalena Lachowicz

and making reparation when those responsible for causing harm are held to account. The analysis has led to the following conclusion.

The level of support for Russian government policies is quite high in Russian society. Although it does not necessarily translate into overt, voluntary and active manifestations of support for the regime, it does indicate the passivity of society which has adopted attitudes ranging from aggressive chauvinism, through those based on fear of an external threat and a desire to protect the Russian-speaking population or on indifference to Russian foreign policy but with full support for the president, to passive conformism. These attitudes are consistent with the logic of an oppressive state, and broad public support for the RF's policy is maintained.

However, we are also witnessing changes in the mentality of Russians and the ways they perceive their surrounding reality. As previously demonstrated, alongside attitudes approving of Russian aggression and state policy, there is a clearly emerging group that expresses a growing desire for putting a speedy end to the war and demobilisation, with a number of groups whose opinions fall in between. However, this does not necessarily result in a widespread recognition of Russia's guilt and the need to make reparations for the wrongs inflicted. The danger of revisionism, combined with lack of accountability for international crimes and the failure to 'de-imperialise' the Russian Federation, could once again push the world into the depths of war.

What completes this patchwork are the attitudes of the opposition to Russia's invasion of Ukraine. The range of political disobedience attitudes on display (methods of peaceful protest and persuasion, social non-cooperation and peaceful intervention) testifies to the process of socio-political socialisation of both Russian citizens and the societies of the Baltic region states; progressing systematically but not very rapidly. In practice, grassroots attitudes of civic participation are being formed, together with a sense of solidarity and a shared responsibility for the future of the present and following generations.

There is currently no satisfactory answer to the fundamental question: Can the publicly expressed civil resistance of Russian Federation citizens both at home and in exile in the states of the Baltic region, and in other countries, lead to developing peaceful ways to end the conflict? This is a process that, if it is initiated at all, will require a complete reconstruction of mentality, acceptance of the criminal nature of the political system and a complete remodelling of the axiological system. It is not impossible, but it will be a long and very painful one, because it must be voluntarily implemented by the Russians themselves.

Notes

1 An application resistant to blocking by Russian censorship, created by the editors of investigative portals Project (Проект), Important Stories (*Важные истории*), The Insider, Bellingcat, and the so-called Navalny Team. Available as *Самиздат* from Google Play Store (United Editors, 2023).

2 After suspension of its activity in Russia in March 2022, and blockade of its new platforms, followed by the RF authorities recognising its editor-in-chief Dmitri Muratov as a 'foreign influence agent' (*инагент*), *Novaya Gazeta* moved its operations to EU territory. See more at https://novayagazeta.ru/.
3 The Russian word for conscription, '*mobilizatsia*' (*мобилизация*) was often changed to '*mogilizatsia*' (*могилизация*), whose root comes from the word '*могила*', that is, a 'grave'.

References

Arendt, H. (1998). *O przemocy. Nieposłuszeństwo obywatelskie*. Trans. A. Łagocka & W. Madej. Fundacja Aletheia.
The Athena Project. (2022, October 9). Russian citizens on the 'special military operation' in Ukraine – independent opinion poll. *ExtremeScan*. www.extremescan.eu/post/1-chronicles-athena-project
Beda Collective. (2022). *It Was Clear to Us That We Would be Made the Front Image of This War: An Interview With Victoria Maladaeva – An Activist from Buryatia and a Co-Founder of the International Anti-War Foundation Free Buryatia*. https://beda.media/en/articles/maladaeva-en
Colta.ru [Website]. (n.d.). www.colta.ru/
The Decision of the Moscow City Court on the Liquidation of the Moscow Helsinki Group Came into Force. (2023, April 27). *Moskovskaya Khel'sinkskaya Gruppa*. www.mhg.ru/news/reshenie-mosgorsuda-o-likvidacii-moskovskoy-helsinkskoy-gruppy-vstupilo-v-silu
A Declaration on the "Russian World" (Russkii mir) Teaching. (2022, March 13). *Public Orthodoxy*. https://publicorthodoxy.org/2022/03/13/a-declaration-on-the-russian-world-russkii-mir-teaching/
Demokraticheskoye soobshchestvo Yugo-vostochnoy Finlyandii [Демократическое сообщество Юго-восточной Финляндии]. (2023, April 23). [Group homepage]. *Facebook*. www.facebook.com/groups/664761104817513
Domańska, M. (2023). Rosyjska emigracja polityczna nowej fali w Niemczech. Struktury, działalność, perspektywy [Report]. *Ośrodek Studiów Wschodnich*. www.osw.waw.pl/pl/publikacje/raport-osw/2023-07-04/rosyjska-emigracja-polityczna-nowej-fali-w-niemczech
Dudek, A. (2022). Reakcje społeczeństwa rosyjskiego na inwazję Rosji na Ukrainę (24.02–24.04.2022). *Instytut Rosji i Europy Wschodniej*. https://rosjoznawstwo.uj.edu.pl/reakcje-spoleczenstwa-rosyjskiego-na-inwazje-rosji-na-ukraine
European Bureau for Conscientious Objection. (n.d.). *Rossiyane protiv voyny s Ukrainoy [Россияне против войны с Украиной]*. https://ebco-beoc.org/node/527
European Parliament Brussels. (2023, January 6). *The Day After: Brussels Dialogue [A Roundtable Talks Programme]*. https://drive.google.com/file/d/1-G4ju-JADBlf-XgDN_gY4Qx60Cp37cVc/view
Flag of the Wonderful Russia of the Future: A Symbol of Freedom and Peace. (n.d.). *Whitebluewhite.info*. https://whitebluewhite.info/english
Foxt, E. (2023, June 12). 'My budem rabotat's Rossiyey: No drugoy Rossiyey'. O chem rossiyskaya oppozitsiya govorila s evropeytsami na konferentsii v Bryussele [Мы будем работать с Россией. Но другой Россией". О чем российская оппозиция говорила с европейцами на конференции в Брюсселе]. *BBC News Russian*. www.bbc.com/russian/features-65877931
Free Buryatia Foundation [Website]. (n.d.). www.freeburyatia.org/?lang=en
Free Yakutia Foundation [Website]. (n.d.). https://kovcheg.live/en/initiatives/free-yakutia-foundation-2/
Grzegorczyk, A. (1984). *Filozofia czasu próby*. Instytut Wydawniczy PAX.

Gulina, R. O. (2023, June). Emigration from Russia after 24 February 2022: Main patterns and developments: Policy brief. *Prague Process*. www.pragueprocess.eu/en/resources/repository/34-briefs/377-emigration-from-russia-after-24-february-2022-main-patterns-and-developments

Guriev, S., & Treisman, D. (2023). *Spin dyktatorzy. Nowe oblicze tyranii w XXI wieku*. Trans. A. Żak. Wydawnictwo Otwarte.

Human Rights Watch. (2022). *Russian Federation: Events of 2022* [Report]. www.hrw.org/world-report/2023/country-chapters/russian-federation

The Insider [Website]. (n.d.). https://theins.ru/

International Centre for Migration Policy Development. (2023). *ICMPD Migration Outlook Eastern Europe and Central Asia 2023: Six Migration Issues to Look Out for in 2023: Origins, Key Events and Priorities for Europe*. www.google.com/url?sa=t&source=web&rct=j&opi=89978449&url=www.icmpd.org/file/download/59104/file/230215_ICMPD_Migration_Outlook_EasternEuropeCentralAsia_2023_final.pdf&ved=2ahUKEwj89Jjl_KqFAxVIKhAIHce0AboQFnoECCQQAQ&usg=AOvVaw3kR3jZngptCFOOV2eCGPUv

Jach, A. (2016). Events of August '91 as an expression of political disobedience in the process of shaping civil conduct. *Kultura i Edukacja*, 4(114), 125–139. DOI: 10.15804/kie.2016.04.09p.125-139

Jach, A. (2019). Pozarządowy sektor niekomercyjny w Rosji w latach 2000–2018. Osobliwości funkcjonowania. *The Non-Governmental, Non-Commercial Sector in Russia in 2000–2018 Peculiarities of Functioning. Неправительственный некоммерческий сектор в России в 2000–2018 гг. Особенности функционирования*. Kraków: Wydawnictwo Księgarnia Akademicka. DOI: 10.12797/9788381380829

Katonina, K. (2022, February 28). Predlagayu flag rossiyskogo protesta – belo-sine-belyy [Предлагаю флаг российского протеста – бело-сине-белый]. [Facebook post]. *Facebook*. www.facebook.com/itsgonnabeokai/posts/10227954032741739

Karwat, M. (2004). Polityka rzeczowa, stronnicza i metapolityka. In T. Klementewicz (Ed.), *Współczesne teorie polityki –od logiki do retoryki. Studia Politologiczne* (Vol. 8). Warszawa.

Karwat, M. (2014). *Podstawy socjotechniki dla politologów, polityków i nie tylko*. Difin SA.

Knockel, J., Dalek, J., Meletti, L., & Ermoshina, K. (2023). *Not OK on VK. An Analysis of In-Platform Censorship on Russia's VKontakte*. The Citizen Lab. https://citizenlab.ca/2023/07/an-analysis-of-in-platform-censorship-on-russias-vkontakte/

Kochkina, K. (2022). Podzhogi voyenkomatov i zheleznodorozhnoye soprotivleniye. Kak deystvuyet antivoyennoye podpol'ye v Rossii [Кочкина К. 2022 Поджоги военкоматов и железнодорожное сопротивление. Как действует антивоенное подполье в России]. *Nastoyaschee Vremia*. www.currenttime.tv/a/podzhogi-voenkomatov-i-zheleznodorozhnoe-soprotivlenie-kak-deystvuet-antivoennoe-podpole-v-rossii-/31846774.html

Krastev, I. (2022, June 13). Politolog Ivan Krastev: "Rossiya – eto ne kollektivnyy Putin" [Политолог Иван Крастев: "Россия – это не коллективный Путин"]. *Radio Svoboda*. www.svoboda.org/a/politolog-ivan-krastev-rossiya-eto-ne-kollektivnyy-putin-/31892880.html

Lenta.ru [Website]. (n.d.). https://lenta.ru/

Levada Center. (2022, June 30). *Konflikt s Ukrainoy [Конфликт с Украиной]*. www.levada.ru/2022/06/30/konflikt-s-ukrainoj-3/

Levada Center. (2023, June 30). *Konflikt s Ukrainoy: otsenki kontsa iyunya 2023 goda [Конфликт с Украиной: оценки конца июня 2023 года]*. www.levada.ru/2023/06/30/konflikt-s-ukrainoj-otsenki-kontsa-iyunya-2023-goda/

Levada-Center [Website]. (n.d.). www.levada.ru/

Makarowa, M. (2022, September 22). Mogilizacja Rosjan. Panika – to najlepiej określa nastroje w Rosji. *OkoPress*. https://oko.press/mogilizacja-rosjan-panikaa

Mediazona [Website]. (n.d.). https://zona.media/

Meduza [Website]. (n.d.). https://meduza.io/

Młodzi Rosjanie: "Jak można inaczej myśleć o tej wojnie?" (2022, March 9). *DW.com*. www.dw.com/pl/m%C5%82odzi-rosjanie-o-swoich-rodzicach-jak-mo%C5%BCna-inaczej-my%C5%9Ble%C4%87-o-tej-wojnie/a-61071536

Nazarov, D. (2022, November 12). Radi mira nel'zya umirat' [Назаров Д. Ради мира нельзя умирать] [Video]. *YouTube*. https://youtu.be/UhT8XdB6Ucg?feature=shared

Novaya Gazeta [Новая газета] [Website]. (n.d.). https://novayagazeta.ru/

Obshchestvenno-politicheskaya organizatsiya Molodёzhnoye Demokraticheskoye Dvizheniye "Vesna" [Vesna] [Общественно-политическая организация Молодёжное Демократическое Движение "Весна"]. (n.d.). https://vesna.democrat/

OVD-Info [Website]. (n.d.). https://ovdinfo.org/

Pavlova, A. (2022, April 26). "Ya nikogo ne khochu otpravit' na voynu". Sotrudnitsa ZHKKH v Peterburge sabotirovala vrucheniye povestok – raznosit' ikh obyazali [Павлова А. "Я никого не хочу отправить на войну". Сотрудница ЖКХ в Петербурге саботировала вручение повесток – разносить их обязали дворников]. *Mediazona*. https://zona.media/article/2022/04/26/draft

Pogruzheniye v voynu: khroniki obshchestvennogo mneniya [Погружение в войну: хроники общественного мнения]. (2023, March 1). *RE: RUSSIA*. https://re-russia.net/expertise/057/

PTS "Memorial" [ПЦ "Мемориал"]. (2023, July 16). *Spisok politzaklyuchёnnykh (bez presleduyemykh za religiyu) [Список политзаключённых (без преследуемых за религию)]*. https://memohrc.org/ru/pzk-list

Radio Sakharov [Радио Сахаров] [Website]. (n.d.). https://radiosakharov.org/

Radio Svoboda [Радио Свобода] [Website]. (n.d.). www.svoboda.org/

Rafaelki, sinyaya kofta i zheltyye bryuki, portrety veteranov i knigi. Za chto zaderzhivali v Moskve 9 maya [Рафаэлки, синяя кофта и желтые брюки, портреты ветеранов и книги. За что задерживали в Москве 9 мая]. (2022, May 9). *BBC*. https://press.lv/post/rafaelki-sinyaya-kofta-i-zheltye-bryuki-portrety-veteranov-i-knigi-za-chto-zaderzhivali-v-moskve-9-maya

Rawls, J. (2009). *Teoria sprawiedliwości*. Trans. A. Romaniuk, M. Panufnik, & J. Pasek. PWN.

RKN ob'yasnil blokirovku saytov "Golosa", Amnesty International i "Vazhnykh istoriy" [РКН объяснил блокировку сайтов "Голоса", Amnesty International и "Важных историй"]. (2022, March 11). www.interfax.ru/russia/827718

Roman-Rawska, K. (2022, October 17). Opór w Rosji przeciw wojnie. „Nastrój protestu rośnie z każdym dniem". *OkoPress*. https://oko.press/opor-w-rosji-przeciw-wojnie-nastroj-protestu-rosnie

Russia's Supreme Court Approves liquidation of International Memorial. (2022, February 28). *Memorial*. www.memo.ru/ru-ru/memorial/departments/intermemorial/news/690

Salenkov, M. (2022). Sotni rossiyskikh voyennykh otkazyvayutsya voyevat' na Ukraine. [Саленков М. Сотни российских военных отказываются воевать на Украине]. *Euronews*. https://ru.euronews.com/2022/04/07/ukraine-war-russians-refusals

Sciences Po Welcomed Political Scientist and Youtube Superstar Ekaterina Schulmann. (2023, April 18). *SciencesPo*. www.sciencespo.fr/en/news/sciences-po-welcomes-political-scientist-and-youtube-superstar-ekaterina-schulmann

Sem'ya protiv voyny. Deti politikov, chinovnikov i krupnykh biznesmenov vyskazyvayutsya protiv napad. [Семья против войны. Дети политиков, чиновников и крупных бизнесменов высказываются против нападения на Украину]. (2022, February 25). *Mediazona*. https://zona.media/article/2022/02/25/no-war

Sharp, G. (2013). *Od dyktatury do demokracji. Drogi do wolności.* Trans. A. Karolak. Fundacja Wolność i Pokój. https://fundacjawip.files.wordpress.com/2013/02/od-dyktatury_a.pdf

Sierocki, R. (2020). Analiza sieci społecznych jako metoda badawcza w naukach społecznych. *Rocznik Antropologii Historii, 13,* 223–255. DOI: 10.25945/rah2020.13.009

Spetsial'naya voyennaya operatsiya na Ukraine otnosheniye rossiyan. 12 volna (16–19 iyunya 2023) ["Специальная военная операция" в Украине: отношение россиян. 12 волна (16–19 июня 2023).] (2023). *Russian Field.* https://russianfield.com/12volna

Spetsial'nyy konkurs [Специальный конкурс]. (2023). *Fond Prezidentskikh Grantov.* https://президентскиегранты.рф/public/fpg/special-competition-2022

Statista. (2022). *Number of Emigrants from Russia in 2022, by Country of Destination.* www.statista.com/statistics/1218477/emigration-by-country-in-russia/

Teluk, T. (2022, May 31). Naród przeciw narodowi. Jak Rosja wykorzystuje mniejszości etniczne. *Trójmorze.* https://trimarium.pl/think_tank/narod-przeciw-narodowi/

Thoreau, H. D. (2017). *Nieposłuszeństwo obywatelskie.* Trans. M. Barski. Wydawnictwo Vis-a-Vis Etiuda.

Turkish Statistical Institute. (2022). *International Migration Statistics, 2022.* https://data.tuik.gov.tr/Bulten/Index?p=International-Migration-Statistics-2022-49457&dil=2

TV Rain [ДО///ДЬ] [Website]. (n.d.). https://tvrain.tv/

United Editors. (2023). Samizdat [Самиздат]. [Mobile app]. *Google Play Store.* https://play.google.com/store/apps/details?id=com.unieditorsmobile&hl=pl&gl=US

Vagner, A. (2023). "Ponimat' rossiyskuyu real'nost'". Antivoyennyy protest – v 220 gorodakh [Вагнер А. (2023). "Понимать российскую реальность". Антивоенный протест – в 220 городах]. *Radio Svoboda.* www.svoboda.org/a/ponimatj-rossiyskuyu-realjnostj-antivoennyy-protest-v-220-gorodah/32414205.html

VCIOM [All-Russian Center for the Study of Public Opinion]. (2023, February 20). *Spetsial'naya voyennaya operatsiya: god spustya [Специальная военная операция: год спустя].* https://wciom.ru/analytical-reviews/analiticheskii-obzor/specialnaja-voennaja-operacija-god-spustja

'Vidimyy protest': gid 3.0 ["*Видимый протест*": гид 3.0]. (2022, June 13). *Vesna.* https://vesna.democrat/2022/06/13/kak-sdelat-protest-zametnee-polnyj-g/

Volkov, V. (2023, June 24). V Rossii zaklyuchennyye ustroili bunty v rostovskoy kolonii i moskovskom SIZO [*Волков, В.* В России заключенные устроили бунты в ростовской колонии и московском СИЗО]. *Vot Tak.* https://vot-tak.tv/novosti/24-06-2023-bunt-sizo-koloniya

Voyna protiv Ukrainy ili genotsid korennykh narodov RF: kak mobilizatsiya v Rossii vliyayet na demografiyu [Война против Украины или геноцид коренных народов РФ: как мобилизация в России влияет на демографию внутри страны]. (2023, April 26). *Freedom.* https://uatv.ua/vojna-protiv-ukrainy-ili-genotsid-korennyh-narodov-rf-kak-mobilizatsiya-v-rossii-vliyaet-na-demografiyu-vnutri-strany/

W Rosji ogłoszono protest przeciwko mobilizacji. "Mają umrzeć dla pałacu Putina?". (2022, September 21). *Onet.* https://wiadomosci.onet.pl/swiat/protest-rosjan-przeciwko-mobilizacji-maja-umrzec-dla-palacu-putina/vrh7p91

Yerpyleva, S. (2023, March 14). Raz nachali, zakanchivat' nel'zya: kak menyayetsya otnosheniye Rossiyan k voyne v Ukraine [Раз начали, заканчивать нельзя: как меняется отношение Россиян к войне в Украине]. *RE: RUSSIA.* https://re-russia.net/expertise/060/

Yudin, G., & Medvedev, S. (2023, July 16). Grigoriy Yudin: "Eta sistema, bezuslovno, budet demontirovana" [Григорий Юдин: "Эта система, безусловно, будет демонтирована"]. *Radio Svoboda.* www.svoboda.org/a/grigoriy-yudin-eta-

sistema-bezuslovno-budet-demontirovana-/32504107.html?fbclid=IwAR0kQhigb
H6jVuEroFQSmDpZBROIJ7mc0oRlFNh_k1NHabaGtav8Y4y5qcw

Zayavleniya predstavitel'_nits narodov Rossiyskoy Federatsii protiv voyny [Заявления
представитель_ниц народов Российской Федерации против войны]. (2022, June 5). *Syg.
ma*. https://syg.ma/@media-resistance-group/zaiavlieniia-priedstavitiel-nits-narodov-
rossiiskoi-fiedieratsii-protiv-voiny

13 Conclusion

Danuta Plecka and Marzena Cichosz

The outbreak of full-scale war in Ukraine was a consequence of the inaction of European states and the United States following the annexation of Crimea by Russia in 2014. The 2022 attack by Russia against Ukraine initiated the growth of awareness among both politicians and societies in Europe (as well as in other regions of the world) has brought recognition of the real threat to peace in the region. By analysing the directions of specific state policies, as well as civic activism in the Baltic region, the authors have discovered information demonstrating the research hypothesis regarding changes to the pre-2022 external and internal strategies of the states of the region, as well as changes in the attitudes of their societies. The hypothesis is confirmed by support for the implementation of the international system of sanctions against the Russian Federation; approval for Sweden's and Finland's NATO membership; the redefinition of energy policies; and military, financial and diplomatic assistance for Ukraine. The main focus of the state's actors in 2022–2023 was a limitation of military operations to the territory of Ukraine; but at the same time, they gradually increased military spending and the combat capabilities of military alliances, and mobilised their societies through the constant presence of a threat of conflict in public debate. These activities could thus be described as the implementation of a strategy for preventing Russia's territorial expansion, deterring potential aggressors and increasing future security (including energy security). Meanwhile, changes in social strategies were expressed through the grassroots activities of individuals and groups who organised themselves around issues related to the armed conflict; including both ad hoc actions, focused for example on helping refugees, and actions with long-term objectives related to government policy. These were expressed through demands to end the war and formulating conditions for restoring peace.

The verification of the research hypotheses set out in individual chapters allows in turn the drawing of the following conclusion.

In the conditions of war, there is a noticeably stronger focus on material values, which in peace time give way to post-material values. There is also a visible confusion of values and 'anti-values', what is considered a value during peace, can become an 'anti-value' during war. A specific case is the autocratic

DOI: 10.4324/9781003558040-16

Conclusion 201

peace theory, which has been used to analyse the Russian-Ukrainian conflict, formulating the conclusion that a non-democratic state will maintain peace with other countries (political system notwithstanding) as long as there is no pressure from the international democratic environment as to the change in the status of its exclusivity. In other words, the principles/norms/values internally recognised by this state, that is if democratic states have no ambitions to change what is non-democratic in others. Furthermore, a non-democratic state will maintain peace with others if it does not need to seek an external enemy to achieve its internal and short-term political goals. Finally, the propaganda of a non-democratic state will not reach and capture the minds of societies in states that have consolidated democratic systems and political elites legitimised on the basis of democratic values. Securing the status quo of non-democratic states guarantees the preservation of autocratic peace in the international arena, while any rationale that disrupts it leads to an unjust war which affects not only its participants but also those neighbouring states and societies closest to the armed conflict area.

An example of such consequences can be found in the states of the Baltic region, forced by the full-scale war in Ukraine to react immediately and widely to Russian aggression. Within the current internal policies of individual states, those concerning foreign and security have been revised, and activities strengthening alliances within the EU and NATO have been undertaken. In the face of a real threat to peace and security in this part of Europe, these states have revised through political action their earlier perception of security in the international arena, reviewing and verifying their security strategies, and this is expected to result in a better preparedness to respond to emerging threats. A further guarantee of security in the region are the strategic plans and actions, especially those of Poland, Lithuania, Latvia and Estonia, aimed at accelerating Ukraine's accession to NATO and EU structures. The war also influenced the economic policies of the Baltic Sea countries. Energy independence from Russian raw materials has become a priority goal, which has intensified efforts for sustainable development and the implementation of the "Green Deal" policy.

Noteworthy in this context is the help provided by Baltic region states for refugees from Ukraine, which undoubtedly required fast and decisive change in order to guarantee funds. Available data reveal this aid to be in the range of 0.5% GDP for Germany to 1.4% GDP for Lithuania (data for June/July 2023). These funds can also be seen as a future investment made by the economies of those countries in the process of rebuilding Ukraine from war destruction.

After 2022, Sweden and Finland found themselves in a specific situation in terms of security. Their decades-long strategy of military neutrality (resulting from quite different reasons) has been revised due to Russian aggression against Ukraine. The legitimacy of changing their security strategy has become a subject for heated debate not only among Swedes and Finns but also in the international arena. The societies of both states realised the necessity of changing their perception of neutrality/engagement in international security-guarding organisations. In the international debates, at the same time, there emerged clear divisions between supporters and opponents of Sweden's and Finland's accession to NATO: the former pointed to the need to strengthen security capabilities through NATO membership, while the latter to possible threats unrelated to the expansionary actions of an imperialistic Russia. Public discourse analysis was used to identify changes in the security strategies of the two countries, with a particular focus on their relevance to changes in the security of the Baltic Sea states. Eventually, both countries became members of NATO: Finland on 4 April 2023 and Sweden on 7 March 2024. This strengthened the defence potential of NATO's eastern flank, comprising all Baltic Sea states.

Undoubtedly, the strategic goals of the Baltic region states are in contradiction with the concept of peace *à la* Putin. While the states analysed recognise Ukraine as a subject of international relations, Russia's narrative in presenting its vision of peace oscillates around the thesis that Ukraine is not a participant in international relations, but only a 'territory' where the interests of the RF and the United States clash. This belief is internally reinforced in Russia by Putin's propaganda presenting a narrative about Ukraine's civilisational ties with Russia and the threats to the RF that come from Western countries. This primarily serves Putin's internal policy of building the image of war as a necessary means for defending Russian territory, language and identity on the international stage. Thus, Putin seeks to shift the narrative's centre of gravity from autocratic peace to a just war.

The Baltic region states do not see peace negotiations with Russia as a politically or economically attractive proposition. On the contrary, realising the possibility that Moscow will use peace negotiations to strengthen its military position, they are sceptical about the chances of engaging in dialogue with Putin to end the war in Ukraine. All the more so because, contrary to Putin's propaganda, they do not consider this war to be just and point to Russia as its initiator and aggressor. Therefore, they assign a very significant role in ensuring accountability for war crimes to international public opinion and the institutions of justice. At the same time, the international narrative not only is dominated by a belief that it is necessary to document Russian crimes in Ukraine after 24 February 2022 but also postulates the necessity of trying the war criminals and, consequently, compensating the Ukrainian people.

Individual countries, groups of states and international organisations have taken initiatives to establish the facts, which includes collecting evidence, identifying the guilty parties, and holding them accountable for violations of international law. As a result, the war in Ukraine is the best documented war in history, which essentially increases the ability of states and the international community to hold the perpetrators of crimes accountable. It is worth noting that activity in the area of documenting and prosecuting crimes has been undertaken by individual Baltic region states on the basis of universal

Conclusion 203

jurisdiction, which complements the activities of the international institutions, particularly the International Criminal Court. However, the conflict in Ukraine has also exposed the gaps and shortcomings of the international criminal system, as exemplified by the inability to hold Russia accountable for the crime of aggression. In this area, the international community is looking for an alternative solution, and this could be the establishment of a tribunal with a jurisdiction limited only to the crime of aggression; however, establishing such an institution would be a long-term process.

It is not only formal settlements and political decisions that impact the direction of engagement of the Baltic region states during the war in Ukraine, as well as in any future peace. This is because such involvement largely depends on the attitudes and actions of their societies. The research results show that the Russian-Ukrainian conflict influenced both the interest in security issues among the inhabitants of the Baltic Sea countries, as well as the models and character of social activism. In this context, it is worth noting that the countries of the Baltic region have diverse experiences which form a foundation for human rights protection. Therefore, while the goal (i.e. civil society acting for security understood as human capital) remains the same, there are different models of social activism. In this case, the main focus should be on the stable financing of instruments for the 'horizontal' cooperative networking of activists from all the Baltic region states and Ukraine. This regards issues related to refugees, Ukrainians who have remained in their homeland, as well as those working to protect human rights in the region. In this context, it is worth mentioning Interreg Baltic Sea Region and European Territorial Cooperation. Other notable initiatives are Swedish Strategy for Regional Cooperation with Eastern Europe, the Western Balkans and Turkey, whose largest recipient is Ukraine, as well as the activities of the Swedish International Development Cooperation Agency (SIDA). No less important is Lithuania's Official Development Assistance (ODA) and the Nordic support instrument in the form of the Nordic-Baltic NGO Programme.

Some of the aid activities for refugees and Ukrainian citizens are aimed at the protection, preservation and development of cultural capital. Assistance in this regard is addressed to three groups of recipients: the primary one being those involved in the arts, opinion leaders as regards initiatives, interpretations of reality and social mobilisation. These make it possible to create a platform for maintaining the unity of the Ukrainian national community. The second group consists of Ukrainian audiences/consumers of culture in a wider sense who have found refuge in the Baltic states following the outbreak of full-scale war. In their case, aid activities have become a form not only of material but above all moral support for Ukraine and its citizens. The third group for whom the activities have proved to be extremely significant is of the residents of the Baltic region countries who need to get used to the presence of a large group of new residents with a different national identity. Assistance in sustaining and developing cultural capital is provided by government entities and the cultural institutions under their supervision (such as museums, galleries, orchestras) as well as NGOs and volunteers. In the initial phase of the war especially, aid actions were spontaneous, only to become institutionalised over time. The assistance provided to arts workers from Ukraine had three main goals: the first was to sustain, develop and popularise embodied cultural capital which involved providing Ukrainian artists with an opportunity to settle down and earn money in Baltic region countries as well as promoting their work. The second goal was to sustain, develop and disseminate objectified cultural capital, which primarily meant ensuring that Ukrainian artists were able to create new work. The third goal was to promote Ukrainian culture among war refugees as well as within communities that now include numerous refugee groups. All of these assistance activities served to strengthen not only Ukrainian identity but also the cultural capital necessary for rebuilding the country after the end of hostilities. However, in the analysis of possible effects of activities in this area, it can be noted that concern for the cultural capital of refugees may potentially bring both benefits and risks for host societies: on the one hand, it integrates, creating opportunities for the formation of group identities; while on the other, it carries the risk of social conflicts and exclusion.

This threat is rising in countries experiencing a rapid growth in movements against state involvement in aid to Ukraine (anti-involvement movement, AIM), who claim that 'this is not our war'. Admittedly, if we assume that the institutionalisation of a social movement is one of the predictors of its success, it should be noted that the level of institutionalisation remains relatively low. However, thanks to modern technology, those 'circles' animating AIMs remain active. The internet has become a place where they can spread disinformation and anti-Ukrainian narratives through Twitter/X, Facebook, YouTube and a variety of other online portals playing a major role. These tools not only allow for the propagation of anti-Ukrainian messages but also foster the rapid mobilisation of groups and individuals; it should be noted, however, that some are quickly blocked by security services and by societies themselves, who have become distrustful and sensitive to certain types of activity.

Characteristically, AIMs use a wide range of arguments to win supporters from different ideological spectra: pacifists, feminists, environmentalists, but nationalists, chauvinists and liberals as well. In this context, it should be noted that despite different emphases, specific to particular nationalities, the narratives of AIM movements are convergent at all levels: diagnostic, prognostic and mobilised. At the same time, the narrative they present reflects the message formulated by the Russian Federation.

Another important form of social behaviour responding to the war in Ukraine are pacifist movements. Their presence is particularly strongly marked in Germany, where demonstrations of opposition to the war, demands for an immediate ceasefire, as well as a relatively low potential for mobilisation, were an expression of objection to the ongoing hostilities. Today their activities focus on campaigns, actions and demonstrations;

Conclusion 205

in Germany, however, the demands and activities of such movements refer directly to slogans from the earlier days of such initiatives in this country. Of course, the demands have been expanded in reaction to the full-scale war in Ukraine, taking the form of opposition to the transfer of additional funds to the Bundeswehr, opposition to the export of arms and heavy equipment to Ukraine, and demands that the government take diplomatic initiatives to end the war. Other important demands involved the protection of energy security and combating climate change.

It is worth noting that despite their rhetoric, pacifist movements do not play a decisive role in the German government's decisions regarding the supply of equipment and weapons to Ukraine, and thus do not change the ideological assumptions of the federal government's policy. Nor do pacifist movements represent the opinion of the majority of the population; the scale of social mobilisation during their actions is relatively low. However, they do have a stake in publicising ethical issues. Due to their demands that the federal government change its orientation from pro-war to pro-peace, the matter of aid to Ukraine, including arms supplies, sanctions imposed on Russia and taking diplomatic action to end the war, have become topical and publicly discussed issues.

In the context of the research issue discussed here, the bipartisan voice of Russian society after the annexation of Crimea in 2014 and the outbreak of full-scale war in 2022 can hardly be overlooked. It is the space where civil disobedience has emerged as a response to the hybrid formula of dictatorship that combines spin activities with feeding fear into society. Notably, three types of Russian public attitude can be distinguished: the first consists of those who support Russia's aggression against Ukraine; the second those who (usually through modern technologies) emphasise their opposition to and disagreement with Putin's actions in Ukraine; and the third those who do not, officially, take a stance on the actions of the authorities. It is difficult to determine which of these attitudes will be dominant in further prospects for both war and peace.

What are therefore the paths to peace chosen by decision-makers in the countries of the region and by the social groups surveyed? The answer to this question is not unequivocal. The states of the Baltic region, as well as the European Union as a whole, have so far not developed a common and coherent strategy for peace. The assumption that the conflict will end and that the pre-war situation will be restored will not come true; the problem of Russia and its concept of 'Russkiy mir' may be postponed for a time, but will return. This leads to the sad reflection that the lack of a communality of goals among the countries of the region and, more broadly, the EU will not allow us to expect that a just peace will come. There may perhaps come an autocratic peace, but it will be immanently fragile and dependent on the whim of Russia's dictator.

Index of persons

Abramovich, Sofia 188
Andersson, Magdalena 67

Babkina, Kateryna 147
Bandera, Stepan 96
Benford, Robert D. 160
Biden, Joe 61
Blåtand ((Bluetooth), Harald 59
Blumer, Herbert 163
Bourdieu, Pierre 137, 138, 140
Braudel, Fernand 56, 66
Buro, Andreas 169

Castañeda, Ernesto 157
Chrupalla, Tino 176
Coleman, James Samuel 138

Dalton, Russell J. 107
Daphi, Priska 169, 172
Deripaska, Oleg 188
Downs, William 158
Drahomanov, Mykhailo 137
Dugin, Alexander 70

Easton, David 169
Eppelmann, Rainer 172, 175
Erästö, Tytti 127
Erdoğan, Recep Tayyip 61

Frank, Peter 88

Gulina, Olga 192

Havemann, Robert 172, 175
Hofstede, Geert 63
Hrushevsky, Mykhailo 137
Huntington, Samuel P. 56, 66

Inglehart, Ronald 4, 5, 13, 17

Janša, Janez 31
Jenssen, Stian 37

Kant, Immanuel 4, 13, 18
Karim, A.A. Khan QC, Karim, Asad
   Ahmad Khan KC 93
Kasyanov, Mikhail 75
Khodorkovsky, Mikhail 190
Kirillov, Viktor Vasil'yevich 71
Kiyanovska, Marianna (Kijanowska
   Marianna) 147
Koneczny, Feliks 56
Konrat, Marek 74
Kozyrev, Andrei 188
Krastev, Ivan 185
Kryuchkov, Yuriy Nikolayevich 71
Kubrakov, Oleksandr 34
Kurkov, Andrey 147
Kurschus, Annette 174

Leistner, Alexander 169, 173
Liberman, Nira 117
Linde, Ann 62, 66
Łukaszenka, Aleksander, Alexander
   Lukashenko 87
Lvova-Belova, Maria 93

Mader, Matthias 108
Makarevich, Andrei 188
Margaret, I. 59
Marin, Sanna 62, 67
Maull, Hanns W. 170
McCarthy, John 123
McFaul, Michael 72
McMahan, Jeff 23

Index of persons 207

Mearsheimer, John 66
Medvedev, Dmitry 70
Meier, Larissa 169, 172
Michel, Charles 31
Morawiecki, Mateusz 31
Moyer, Bill 124
Muratov, Dmitri 195

Navalny, Alexei 188
Nemtsova, Zhanna 190
Neubert, Ehrhart 171

Orban, Viktor 60, 61, 62
Ovsyannikova, Marianna 188

Paleckis, Algidras 157
Paludan, Rasmus 61
Pasikowska-Schnass, Magdalena 139
Person, Robert 72
Peskova, Yelizaveta 188
Peterson, Aivo 161
Pipes, Richard 65
Poroshenko, Petro 71
Prigozhin, Yevgeny 27
Pugacheva, Alla 188
Putin, Władimir, Vladimir Putin 6, 16,
    19, 20, 21, 22, 23, 30, 62, 65, 70,
    71, 72, 74, 76, 77, 78, 79, 87, 93,
    184, 187, 188, 189, 190, 202, 205
Putnam, Robert 138

Riabczuk, Mykola/ Riabchuk Mykola
    122, 123
Riesenberger, Dieter 169
Rotfeld, Adam 70

Schmitt, Rüdiger 169
Scholz, Olaf 31, 37, 168, 176

Scholzman, Daniel 163
Schulze, Svenja 34
Schwarzer, Alice 176
Sergeytsev, Timofey 84
Shevchenko, Taras 137
Shulman, Yekateryna 192
Smyha, Denys 34
Snow, David A. 160
Sobchak, Ksenia 188
St. Augustine 13
Stalin, Josef 74
Stoltenberg, Jens 58, 61
Stoltenberg, Thorvald 58

Tarrow, Sidney 123
Tempel, Konrad 171
Tilly, Charles 123
Trope, Yaacov 117

Utkin, Sergey 192

Wagenknecht, Sahra 176
Wasmuht, Ulrike C. 169
Waszczykowski, Stanislaw
    85, 86
Wetterberg, Gunnar 59

Yanukovych, Viktor 20, 71
Yeltsin, Boris 188
Yumasheva, Maria 188
Yumasheva, Tatiana 188

Zakharova, Maria 74
Zald, Mayer 123
Zarhkov, Vasilyj 192
Zelenskyy, Volodymyr 33, 75
Zhadan, Serhyi 147
Żuradzki, Tomasz 23

Milton Keynes UK
Ingram Content Group UK Ltd.
UKHW031330071224
451979UK00005B/70